Learning Aid for use with

Basic Marketing

A Managerial Approach Ninth Edition

E. Jerome McCarthy
Michigan State University

William D. Perreault, Jr.
University of North Carolina

1987

IRWIN

Homewood
Illinois 60430

©Richard D. Irwin, Inc., 1971, 1975, 1978, 1981, 1984, and 1987

Printed in the United States of America.

ISBN 0-256-03650-0

1 2 3 4 5 6 7 8 9 0 VK 4 3 2 1 0 9 8 7

Contents

Introduction   5

1. Marketing's role in society   1-1
    Exercise 1-1   What is marketing?   1-7
    Exercise 1-2   How markets and marketing middlemen develop to
                   facilitate exchange   1-9
    Exercise 1-3   How marketing functions create economic utility   1-15
    Exercise 1-4   Revenue, cost, and profit relationships   1-21

2. Marketing's role within the firm   2-1
    Exercise 2-1   Marketing-oriented vs. production-oriented firm   2-7
    Exercise 2-2   Mass marketing vs. target marketing   2-13
    Exercise 2-3   Developing a unique marketing mix for each target
                   market   2-17
    Exercise 2-4   Target marketing   2-21

Appendix A. Economics fundamentals   A-1
    Exercise A-1   Estimating and using demand elasticity   A-7

3. Finding target market opportunities with market segmentation   3-1
    Exercise 3-1   Product-markets vs. generic markets   3-9
    Exercise 3-2   Seven-step approach to segmenting markets   3-11
    Exercise 3-3   Using positioning to evaluate marketing opportunities   3-15
    Exercise 3-4   Segmenting customers   3-19

4. Evaluating opportunities in uncontrollable environments   4-1
    Exercise 4-1   How uncontrollable variables affect marketing strategy
                   planning   4-9
    Exercise 4-2   Analyzing the competitive environment   4-11
    Exercise 4-3   How the legal environment affects marketing strategy
                   planning   4-15
    Exercise 4-4   Company resources   4-19

5. Getting information for marketing decisions   5-1
    Exercise 5-1   Locating sources of secondary data   5-9
    Exercise 5-2   Evaluating marketing research   5-13
    Exercise 5-3   Marketing research   5-17

6. Demographic dimensions of the U.S. consumer market   6-1
    Exercise 6-1   How demographic trends affect marketing strategy
                   planning   6-7
    Exercise 6-2   Marketers must know their markets   6-11
    Exercise 6-3   Demographic analysis   6-15

7. Behavioral dimensions of the consumer market 7-1
    Exercise 7-1   Psychological variables and social influences affect consumer buying behavior 7-9
    Exercise 7-2   Consumer behavior is a problem-solving process 7-13
    Exercise 7-3   Selective processes 7-15

8. Industrial and intermediate customers and their buying behavior 8-1
    Exercise 8-1   Analyzing industrial buying behavior 8-7
    Exercise 8-2   Using SIC codes to analyze industrial markets 8-11
    Exercise 8-3   Vendor analysis 8-15

9. Elements of product planning 9-1
    Exercise 9-1   Classifying consumer products 9-13
    Exercise 9-2   Classifying industrial products 9-17
    Exercise 9-3   Achieving brand familiarity 9-21
    Exercise 9-4   Comparing branded product offerings 9-23
    Exercise 9-5   Branding decision 9-25

10. Product management and new-product development 10-1
    Exercise 10-1   Identifying a product's stage in the product life cycle 10-7
    Exercise 10-2   New-product development process 10-11
    Exercise 10-3   Growth stage competition 10-15

11. Place and development of channel systems 11-1
    Exercise 11-1   Evaluating the costs of adjusting discrepancies of quantity and assortment in channel systems 11-7
    Exercise 11-2   Determining market exposure policies 11-11
    Exercise 11-3   Intensive vs. selective distribution 11-15

12. Retailing 12-1
    Exercise 12-1   Analyzing store-product combinations 12-9
    Exercise 12-2   Identifying and analyzing retail stores 12-13
    Exercise 12-3   Mass merchandising 12-17

13. Wholesaling 13-1
    Exercise 13-1   Choosing the right kind of wholesaler 13-7
    Exercise 13-2   Analyzing channels of distribution 13-11
    Exercise 13-3   Merchant vs. agent wholesaler 13-15

14. Physical distribution 14-1
    Exercise 14-1   Evaluating physical distribution alternatives 14-7
    Exercise 14-2   Strategic planning for customer service level 14-11
    Exercise 14-3   Total distribution cost 14-15

15. Promotion-Introduction 15-1
    Exercise 15-1   The communication process in promotion 15-7
    Exercise 15-2   Using the adoption curve to develop promotion blends 15-11
    Exercise 15-3   Sales promotion 15-17

16. Personal selling   16-1
     Exercise 16-1   Analyzing the nature of the personal selling task   16-7
     Exercise 16-2   Selecting the appropriate kind of salesperson   16-11
     Exercise 16-3   Sales compensation   16-15

17. Mass selling   17-1
     Exercise 17-1   Identifying differnt kinds of advertising   17-7
     Exercise 17-2   Determining advertising objectives and the appropriate
                      kind of advertising   17-9
     Exercise 17-3   Advertising media   17-13

18. Pricing objectives and policies   18-1
     Exercise 18-1   Using discounts and allowances to improve the
                      marketing mix   18-11
     Exercise 18-2   How legislation affects pricing policies   18-15
     Exercise 18-3   Cash discounts   18-19

Appendix B. Marketing arithmetic   B-1
     Exercise B-1   Marketing arithmetic   B-7

19. Price setting in the real world   19-1
     Exercise 19-1   Elements of cost-oriented price setting   19-13
     Exercise 19-2   Using break-even analysis to evaluate alternative prices   19-19
     Exercise 19-3   Setting the most profitable price and quantity to
                      produce   19-23
     Exercise 19-4   Using marginal analysis to set the most profitable price
                      and quantity to produce   19-27
     Exercise 19-5   Break-even/profit analysis   19-29

20. Planning and implementing marketing programs   20-1
     Exercise 20-1   Using the "Survey of Buying Power" to estimate market
                      and sales potential   20-9
     Exercise 20-2   Using response functions to help plan marketing mixes   20-13
     Exercise 20-3   Adjusting marketing strategies over the product life
                      cycle   20-17
     Exercise 20-4   Comparing marketing mixes   20-21

21. Controlling marketing plans and programs   21-1
     Exercise 21-1   Sales and performance analysis   21-7
     Exercise 21-2   Controlling marketing plans and programs with
                      marketing cost analysis   21-11
     Exercise 21-3   Marketing cost analysis   21-15

22. Marketing strategy planning for international markets   22-1
     Exercise 22-1   Strategy planning for international markets: Consumer
                      products   22-7
     Exercise 22-2   Strategy planning for international markets: Industrial
                      products   22-11
     Exercise 22-3   Export opportunities   22-15

23. Marketing in a consumer-oriented society: appraisal and challenges   23-1
     Exercise 23-1   Does micro-marketing cost too much?   23-5
     Exercise 23-2   Does macro-marketing cost too much?   23-9

McCarthy and Perreault

Introduction

This *Learning Aid* is designed to help you organize and learn all of the material that is presented in *Basic Marketing*, 9th edition. Feedback from marketing instructors--and students--indicates that students who use the *Learning Aid* regularly do tend to learn the material better--and also tend to do better on examinations.

Please note, however, that the *Learning Aid* is intended to be used along with *Basic Marketing*. *It is not a substitute for reading and carefully studying the text!*

How the Learning Aid Is Organized

The *Learning Aid* is divided into 23 chapters--one chapter for each corresponding chapter in *Basic Marketing*. There are also separate chapters for Appendix A: Economics Fundamentals and Appendix B: Marketing Arithmetic.

Each chapter in the *Learning Aid* contains the following five sections:

> A. What this chapter is about
> B. Important terms
> C. True-false questions
> D. Multiple-choice questions
> E. Application exercises

The purpose of each of these sections is explained below. Please note that some sections are designed to be used *before* you read each chapter in *Basic Marketing*.

What This Chapter Is About

This section provides a brief introduction to each chapter in *Basic Marketing*. It should be read *before* you read the text--to help you focus on the important points in each chapter.

Important Terms

This section lists the important new terms introduced in each chapter of *Basic Marketing*--and the page on which each term first appears. (These terms are shown in red in the text to help you find them.)

You should look over the list of important terms *before* reading each chapter--to help you focus on the key points in the chapter. *After* reading each chapter, you should review the list of important terms to make sure you understand each term. If you have any doubts about what a particular term means, use the indicated page number to find and restudy its definition in the text--or look up the term's definition in the Glossary at the end of the text. Some students even write out the definitions of each important term on 3 x 5 cards--to help them study for exams.

True-False Questions

This section provides a series of *self-testing* true-false questions--to test your understanding of the material presented in *Basic Marketing*. The correct answer for each question is given at the end of the test--along with a page number showing where the correct answer can be found in the text.

After reading each chapter in the text and reviewing the important terms, try to answer all of the true-false questions *before* looking at the correct answers. Then check. your answers--and for each question that you answered wrong, review the related text material to find out *why* your answer is wrong. This is an important step! Simply memorizing the correct answers is *not* likely to improve your exam performance!

Multiple-Choice Questions

This section contains a series of *self-testing* multiple-choice questions--to further test your understanding and comprehension of the material presented in *Basic Marketing*. Again, the correct answer for each question is given at the end of the questions--along with a page number showing where the correct answer can be found in the text.

Ideally, you should take the multiple-choice tests only *after* you have read the text, reviewed the important terms, and tried the true-false questions. Again, you should try to answer all of the questions *before* looking at the correct answers--and make sure you review the text material to learn *why* your wrong answers were wrong!

Finally, keep in mind that the self-testing true-false and multiple-choice questions are just a *sample* of what you might expect on an exam. They do not cover every single concept discussed in the text--nor do they cover every possible type of question that might be asked. In other words, *simply answering these self-testing questions is not adequate preparation for exams.* You must also read and study the text!

Application Exercises

This section includes two or more exercises for each of the chapters in *Basic Marketing* (not including the appendices). One of the exercises for each chapter is based on the *Computer-Aided Problems to Accompany Basic Marketing*. Each exercise is designed to illustrate and apply some of the more important concepts and analytical approaches introduced in the text.

Although these exercises are designed mainly to be discussed in class and/or assigned as homework--*you can still benefit from doing them even if your instructor does not assign them.* Many students find the "Introductions" to each exercise quite helpful in understanding the related text material. And many of the exercises contain short "caselets" which show how concepts discussed in the text can be applied in the "real world." Doing these exercises will not only improve your understanding of the text material--but will also better prepare you for more advanced marketing and business case courses.

Note: Your instructor has been supplied with suggested answers for each of the application exercises--and with software that can be used to work the computer-aided exercises. So even if the exercises are not formally assigned, you can still do them--and ask your instructor to show you the suggested answers so you can check your answers. Your instructor will surely be impressed by your dedication to learning!

How to Study for Examinations

While no study routine works best for everyone, the following suggestions are based on proven learning principles and should be of benefit to most students. *For every chapter your instructor assigns in Basic Marketing:*

1. Read the *what this chapter is about* section in the *Learning Aid*.

2. Look over the *important terms* section in the *Learning Aid*.

3. Read the learning objectives listed at the beginning of the chapter.

4. Read the chapter from beginning to end without any interruptions--and *without doing any underlining or note-taking.* (Underlining key points while you read interrupts your flow of thought and tends to reduce reading comprehension.)

5. Read the chapter again--this time underlining key points and/or writing notes in the page margins. Look at the exhibits and illustrations, and think about how they relate to the text material.

6. Review the *important terms* section in the *Learning Aid* to make sure you can define each term.

7. Take the self-testing true-false test in the *Learning Aid*--and go back to the text to study any questions you answered wrong.

8. Take the self-testing multiple-choice test in the *Learning Aid*--and go back to the text to study any questions you answered wrong.

9. Take detailed classroom lecture notes--and review them *immediately after class* to make sure that they are complete and that you understand everything your instructor said.

10. Do any *application exercises* that your instructor assigns.

11. *Optional:* Do the *application exercises* that were not assigned.

12. Just before the examination--review:

    a.   the points you underlined in the text and/or your notes in the page margins.

    b.   the *important terms* in the *Learning Aid*.

    c.   the self-testing true-false and multiple-choice questions in the *Learning Aid*--especially the questions you answered wrong the first time.

    d.   any *application exercises* that were assigned.

    e.   your lecture notes.

Good luck!

Acknowledgment

Professor Andrew Brogowicz of Western Michigan University contributed many creative ideas to earlier editions of this *Learning Aid*. His earlier contributions have continued to influence many of the new, revised, and/or updated exercises that appear in this edition.

We also appreciate the contributions of Ms. Linda G. Davis. She did all of the word processing work for several drafts of all of the materials in this edition--and was also responsible for preparing the final manuscript in "camera ready" form.

McCarthy and Perreault

Chapter 1

Marketing's role in society

What This Chapter Is About

Chapter 1 introduces the concept of marketing. First, we show how marketing relates to production--and why it is important to you and to society. Then the text shows that there are two kinds of marketing--micro-marketing and macro-marketing. The importance of a macro-marketing system in any kind of economic system is emphasized.

The vital role of marketing functions is discussed. It is emphasized that producers, consumers, *and* marketing specialists perform marketing functions. You will learn that responsibility for performing the marketing functions can be shifted and shared in a variety of ways, but that from a macro viewpoint all of the functions must be performed by someone. No function can be completely eliminated.

The main focus of *this chapter* is on macro-marketing--to give you a broad introduction. But the focus of *this text* is on management-oriented micro-marketing--beginning in Chapter 2.

Important Terms

production, p. 5
utility, p. 6
form utility, p. 6
possession utility, p. 6
time utility, p. 6
place utility, p. 6
micro-marketing, p. 8
macro-marketing, p. 10
economic system, p. 11
planned economic system, p. 11
market-directed economic system, p. 11
micro-macro dilemma, p. 12
pure subsistence economy, p. 14
market, p. 14

central market, p. 14
middleman, p. 15
economies of scale, p. 17
universal functions of marketing, p. 18
buying function, p. 18
selling function, p. 18
transporting function, p. 18
storing function, p. 18
standardization and grading, p. 18
financing, p. 18
risk taking, p. 18
market information function, p. 18
facilitators, p. 20
innovation, p. 21

True-False Questions

__F__ 1. According to the text, marketing means "selling" or "advertising."

__F__ 2. Production is a more important economic activity than marketing.

F   3.   Actually making goods or performing services is called marketing.

T   4.   Marketing provides time, place, and possession utility.

T   5.   It is estimated that marketing costs about 50 percent of each consumer's dollar.

T   6.   Marketing is both a set of activities performed by organizations and a social process.

T   7.   Micro-marketing is the performance of activities which seek to accomplish an organization's objectives by anticipating customer or client needs and directing a flow of need-satisfying goods and services from producer to customer or client.

F   8.   Micro-marketing activities should be of no interest to a nonprofit organization.

T   9.   Macro-marketing is a set of activities which direct an economy's flow of goods and services from producers to consumers in a way which effectively matches supply and demand and accomplishes the objectives of society.

T   10.   Macro-marketing emphasizes how the whole system works, rather than the activities of individual organizations.

F   11.   Only market-directed societies need an economic system.

F   12.   In a market-directed economy, government planners decide what and how much is to be produced and distributed by whom, when, and to whom.

T   13.   In a market-directed economy, the prices of consumer goods and services serve roughly as a measure of their social importance.

T   14.   Sometimes micro-macro dilemmas arise because what is "good" for some producers and consumers may not be "good" for society as a whole.

F   15.   The American economy is entirely market-directed.

T   16.   A pure subsistence economy is an economy in which each family unit produces everything it consumes.

T   17.   Marketing takes place whenever a person needs something of value.

T   18.   The term marketing comes from the word market--which is a group of sellers and buyers who are willing to exchange goods and/or services for something of value.

F   19.   While central markets facilitate exchange, middlemen usually complicate exchange by increasing the total number of transactions required.

T   20.   More effective macro-marketing systems are the result of greater economic development.

T 21. Without an effective macro-marketing system, the less-developed nations may be doomed to a "vicious circle of poverty."

T 22. "Economies of scale" means that as a company produces larger numbers of a particular product, the cost for each of these products goes down.

F 23. "Universal functions of marketing" consist only of buying, selling, transporting, and storing.

F 24. Achieving effective marketing in an advanced economy is simplified by the fact that producers are separated from consumers in only two ways: time and space.

T 25. In a market-directed economy, marketing functions are performed by producers, consumers, and a variety of marketing institutions.

F 26. Marketing facilitators are any firms which provide the marketing functions of buying and selling.

T 27. Responsibility for performing the marketing functions can be shifted and shared in a variety of ways, but no function can be completely eliminated.

F 28. Our market-directed macro-marketing system discourages the development and spread of new ideas and products.

Answers to True-False Questions

1. F, p. 3	11. F, p. 11	21. T, p. 16
2. F, p. 5	12. F, p. 11	22. T, p. 17
3. F, p. 5	13. T, p. 16	23. F, p. 18
4. T, p. 6	14. T, p. 12	24. F, p. 18
5. T, p. 6	15. F, p. 12	25. T, p. 19
6. T, p. 8	16. T, p. 14	26. F, p. 20
7. T, p. 8	17. F, p. 14	27. T, p. 21
8. F, p. 8	18. T, p. 14	28. F, p. 21
9. F, p. 10	19. F, p. 15	
10. T, p. 10	20. F, p. 16	

Multiple-Choice Questions (Circle the correct response)

1. According to the text:
   a. marketing is much more than selling or advertising.
   b. the cost of marketing is about 25 percent of the consumer's dollar.
   c. production is a more essential economic activity than marketing.
   d. only marketing creates economic utility.
   e. all of the above are true statements.

2. When a "fruit peddler" drives his truck through residential neighborhoods and sells fruits and vegetables grown by farmers, he is creating:
   a. form utility.
   b. time and place utility.
   c. possession utility.
   d. all of the above.
   e. all of the above, *except* a.

3. The text stresses that:
   a. advertising and selling are not really part of marketing.
   b. marketing is nothing more than a set of business activities performed by individual firms.
   c. marketing techniques have no application for nonprofit organizations.
   d. marketing is a social process and a set of activities performed by organizations.
   e. a good product usually sells itself.

4. *Micro*-marketing:
   a. is concerned with need-satisfying goods, but not with services.
   b. involves an attempt to anticipate customer or client needs.
   c. is primarily concerned with efficient use of resources and fair allocation of output.
   d. includes activities such as accounting, production, and financial management.
   e. is the process of selling and distributing manufactured goods.

5. *Macro*-marketing:
   a. is not concerned with the flow of goods and services from producers to consumers.
   b. seeks to match homogeneous supply capabilities with homogeneous demands for goods and services.
   c. refers to a set of activities performed by both profit and nonprofit organizations.
   d. focuses on the objectives of society.
   e. All of the above are true statements.

6. Which of the following statements about economic decision making is *true*?
    a. In a market-directed system, the micro-level decisions of individual producers and consumers determine the macro-level decisions.
    b. Government planning usually works best when economies become more complex and the variety of goods and services produced is fairly large.
    c. The United States may be considered a pure market-directed economy.
    d. Planned economic systems usually rely on market forces to determine prices.
    e. All of the above are true statements.

7. Marketing cannot occur unless:
    a. an economy is market-directed rather than planned.
    b. producers and consumers can enter into face-to-face negotiations at some physical location.
    c. an economy has a money system.
    d. there are two or more parties who each have something of value they want to exchange for something else.
    e. middlemen are present to facilitate exchange.

8. The development of marketing middlemen:
    a. tends to make the exchange process more complicated, more costly, and harder to carry out.
    b. usually reduces the total number of transactions necessary to carry out exchange.
    c. tends to increase place utility but decrease time utility.
    d. becomes less advantageous as the number of producers and consumers, their distance apart, and the number and variety of products increase.
    e. All of the above are true statements.

9. In advanced economies:
    a. mass production capability is a necessary and sufficient condition for satisfying consumer needs.
    b. exchange is simplified by discrepancies of quantity and assortment.
    c. the creation of time, place, and possession utilities tends to be easy.
    d. both supply and demand tend to be homogeneous in nature.
    e. producers and consumers experience a separation of values.

10. Which of the following is *not* one of the "universal functions of marketing"?
    a. Production
    b. Standardization
    c. Financing
    d. Buying
    e. Transporting

11. Which of the following is a *true* statement?
    a. Since marketing is concerned with many thousands of different products, there is no one set of marketing functions that applies to all products.
    b. Responsibility for performing marketing functions can be shifted and shared, but no function can be completely eliminated.
    c. From a micro viewpoint, every firm must perform all of the marketing functions.
    d. Marketing functions should be performed only by marketing middlemen or facilitators.
    e. Many marketing functions are not necessary in planned economies.

Answers to Multiple-Choice Questions

1. a, p. 3
2. e, p. 6
3. d, p. 8
4. b, p. 9

5. d, p. 10
6. a, p. 11
7. d, p. 14
8. b, p. 15

9. e, p. 18
10. a, p. 18
11. b, p. 21

Exercise 1-1

What is marketing?

Introduction

Society ignored or even criticized the contributions of marketing until the beginning of the 20th century. At that time, economies once marked by a scarcity of goods began to enjoy an abundance of goods. Marketing skills were needed to solve the distribution problems that resulted. Thus, it was not until the early 1900s that the importance of marketing was realized--and that marketing was accepted as a separate academic subject in schools and colleges.

Even today, many people do not have a very clear understanding of marketing. No one single definition of marketing will satisfy everyone. Many people--including some students and business managers--tend to think of marketing as "selling" or "advertising." Others see marketing as an all-inclusive social process that can solve all the world's problems. Some critics, meanwhile, seem to blame marketing for most of society's ills!

This exercise is intended to help you see more clearly what marketing is all about. One way to learn about marketing is to study the definitions in the text. Another way is to use these definitions. This is the approach you will follow in this exercise.

Assignment

Listed below are some commonly asked questions about marketing. Answer each of these questions in a way which shows your understanding of marketing.

1. Do "marketing" and "selling" mean the same thing?

2. What activities does marketing involve besides selling?

3. Would there be any need for marketing activities if manufacturers would just try to produce better products? Why or why not?

4. Is marketing useful for non-profit organizations? Explain.

5. If marketing activities are so important, why are they found only in market-directed economic systems?

6. How do consumers in a market-directed economy influence what products will be produced and by whom?

Question for Discussion

Should marketing be viewed as a set of activities performed by business and nonprofit organizations, or alternately as a social process? Why is it important to make this distinction?

McCarthy and Perreault

Exercise 1-2

How markets and marketing middlemen develop to facilitate exchange

Introduction

The functions of exchange--buying and selling--are at the heart of the marketing process. Generally, as economies become more advanced, exchange becomes more complicated. In modern economies, markets and marketing middlemen develop to smooth exchange. How well exchange is carried out affects consumer welfare. This is because goods take on value only when they are in the right place at the right time so that the customer can take possession of them.

The purpose of this exercise is to look at the way exchange works as it moves from its simplest stage to more complex stages. We will focus on three basic forms of exchange: (a) decentralized exchange, (b) centralized exchange, and (c) centralized exchange through marketing middleman.

To simplify our study, we will look at the way exchange evolves in a small barter economy. A money system would speed trading, but it would not change the basic nature of how and why markets and marketing middlemen develop.

Assignment

The following case about the "Banana Republic" shows important aspects of the evolution of exchange. Questions appear at various points throughout the case to test your understanding of the material--and especially the implications for a highly developed economy like the United States. Read the case carefully and answer the questions--*as they appear*--in the space provided.

BANANA REPUBLIC

Banana Republic is a small, developing nation whose population is mostly self-sufficient family units. Most of the goods used in a household are produced by members of the household. Sometimes, some families manage to produce a small surplus of goods and want to exchange their extra goods with other families who also have extra goods.

Recently, the people of Banana Republic began to see that some household needs could be filled better by exchange than by production. For example, one family might be better at making shoes and another at growing vegetables. If both families were to concentrate on producing the goods they can make best and then trade, both may get better quality products in larger quantities. In other words, exchange provides a way of getting the advantages of specialization in production.

Decentralized Exchange

Garden Village, a small town located within the Banana Republic, consists of five widely scattered families. Each family specializes in producing only the kinds of goods that it can make best. So, each family has to exchange its goods directly with four other families to get needed articles. The network of exchange in Garden Village is shown in Figure 1-1a. Ten separate transactions are needed to carry out decentralized exchange--with the five families having to seek each other out to complete each transaction.

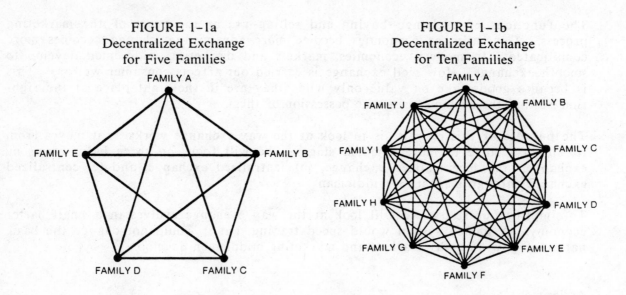

FIGURE 1-1a
Decentralized Exchange
for Five Families

FIGURE 1-1b
Decentralized Exchange
for Ten Families

1. Decentralized exchange becomes extremely complex as the population increases in size. For example, Figure 1-1b shows what the network of exchange would look like in Garden Village if there were ten families instead of five. If you were to count all of the connecting lines, you would find that 45 separate transactions would be required to carry out decentralized exchange among the ten families. (Picture in your mind what the network of decentralized exchange would look like for a city of 1,000,000 people!) Calculate the number of separate transactions that would be required to carry out decentralized exchange if there were: (a) 100 families living in Garden Village; (b) 2,500 families. Show your work.

    Hint: The number of transactions (T) necessary to carry out decentralized exchange is:

$$T = \frac{n(n-1)}{2},$$

where n is the number of producers and each makes only one article. For example, we saw in Figure 1-1a that ten transactions were required when there were five families engaged in decentralized exchange. This fact could also have been determined mathematically using the above formula as follows:

$$T = \frac{5(5 - 1)}{2} = 10.$$

a)   100 families:

b)   2,500 families:

Centralized Exchange

The people in Garden Village soon saw that in spite of the benefits of specialization, the process of decentralized exchange was most inefficient and inconvenient. For one thing, all five traders probably had to travel and seek each other out to complete each transaction. Also, there was no guarantee that each family would be home and would have goods to trade at any given time. Long-distance trips were often wasted when no exchange could take place.

To remedy this situation, the villagers created a *central market* to make exchange easier and allow greater time for production. All agreed to meet together at the marketplace each Saturday at noon to trade goods. Exchange was easier when all five traders met at the same time and place. A total of only five trips were required--one by each family--although ten separate transactions were still needed as shown in Figure 1-2.

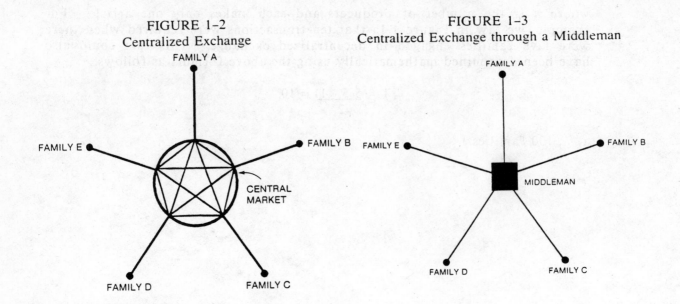

FIGURE 1-2
Centralized Exchange

FIGURE 1-3
Centralized Exchange through a Middleman

Centralized Exchange through Middlemen

The process of exchange was made much easier in Garden Village by the use of a central market. Soon, however, the operation of the market was taken over by a new resident--called a "middleman." The new villager came to town without any special production skills. Trying to develop some specialty to provide for the needs of his family, he noticed that while the villagers benefited a lot from specialization in production, the exchange process was very complicated. Even with a central market, much time and effort were needed to complete all transactions between families. So, he decided to open up a trading business to serve the local market.

The five producing families of Garden Village now exchange with the middleman rather than with each other. The families bring all they want to trade to the middleman--trading with him for different goods. The baker, for example, exchanges bread for other items needed by his household. And he does this all in a single transaction--rather than through four separate transactions with the other producers in Garden Village. The total number of transactions for the entire village is cut in half from ten to five--as each family trades only with the middleman. This is shown in Figure 1-3.

By specializing in trading, the middleman transfers goods from producer to consumer with less effort than would be involved in direct trading. He does this by reducing the number of transactions involved in creating complete assortments of goods for every household. In payment for his services, the middleman keeps a small portion of each producer's output to satisfy the needs of his own family.

2. In our simple example of an economy with five producers, the presence of a marketing middleman reduced the number of exchange transactions from 10 to 5. Had there been ten producing families, the number of transactions would have been reduced from 45 to 10. What would the reduction have been if there were: (a) 100 producing families; (b) 2,500 producing families?

Hint: You may have noticed that the number of transactions required in a central market using a marketing middleman is always equal to *n*, the number of producers in the market. Recall how the number of transactions, (T), needed to carry out decentralized exchange was calculated in Question 1. The reduction in transactions, (R), which is due to a marketing middleman is simply the difference between the transactions necessary in a decentralized market and the transactions using a middleman, or:

$$R = \frac{n(n-1)}{2} - n.$$

a)   100 families:

b)   2,500 families:

3.   Which of the three forms of exchange--decentralized, centralized, or centralized through middlemen--created the greatest amount of economic utility for Garden Village? Explain your answer.

4. From a macro-marketing viewpoint, would you say that exchange tends to be carried out *more* or *less* efficiently when it takes place through marketing middlemen rather than directly between producers and consumers? Why?

Question for Discussion

If there are advantages--from a macro-marketing viewpoint--in using marketing middlemen, why do so many people wish to "eliminate the middleman"?

Exercise 1-3

How marketing functions create economic utility

Introduction

Marketing has been defined as the "creation and delivery of a standard of living." In economic terms, marketing contributes to the consumer welfare through the creation of three of the four basic kinds of economic utility--*time*, *place*, and *possession* utility. Further, marketing may also guide development of *form* utility.

The marketing process does not take place automatically. It requires that certain marketing functions or activities be performed by various marketing institutions-- and by *consumers* themselves. The following eight functions are essential to the marketing of all goods: buying, selling, transporting, storing, grading, financing, risk-taking, and market information. No matter how simple or complex the marketing process is, these functions must be performed. Some functions may be performed several times to facilitate the marketing of a given product, while others may be performed only once. At times, the performance of a function may be shifted from one member of a marketing system to another. For example, some modern wholesalers and retailers shift the burden of storing goods back to manufacturers. But, the fact remains that each of the eight functions must be performed by someone at least once before any good can be marketed--none can be eliminated.

Assignment

This assignment illustrates how the performance of marketing functions creates economic utility. Read the following case carefully and then answer the questions that follow in the space provided.

FOOD LAND GROCERY STORE

Mary and Jim Lattin are a young couple who live and work in a large city. They shop for most of their food--including meat--at Food Land, a small grocery store located near their apartment. The Lattins inspect the packages of meat and select the amount and type of meat they want for their meals that week. They have always been happy with the quality and selection of meat at Food Land--and they like the store's "satisfaction or your money back" guarantee.

Food Land is too small to have a big butcher department and meat freezer. Instead, the manager of the Food Land meat counter buys fresh meat from Meat

Specialties, a wholesale butcher. The wholesaler keeps a large quantity of bulk meat in cold storage--and then cuts grade-A stew beef, steaks, roasts, hamburger, and other selections to fill orders from Food Land and its other grocery store customers. The wholesaler delivers the meat to Food Land each morning before the store opens. At the end of the month the wholesaler bills Food Land for its purchases.

This arrangement seems to work well. The meat counter manager pays close attention to what cuts of meat his local customers want--and he orders carefully. He packages the meat in convenient serving sizes. He is also happy to handle special requests. As a result, Food Land can offer a selection that meets most customers' needs. If the manager orders too much of a certain type of meat and it has not sold within a few days, he marks down the price--to prompt a quicker sale.

Based on your analysis of this description, answer the following questions.

1.   What kind(s) of economic utility is created by Food Land for its customers?

   _____

   _____

   _____

2.   Does Food Land help to resolve discrepancies of assortment between food producers and consumers? Briefly explain your answer.

   _____

   _____

   _____

   _____

3.   The eight basic marketing functions are listed below. Check Yes or No whether each function is performed by someone in this description. If "Yes," explain *when* and *by whom* each function was performed. If "No," explain why not.

   a)   Buying: Yes _____   No _____   Explain.

   _____

   _____

   _____

   _____

b)   Selling: Yes _____ No _____ Explain.

_____

_____

_____

c)   Transporting: Yes _____ No _____ Explain.

_____

_____

_____

d)   Storing: Yes _____ No _____ Explain.

_____

_____

_____

e)   Grading: Yes _____ No _____ Explain.

_____

_____

_____

f)   Financing: Yes _____ No _____ Explain.

_____

_____

_____

g) Risk-taking: Yes _____ No _____ Explain.

_____

_____

_____

_____

h) Market information: Yes _____ No _____ Explain.

_____

_____

_____

_____

Like most young couples, the Lattins are always interested in ways to make their budget stretch further. Recently, a friend told them about a meat packing plant that is about 30 miles from their city. The packing plant will sell direct to a consumer--if the consumer buys a whole side of beef. It works like this. The customer calls the meat packing plant and agrees on a price and time he will pick up the purchase. The packing plant then cuts the side of beef into large pieces and wraps them in freezer paper. The customer must pay with cash when he picks up the meat.

The Lattins' friend has never actually purchased meat this way--but has heard that on a per pound basis the price is about 20 percent cheaper than the same selection of meat would be at a grocery store.

4. If the Lattins were to buy meat directly from the packing plant, they would probably need to perform some of the basic marketing functions themselves. Each of the basic marketing functions is listed below. For each function, check "yes" or "no" to indicate if the Lattins would need to perform this function. In addition, briefly explain any difficulties you think the Lattins might face in trying to perform the function.

a) Buying: Yes _____ No _____ Explain:

_____

_____

_____

_____

b)   Selling: Yes _____ No _____ Explain:

_____

_____

_____

_____

c)   Transporting: Yes _____ No _____ Explain:

_____

_____

_____

_____

d)   Storing: Yes _____ No _____ Explain:

_____

_____

_____

_____

e)   Grading: Yes _____ No _____ Explain:

_____

_____

_____

f)   Financing: Yes _____ No _____ Explain:

_____

_____

_____

g) Risk-taking: Yes _____ No _____ Explain:

_____

_____

_____

_____

h) Market information: Yes _____ No _____ Explain:

_____

_____

_____

_____

Question for Discussion

Name a product for which all eight marketing functions do *not* need to be performed by someone somewhere in the marketing system.

Exercise 1-4

Revenue, cost, and profit relationships

This exercise is based on computer-aided problem number 1--Revenue, Cost and Profit Relationships. A complete description of the problem appears on page 15 of *Computer-Aided Problems to Accompany Basic Marketing.*

This is a practice problem--to get you started with the PLUS computer program and help you see how spreadsheet analysis will help you with more complicated problems.

The marketing manager for Firm B is interested in increasing profits. He knows that he can do this by increasing revenue, by decreasing costs--or, more generally, developing a marketing mix that results in a greater difference between revenue and cost.

1. Write down Firm B's quantity sold, price, revenue, cost, and profit as it appears on the initial spreadsheet.

    Price: _____   Cost: _____

    Quantity: _____   Profit: _____

    Revenue: _____

2. Revenue will increase if a higher price can be charged and the quantity sold remains unchanged. Change Firm B's price to $15.00 and record the resulting profit.

    Profit: _____

3. Revenue will increase if a larger quantity can be sold at the same price. Change the price on the spreadsheet back to $12.00, and increase the quantity sold to 1,250. Record the resulting profit.

    Profit: _____

4. Profit will increase if the same revenue can be achieved at lower cost. Change the quantity sold back to 1,000 and decrease the total cost amount to $7,000. Record the result profit.

    Profit: _____

5. The marketing manager for Firm B would like to increase profits. He is thinking about lowering his price in the hope of selling a larger quantity. He thinks that he might sell 1,100 units at a price of $11.75, 1,150 units at $11.25, or 1,170 units at $10.75. If he is right about these price-quantity relationships, what price would you recommend? Why?

6. As another alternative, the manager is thinking of improving his product and charging a higher price--about $14.00 a unit. To improve the product, he will have to spend money to modify the machine that makes the product. His total cost will increase to $14,000. In addition, he will only be able to produce a maximum of 1,200 units. Assuming that he could sell all 1,200 units, approximately what price would he have to be able to charge to make at least as much profit as in the best alternative from the question above. (Hint: change the quantity sold and total cost values on the spreadsheet, and then do a What If analysis. In the What If analysis, select price for Firm B as the variable to vary and vary it between a minimum of $14.00 and a maximum of $14.20. Select profit as the value to display. Study the results and compare them to your answer to question 5.)

   Approximate price he would have to charge: _____, which would result in a profit of _____.

7. If the manager for Firm B decided that customers would only pay $14.00 for the improved product, approximately how many would he have to sell to make some profit (that is, profit greater than 0)? Hint: change Firm B's price to $14.00 on the spreadsheet, and then do a What If analysis--selecting quantity as the value to vary and profit as the value to display.

   Quantity he would have to sell: _____ units.

Chapter 2

Marketing's role within the firm

What This Chapter Is About

Chapter 2 shows how important micro-marketing can be within a firm. In particular, the "marketing concept" and the evolution of firms from a production to a marketing orientation is explained. Then, the importance of understanding the difference between a production orientation and a marketing orientation is discussed.

The nature of the marketing management process is introduced--and the importance of marketing strategy planning is explained. The four Ps--Product, Price, Place, and Promotion--are introduced as the controllable elements which the marketing manager blends into a marketing mix to satisfy a particular target market. It is very important for you to understand the four Ps--because planning the four Ps is the major concern of the rest of the text.

The chapter gives a very necessary overview to what is coming. Study it carefully so you can understand how the material in the following chapters will fit together.

Important Terms

simple trade era, p. 26
production era, p. 26
sales era, p. 27
marketing department era, p. 27
marketing company era, p. 27
marketing concept, p. 28
production orientation, p. 28
marketing orientation, p. 28
marketing management process, p. 34
strategic (management) planning, p. 35
marketing strategy, p. 35
target market, p. 35
marketing mix, p. 35

target marketing, p. 36
mass marketing, p. 36
channel of distribution, p. 39
personal selling, p. 39
mass selling, p. 39
advertising, p. 39
publicity, p. 39
sales promotion, p. 39
marketing plan, p. 42
implementation, p. 43
operational decisions, p. 43
marketing program, p. 44

True-False Questions

___ T 1. The simple trade era was a time when families traded or sold their "surplus" output to local middlemen who sold these goods to other consumers or distant middlemen.

F ~~T~~ 2. Marketing departments are usually formed when firms go from the "production era" to the "sales era."

T 3. A company has moved into the "marketing company era" when, in addition to short run marketing planning, the total company effort is guided by the marketing concept.

F 4. The marketing concept says that a firm should aim all its efforts at satisfying customers, even if this proves to be unprofitable.

F 5. The term "marketing orientation" means making products which are easy to produce and then trying to sell them.

F 6. The three basic ideas included in the definition of the marketing concept are: a customer orientation, a total company effort, and sales as an objective.

F 7. There are no functional departments in a firm that has adopted the marketing concept.

F 8. The marketing concept was very quickly accepted, especially among producers of industrial products.

T 9. In the last decade, service industries have adopted the marketing concept more and more.

F 10. Because they don't try to earn a profit, the marketing concept is not very useful for nonprofit organizations.

T 11. The marketing management process consists of (1) planning marketing activities, (2) directing the implementation of the plans, and (3) controlling these plans.

F ~~T~~ ~~F~~ 12. Strategic (management) planning is a managerial process of developing and maintaining a match between the resources of the production department and its product opportunities.

F 13. Marketing strategy planning is the process of deciding how best to sell the products the firm produces.

T 14. A marketing strategy specifies a target market and a related marketing mix.

F 15. A target market consists of a group of consumers who are usually quite different.

T 16. A marketing mix consists of the uncontrollable variables which a company puts together to satisfy a target market.

T 17. Target marketing aims a marketing mix at some specific target customers.

F ~~18.~~ The mass marketing approach is more production-oriented than marketing-oriented.

F 19. The terms "mass marketing" and "mass marketer" mean the same thing.

F 20. The problem with target marketing is that it limits the firm to small market segments.

F 21. The four "Ps" are: Product, Promotion, Price, and Personnel.

T ~~22.~~ The customer should not be considered part of a "marketing mix."

T 23. The Product area is concerned with developing the right physical good, service, or blend of both for the target market.

F 24. A channel of distribution must include several kinds of middlemen and specialists.

T ~~25.~~ Personal selling and advertising are both forms of sales promotion.

F 26. Price is the most important of the four Ps.

F 27. The marketing mix should be set before the best target market is selected.

F 28. A marketing plan and a marketing strategy mean the same thing.

T 29. Implementation means putting the marketing plan into operation.

F 30. Short-run decisions that stay within the overall guidelines set during strategy planning are called implementation decisions.

T 31. A marketing program may consist of several marketing plans.

T 32. An extremely good marketing plan may be carried out badly and still be profitable, while a poor but well-implemented plan can lose money.

F 33. Henry Ford was "production-oriented" because he decided to mass produce cars before he asked whether there was a market for such cars.

T 34. In the last decade, the airline industry has become much more marketing-oriented.

F 35. Well-planned marketing strategies usually can ignore the uncontrollable variables.

1. T, p. 26	13. F, p. 35	25. F, p. 39
2. F, p. 27	14. T, p. 35	26. F, p. 39
3. T, p. 27	15. F, p. 35	27. F, p. 40
4. F, p. 28	16. F, p. 35	28. F, p. 42
5. F, p. 28	17. T, p. 36	29. T, p. 43
6. F, p. 28	18. T, p. 36	30. F, p. 43
7. F, p. 29	19. F, p. 36	31. T, p. 44
8. F, p. 32	20. F, p. 36	32. T, p. 45
9. T, p. 32	21. F, p. 37	33. F, p. 45
10. F, p. 32	22. T, p. 38	34. T, p. 47
11. T, p. 34	23. T, p. 38	35. F, p. 47
12. F, p. 35	24. F, p. 39	

Multiple-Choice Questions (Circle the correct response)

1. A firm that focuses its attention primarily on "selling" its present products in order to meet or beat competition is operating in which of the following "management eras"?
   a. Production era
   b. Sales era
   c. Marketing department era
   d. Marketing company era
   e. Advertising era

2. Which of the following best explains what the "marketing concept" means:
   a. Firms should spend more money on marketing than they have in the past.
   b. A firm's main emphasis should be on the efficient utilization of its resources.
   c. All of a firm's activities and resources should be organized to satisfy the needs of its customers--at a profit.
   d. A company's chief executive should previously have been a marketing manager.
   e. A firm should always attempt to give customers what they need regardless of the cost involved.

3. The difference between "production orientation" and "marketing orientation" is best explained as follows:
   a. there are no separate functional departments in a marketing-oriented firm.
   b. in a marketing-oriented firm, the total system's effort is guided by what individual departments would like to do.
   c. production-oriented firms usually do not have a marketing manager.
   d. in a marketing-oriented firm, every department's activities are guided by what customers need and what the firm can deliver at a profit.
   e. all major decisions are based on extensive marketing research studies in marketing-oriented firms.

4. Which of the following is one of three basic marketing management jobs?
   a. To direct the implementation of plans
   b. To control the plans in actual operation
   c. To plan marketing activities
   d. All of the above

5. The marketing management process:
   a. includes the on-going job of planning marketing activities.
   b. is mainly concerned with obtaining continuous customer feedback.
   c. involves finding opportunities and planning marketing strategies, but does not include the management tasks of implementing and control.
   d. is called "strategic planning."
   e. Both a and d are true statements.

6. A marketing strategy consists of two interrelated parts. These are:
   a. selection of a target market and implementing the plan.
   b. selection of a target market and development of a marketing mix.
   c. selection and development of a marketing mix.
   d. finding attractive opportunities and developing a marketing mix.
   e. finding attractive opportunities and selecting a target market.

7. Marketing strategy planners should recognize that:
   a. target markets should not be large and spread out.
   b. mass marketing is often very effective and desirable.
   c. firms like General Electric, Sears Roebuck, and Procter & Gamble are too large to aim at clearly defined markets.
   d. target marketing is not limited to small market segments.
   e. the terms "mass marketing" and "mass marketers" mean essentially the same thing.

8. A marketing mix consists of:
   a. policies, procedures, plans, and personnel.
   b. the customer and the "four Ps."
   c. all variables, controllable and uncontrollable.
   d. product, price, promotion, and place.
   e. none of the above.

9. Which of the following statements about marketing mix variables is *false*?
   a. "Promotion" includes personal selling, mass selling, and sales promotion.
   b. The term "Product" refers to services as well as physical goods.
   c. A channel of distribution does not have to include any middlemen.
   d. Generally speaking, "Price" is more important than "Place."
   e. The needs of a target market virtually determine the nature of an appropriate marketing mix.

10. A "marketing plan":
    a. is just another term for "marketing strategy."
    b. consists of several "marketing programs."
    c. includes the time-related details for carrying out a marketing strategy.
    d. is a strategy without all the operational decisions.
    e. ignores implementation and control details.

11. A "marketing program":
   a. is another name for a particular marketing mix.
   b. blends several different marketing plans.
   c. consists of a target market and the marketing mix.
   d. is primarily concerned with all of the details of implementing a marketing plan.
   e. must be set before a target market can be selected.

12. The Ford and General Motors examples in the text all serve to illustrate that:
   a. good implementation and control is usually more important than good planning.
   b. strategy planning is not relevant for nonmarketing people.
   c. an effective marketing strategy guarantees future success.
   d. consumers want only high-quality products.
   e. creative strategy planning is needed for survival.

Answers to Multiple-Choice Questions

1. b, p. 27
2. c, p. 28
3. d, p. 28
4. d, p. 34

5. a, p. 34
6. b, p. 35
7. d, p. 36
8. d, p. 37

9. d, p. 39
10. c, p. 42
11. b, p. 44
12. e, p. 47

Exercise 2-1

Marketing-oriented vs. production-oriented firms

Introduction

Business firms can be classified as either "production-oriented" or "marketing-oriented," depending on whether they have adopted the "marketing concept." The marketing concept is a modern business philosophy which simply states that a firm should aim all its efforts at satisfying its customers--at a profit. This philosophy implies a total management commitment to (1) a customer orientation, (2) a total company effort, and (3) profit, not just sales, as an objective of the firm.

In general, a production-oriented firm tries to get customers to buy what the firm has produced, while a marketing-oriented firm tries to produce and sell what customers need. Actually, the terms "production-oriented" and "marketing-oriented" should be viewed as opposite ends of a continuum along which different firms could be placed. But it is often useful to classify a firm as being *mainly* production- or marketing-oriented.

In practice, however, there is no simple way of identifying the two types of firms. Instead, one must look for subtle "clues" to help decide whether a firm is production-oriented or marketing-oriented. These clues can take many forms, such as the attitudes of management toward customers, the firm's organization structure, and its methods and procedures.

Assignment

This exercise gives you some practice in identifying production-oriented and marketing-oriented firms. You will be given pairs of firms--and a "clue" about each firm. On the basis of these clues, you must decide which one of the two firms is more marketing-oriented and which is more production-oriented.

For each pair of firms, print an *M* before the firm that you think is marketing-oriented and a *P* before the firm that is production-oriented--and then briefly explain your answers. (Note: each set should have an *M* and a *P*--you *must* make a choice.) The first pair is answered for you as an example.

Orientation		Clues

1.   **P**   Firm A: "We try to sell the products that we make."

      M   Firm B: "We try to make the products that customers need and want to buy."

Firm A is interested in "doing its own thing," while Firm B has focused its efforts on producing what customers want and need.

2.   _____   Firm A: "It costs at least $15.00 to produce a high quality dress shirt."

  _____   Firm B: "Our customers don't always want to pay the high price that usually goes with a really high quality dress shirt."

3.   _____   Firm A: "Our transportation costs are too high. We'll have to use a cheaper mode of transportation, even if it means that it will take customers longer to get their orders."

  _____   Firm B: "Sure our transportation costs are high. But how many customers would we lose if we were frequently late in getting products to customers?"

4. _____ Firm A: "It would cost us too much to lease a store in the shopping center. We'll locate our supermarket a few blocks away where the land is cheaper. We can depend on our low prices and the popularity of our own brands to bring the customers to us."

_____ Firm B: "People today want the convenience of one-stop shopping and we've got to go where the customers are. It will cost us more to lease a building in the shopping center, but we'll do a larger volume and that's the key to profit in the food business."

5. _____ Firm A: "As finance manager, my job is to determine how many units it will be profitable for us to sell at the price customers are willing to pay."

_____ Firm B: "As advertising manager, my job is to develop an advertising campaign that will create demand for as many units as we can produce. After all, the higher the sales, the higher the profits."

6. _____ Firm A: "Our Research and Development group has developed a new type of potato chip that we could produce at low cost with the excess capacity in our cereal plant. Let's see if the sales force can sell it at a profit."

_____ Firm B: Marketing research shows that some customers want potato chips that are thicker and crunchier. Let's see if our Research and Development group can develop a product that can meet this need, and at the same time make better use of our company resources."

7. _____ Firm A: "How much money will we save if we do not build the new warehouse?"

_____ Firm B: "How much will it improve our customer service if we build the new warehouse?"

8. _____ Firm A: "Our inventories are too high. Let's ask our salespeople why middlemen have stopped buying our product."

_____ Firm B: "Our inventories are too high. Perhaps we could use our most persuasive sales people to recruit some new middlemen."

9. _____ Firm A: "We've given the people in this city one of the finest rapid transit systems in the world, but hardly anyone takes advantage of this energy efficient way of getting around. It's a case of misplaced social values--and something must be done about it."

_____ Firm B: "We've got to find out what it is about our rapid transit system that turns people away. It's a case of the system needing to do a better job of meeting people's needs-- rather than sitting back and waiting for people to see the light."

10. _____ Firm A: "Our profits have been declining. Perhaps we should search for new opportunities to satisfy unfulfilled needs."

_____ Firm B: "Our profits have been declining. Perhaps we should search for ways to cut costs and make more efficient use of our resources."

11. _____ Firm A: "What consumer needs would the proposed new product satisfy?"

_____ Firm B: "I think this new product is a great idea. Let's see what consumers think of it."

12. _____ Firm A: "Our sales have nearly doubled since the sales manager was promoted to president. He's tripled the amount we spend on advertising and personal selling, and he's told the engineers to stick to production and leave product planning to him."

_____ Firm B: "It helps to have an accountant as president. When he took over the company, he found that only 20 percent of our customers accounted for over 80 percent of our sales. We've dropped many of our smaller customers, and now our sales force concentrates its efforts on satisfying those larger accounts that contribute the most to our profits."

Question for Discussion

If, as the text emphasizes, it is so important that firms be marketing-oriented, how is it that many production-oriented firms are not only surviving but apparently operating profitably?

Exercise 2-2

Mass marketing vs. target marketing

Introduction

A marketing manager's planning job is to find attractive market opportunities and develop effective marketing strategies. A "marketing strategy" consists of two interrelated parts: (1) a *target market*--a fairly homogeneous group of customers to whom a company wishes to appeal, and (2) a *marketing mix*--the controllable variables which the company puts together to satisfy this target group.

Here, it is important to see the difference between *mass marketing* and *target marketing* in planning marketing strategies.

Production-oriented firms typically assume that everyone's needs are the same. They try to build universal appeals into a marketing mix which--it is hoped--will attract "everyone." This approach we will call "mass marketing." Marketing-oriented firms, on the other hand, recognize that different customers usually have different needs--so they try to satisfy the needs of some particular group of customers--whose needs are fairly similar--rather than trying to appeal to everyone. This "target marketing" approach--a logical application of the marketing concept--simply means that a marketing strategy should aim at *some* target market.

Assignment

This exercise is designed to illustrate the difference between mass marketing and target marketing. Read each of the following cases carefully, and then (1) indicate in the space provided whether each firm is following a mass-marketing or a target-marketing approach and (2) briefly explain your answers.

1. Acme Products, Corp. has just introduced a new type of lawn sprinkler called "Grow-All Sprinkler" and it is being promoted as the "ultimate lawn sprinkler--more convenient than rain." According to Rainmaker's president, the sprinkler is "absolutely guaranteed" not to leak, rust, or break. Moreover, "it has a unique mechanical timer so that it turns itself off automatically after a set period of time--and when it is on, the water pressure makes it 'crawl' along the hose so that different areas get watered without having to touch or move the sprinkler." Available in several models ranging in price from $40 to $70, the "Grow-All Sprinkler" is expected to sell "in the millions." "This product is so superior," say company officials, "that no household in the United States will want to be without one."

a) Mass marketing _____ Target marketing _____

b) Comments: _____

_____

_____

_____

_____

_____

2. Campbell's, the world's largest soup manufacturer, recently introduced a new line of premium priced, heat-and-serve foods under the "Singles" label. The single-serving package for the foods was designed so that it would work well in microwave ovens--for fast, no-mess cooking. "Singles" foods are aimed primarily at single-person households in the United States--in which the company estimates that the number of main meals eaten alone each day totals more than 22 million. The new product line is also expected to appeal to two-person households. Thus, Campbell's believes that the potential market for "Singles" includes almost one half of the nation's households--but especially those persons who want and can afford the convenience of easily prepared meals in small, no-leftover quantities.

a) Mass marketing _____ Target marketing _____

b) Comments: _____

_____

_____

_____

_____

_____

3. Consumers may eventually enjoy "personalized" magazines--magazines which are tailored to each individual reader's interests in both editorial and advertising content. By combining detailed survey information about respondents with U/Stat Inc.'s computerized collating system, consumer and trade magazine publishers may be able to publish magazines which will be read from cover to cover because every article and ad in the magazine will appeal to each

reader's self-identified interests. Thus, nonsmokers will never receive a magazine with cigarette ads, while smokers will. And skiers can look forward to a lot of articles about skiing, while camera buffs can look forward to many articles about photography. Because of equipment limitations, the "personalized" magazines would have to be limited to a 300,000-500,000 circulation range.

a) Mass marketing _____ Target marketing _____

b) Comments: _____

_____

_____

_____

_____

_____

_____

4. Mac Fitch recently retired after 20 years of service as a cook in the Navy. His long tour of duty took him to almost every part of the world. In the process, he learned to prepare the favorite dishes of many different countries. Mac and his wife--also an outstanding cook--have decided to use their savings to open an "ethnic" restaurant, but with a difference. Customers will be able to try authentic recipes from all over the world. Paul is sure that their restaurant will be an outstanding success. "After all," he says, "one thing you can count on is that everybody enjoys good food. And where else can people get the variety and quality that we can offer?"

a) Mass marketing _____ Target marketing _____

b) Comments: _____

_____

_____

_____

_____

_____

_____

Question for Discussion

A marketing strategy should aim at some target market. But does "target marketing" guarantee that a firm's marketing strategy will be successful?

Exercise 2-3

Developing a unique marketing mix
for each target market

Introduction

Developing a marketing strategy consists of two *interrelated* tasks: (1) selecting a target market and (2) developing the best marketing mix for that target market.

Marketing-oriented firms recognize that not all potential customers have the same needs. Thus, rather than first developing a marketing mix and *then* looking for a market to sell that mix to, marketing-oriented firms first try to determine what kind of mix each possible target market may require. Then they select a target market based on their ability to offer a good marketing mix at a profit.

Assignment

This exercise assumes that different groups of customers in a general market area may have different needs--and therefore may require different marketing mixes. Three possible target markets and alternative marketing mixes are described below for each of four different product types. For each product type, select the marketing mix which would be best for each target market. (*All alternatives must be used, i.e., you cannot use one alternative for two target markets.*) Indicate your selection by writing the letter of the marketing mix in front of the target market you select.

Note: To make it easier for you, each target market consists of only one individual or family, but it should be clear that each individual or family really represents a larger group of potential customers who have similar needs.

I. Product type: Food

Possible Target Markets

_____ (1) Career woman who has just arrived back from an out-of-town business trip at 6:30 pm.

_____ (2) Middle-aged low-income housewife concerned with feeding her large family a well-balanced meal, while operating on a tight budget.

_____ (3) Young housewife who has spent the morning playing tennis and has to rush to pick up her two grade-school children for lunch.

Alternative Marketing Mixes

(a) A box of fried chicken, fries, and some soft drinks at the nearby Kentucky Fried Chicken Restaurant.

(b) Nationally advertised brand of frozen "gourmet" frozen dinners on display in the frozen-food case of a "7-Eleven" convenience food store.

(c) "Market basket" of perishables and canned goods purchased at a large supermarket that features "low everyday prices."

II. Product type: Computer

Possible Target Markets

_____ (1) Sales rep who wants to keep records of his sales calls and prepare short reports for the home office while he travels.

_____ (2) Young working couple who want their child to learn about computers by using educational game programs.

_____ (3) Large insurance firm that frequently has to make many copies of company records, reports, and other documents.

Alternative Marketing Mixes

(a) Powerful mini-computer leased from a manufacturer--such as Digital Equipment--that uses knowledgeable sales people to help the customer decide on the right equipment.

(b) Inexpensive computer that can be connected to a television screen--sold by a mass merchandiser that advertises its discount prices.

(c) Well known brand of portable lap-top computer with built in software--sold through a dealer who provides service and a "loaner" if repairs are needed.

III. Product type: Wine

Possible Target Markets

_____ (1) Wealthy couple planning a dinner for some socially prominent guests.

_____ (2) Young college student going to a "bring your own bottle" party at a friend's apartment.

_____ (3) Young, middle-income, married couple who have invited some friends over for the evening.

Alternative Marketing Mixes

(a) Low-priced, wine cooler, heavily promoted over the radio and sold at a conveniently located party store.

(b) Expensive French wine stocked at a wine store whose owner is a well-known wine expert.

(c) Popular brand of a medium-priced California wine on display in the wine section of a large supermarket.

IV. Product type: Stereo Equipment

Possible Target Markets

_____ (1) Affluent young executive who wants to install a stereo in her penthouse, but doesn't know much about stereo equipment.

_____ (2) Middle-class married couple who are looking for a stereo that will blend in with their living room furniture.

_____ (3) Do-it-yourself enthusiast who wants to add a stereo to the basement recreation room he has just built.

Alternative Marketing Mixes

(a) Popular brand of an AM/FM console stereo with an attractive wood cabinet purchased on credit at a large department store.

(b) Expensive component stereo system, manufactured by a firm with a reputation for high quality and sold by a dealer who specializes in stereo equipment.

(c) Build-it-yourself component stereo kit featured in a catalog published by a large mail-order distributor of electronic equipment.

Question for Discussion

Assuming that a firm cannot satisfy all the needs of all potential customers, what factors should a marketing manager consider before selecting a target market?

Exercise 2-4

Target marketing

This exercise is based on computer-aided problem number 2--Target Marketing. A complete description of the problem appears on page 16 of *Computer-Aided Problems to Accompany Basic Marketing*.

1. Marko's marketing manager is interested in ways to reduce distribution cost-- to increase profits. Marko knows that many customers in the target market want products quickly once they decide to buy. And at present no competitor provides really fast delivery. Marko could switch to air transportation--and that would get products delivered faster and increase the percent of purchasers who would buy its product. But better delivery service would also increase distribution cost per unit sold to $2.50. If Marko were to change to the new distribution system, approximately what share of the target market's purchases would it need to get to earn a total profit of $41,800? (Hint: Set the distribution cost per unit to $2.50 on the spreadsheet, and then do a What If analysis--varying the firm's share of purchases and displaying profit.)

    Market share to earn a profit of $41,800: _____ percent

2. If Marko won this share of the target market's purchases, how many units would it expect to sell? What would its total cost be? What would its total revenue be?

    Quantity sold: _____ units

    Total cost at this quantity: $_____

    Total revenue at this cost: $_____

3. If Marko implemented this strategy, but only won a share of the purchases that was 5 percent less than the percent needed to earn $41,800, what would happen to total profit?

    Profit: _____

4. If Marko were to use air transportation with the mass marketing approach and this added $.50 a unit to distribution cost--resulting in a unit distribution cost of $3.00--approximately what share of purchases would Marko have to win to earn a profit of $41,800? (Hint: change the unit distribution cost on the spreadsheet, and then do a What If analysis as described above. If the first What If analysis does not provide an answer to the question, continue with the What If Analysis using a larger or smaller minimum and maximum value for the share value until you get closer to the answer. In other words, use the What If analysis to help "search" for the answer you need.)

Share of customer purchases: _____ percent

5. If Marko implemented this approach, but only won a share of purchases that was 5 percent less than the percent needed to earn about $41,800, what profit would be earned?

Profit: _____

6. Marko is thinking about doing additional marketing research to help "fine tune" the promotion it is thinking about using with its target marketing strategy. The marketing research will add $4,000 to the total promotion cost, but Marko thinks that the more precisely targeted promotion might increase its share of purchases to 55 percent. If Marko's estimates are correct, would it make sense to spend the extra money on marketing research? Briefly explain the reason for your answer. (Note: do your analysis assuming that distribution cost will be $2.00 per unit, and that other values are as originally planned-- that is, as they appeared on the original spreadsheet.)

_____

_____

7. If the marketing research above cost $10,000 and Marko managers estimated that the improved promotion might increase their share of market to as much as 56 percent of the market, would it make sense to spend the money on the additional marketing research? Why?

_____

_____

8. Marko thinks that it would have to charge an even lower price of $13.70 a unit to win a larger share of the "mass market." If it charged a price $13.70 and its share of purchases in the mass market increased to 25 percent, what profit would be earned?

Profit: $_____

9. If other competitors reacted to Marko's price cut with price cuts of their own, and Marko's share of purchases in the mass market fell back to 20 percent, what profit would be earned?

Profit: $_____

10. Briefly discuss the profit implications of firms trying to compete with each other in the mass market by offering lower and lower prices?

_____

_____

Appendix A

Economics fundamentals

What This Chapter Is About

Appendix A is important to understanding how buyers and sellers look at products and markets. Some of the economist's tools are shown to be useful. In particular, demand and supply curves, and their interaction are discussed. Also, elasticity of demand and supply are explained. They help us understand the nature of competition.

The material in this Appendix is not easy--but it is very important. A good marketing manager does not always "win" in every market because consumers' attitudes are continually changing. But an understanding of the nature of demand and competition in different markets will greatly increase your chances for success. Careful study of this Appendix will build a good economics base for this text (especially Chapters 3, 4, 18, and 19).

Important Terms

law of diminishing demand, p. 51

demand curve, p. 52

inelastic demand, p. 53

elastic demand, p. 54

substitutes, p. 55

supply curve, p. 57

inelastic supply, p. 58

elastic supply, p. 58

equilibrium point, p. 59

consumer surplus, p. 60

True-False Questions

____ 1. Economists usually assume that customers evaluate a given set of alternatives in terms of whether they will make them feel better (or worse) or in some way improve (or change) their situation.

____ 2. "The law of diminishing demand" says that if the price of a product is raised, a greater quantity will be demanded--and if the price of a product is lowered, a smaller quantity will be demanded.

____ 3. A demand schedule may indicate that as prices go lower, the total unit sales increase, but the total revenue decreases.

____ 4. A demand curve is a "picture" of the relationship between price and quantity in a market.

____ 5. Most demand curves slope upward.

___ 6. If total revenue would decrease if price were raised, then demand is said to be elastic.

___ 7. If total revenue would increase if price were lowered, then demand is said to be inelastic.

___ 8. Unitary elasticity of demand means that total revenue remains the same when prices change, regardless of whether price is increased or decreased.

___ 9. A demand curve must be entirely elastic or inelastic; it cannot be both.

___ 10. Whether a product has an elastic or inelastic demand depends on many factors including the availability of substitutes, the importance of the item in the customer's budget, and the urgency of the customer's need in relation to other needs.

___ 11. When only a small number of good "substitutes" are available, demand tends to be quite inelastic.

___ 12. A supply curve shows the quantity of products that will be offered at various possible prices by all suppliers together.

___ 13. An extremely steep or almost vertical supply curve is called elastic because the quantity supplied would not change much if the price were raised.

___ 14. The intersection of demand and supply determines the size of a market and the market price.

___ 15. A market is in equilibrium if the quantity and the price that sellers are willing to offer are equal to the quantity and the price that buyers are willing to accept.

___ 16. "Consumer surplus" is the difference between the value of a purchase and the price the consumer has to pay.

Answers to True-False Questions

1. T, p. 51	7. F, p. 54	13. F, p. 58
2. F, p. 51	8. T, p. 54	14. T, p. 59
3. T, p. 51	9. F, p. 55	15. T, p. 59
4. T, p. 52	10. T, p. 55	16. T, p. 60
5. F, p. 52	11. T, p. 56	
6. T, p. 54	12. T, p. 57	

Multiple-Choice Questions (Circle the correct response)

1. The "law of diminishing demand" says that:
    a. if the price of a product were lowered, a greater quantity would be demanded.
    b. if the price of a product were raised, a greater quantity would be demanded.
    c. the demand for any product will tend to decline over time.
    d. if the price of a product were lowered, a smaller quantity would be demanded.
    e. the more of a product a person buys, the less utility that particular product offers him.

2. A demand curve:
    a. is generally up-sloping from left to right.
    b. is formed by plotting the points from a supply schedule.
    c. shows what quantities would be demanded by potential customers at various possible prices.
    d. shows how total revenue increases as prices decrease.
    e. All of the above are true statements.

3. If a firm's total revenue increases when the price of its product is reduced from $15 to $10, the demand for this product is:
    a. elastic.
    b. inelastic.
    c. unitary elastic.
    d. cannot be determined without looking at the demand curve.

4. Study the following demand schedule:

PRICE	QUANTITY DEMANDED	TOTAL REVENUE
$500	1,000	$500,000
400	2,000	800,000
300	3,000	900,000
200	4,000	800,000
100	5,000	500,000

    This demand schedule shows that the demand for this product is:
    a. elastic.
    b. inelastic.
    c. unitary elastic.
    d. both elastic and inelastic.
    e. This demand schedule cannot be correct because it violates the "law of diminishing demand."

5. The elasticity of demand for a particular product does *not* depend upon:
   a. the availability of substitutes.
   b. the importance of the item in the customer's budget.
   c. the urgency of the customer's need.
   d. how much it costs to produce the product.
   e. All of the above affect the elasticity of demand.

6. Which of the following products would have the most *inelastic* demand for most potential customers?
   a. A home computer
   b. A vacation trip to France
   c. A one-pound package of salt
   d. A pair of designer jeans
   e. A "Big Mac" hamburger

7. A supply curve:
   a. is generally flatter than its supply schedule.
   b. is not affected by production costs.
   c. is generally up-sloping from left to right.
   d. is a picture of the quantities of goods that would be demanded at various possible prices.
   e. All of the above are true statements.

8. Which of the following statements about elasticity of supply is *true*?
   a. If a product's demand curve is elastic, then its supply curve also must be elastic.
   b. A product's elasticity of supply determines its elasticity of demand.
   c. In the short run, the supply curve for most agricultural products is highly elastic.
   d. In the long run, the supply curve for most products is highly inelastic.
   e. None of the above statements are true.

9. Which of the following statements about demand and supply interaction is *true*?
   a. Demand is the sole determiner of price.
   b. A market is said to be in equilibrium when the elasticity of demand equals the elasticity of supply.
   c. The interaction of supply and demand determines the size of the market and the market price.
   d. For a market to be in equilibrium, the price and quantity that buyers are willing to accept must be greater than the price and quantity that suppliers are willing to offer.
   e. All of the above statements are true.

10. Given a situation where there is elastic demand and elastic supply, an *increase* in the quantity suppliers are willing to supply at all possible prices will:
    a. decrease price, but not change quantity demanded.
    b. increase price and decrease quantity demanded.
    c. lower price and increase quantity demanded.
    d. increase price and increase quantity demanded.

11.   The term "consumer surplus" means that:
   a.   consumers never get their money's worth in any transaction.
   b.   there are more needs than there are products to satisfy them.
   c.   consumers don't consume all the products they buy.
   d.   some consumers would be willing to pay more than the market equilibrium price if they had to.
   e.   there are more consumers than there are producers.

Answers to Multiple-Choice Questions

1. a, p. 51
2. c, p. 52
3. a, p. 54
4. d, p. 55

5. d, p. 55
6. c, p. 56
7. c, p. 57
8. e, p. 58

9. c, p. 59
10. c, p. 59
11. d, p. 60

Exercise A-1

Estimating and using demand elasticity

Introduction

"Demand elasticity" is a very useful concept for analyzing the nature of demand and competition in markets. As explained in Appendix A in the text, demand elasticity can be defined in terms of what happens to total revenue when the price of a product is lowered.

a. If total revenue would increase if the price were lowered, then demand is said to be *elastic*.

b. If total revenue would decrease if the price were lowered, then demand is said to be *inelastic*.

c. If total revenue would stay the same if the price were lowered, then we have a special case called *unitary elasticity of demand*.

Different products have different demand elasticities because of factors such as the availability of substitutes, the importance of the item in the customer's budget, and the urgency of the customer's need in relation to other needs.

The elasticity of a firm's demand curve is extremely important to a marketing strategy planner. It provides a shorthand description of the nature of competition and demand facing a firm--often suggesting necessary changes in strategies. For example, a firm with a highly elastic demand curve might have many competitors and would have very little control over the price it could charge for its product. In this case, perhaps the firm should plan a new strategy--one aimed at a different target market with fewer competitors and less elastic demand.

Assignment

This exercise has three parts and is designed to increase your understanding of demand elasticity. The first part focuses on the relationship of demand elasticity to changes in total revenue. The second part shows how demand elasticity can vary in different market situations. The third part shows how product and price are related through demand elasticity.

1. Demand elasticity was defined above in terms of what happens to total revenue when price is lowered. Now complete the following table--showing what happens to total revenue *(TR)* when price is *raised* instead of lowered.

	Elastic demand	Inelastic demand	Unitary elasticity of demand
Price lowered	TR increases	TR decreases	TR remains the same
Price raised			

2. Figure A-1 shows three demand curves--each with a different degree of elasticity. Each of the demand curves represents *one* of the following situations:

a) The demand for one firm's "quality" home computer.
b) The demand for an individual farmer's wheat crop.
c) The demand for natural gas to heat homes during a long cold spell.

In the space provided, state which of the three situations each demand curve most likely represents. Then briefly explain each answer in terms of the factors which can cause demand elasticity to vary in different market situations.

FIGURE A-1

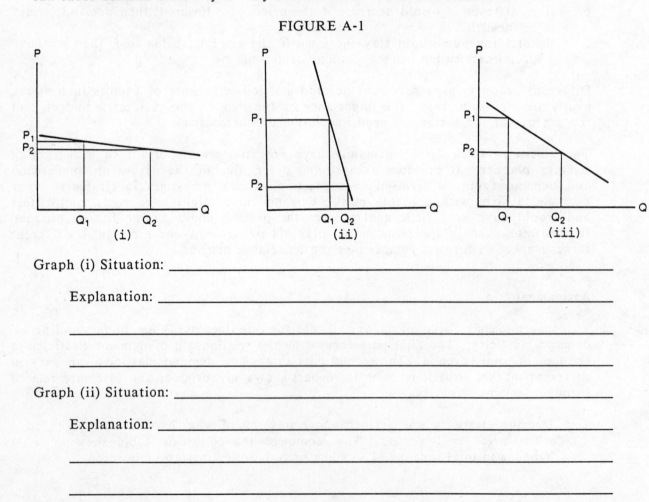

(i) (ii) (iii)

Graph (i) Situation: _____

Explanation: _____

_____

_____

Graph (ii) Situation: _____

Explanation: _____

_____

_____

Graph (iii) Situation: _____

Explanation: _____

_____

_____

3. Read the following paragraph and then answer questions (a) through (c).

Auto-Control Corporation produces and sells computer control devices that are used by industrial firms to automate their equipment. Auto-Control's management is seeking a larger share of the market. Thus, its objective for the coming year is to increase both its dollar sales volume and its market share for the devices--which are currently priced at $3,200. Auto-Control's estimated demand curve for the next year is shown in Figure A-2.

FIGURE A-2

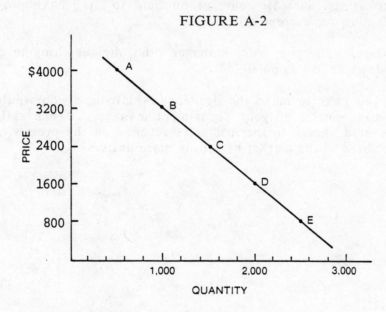

a) Use Figure A-2 to complete the following table:

Demand Schedule of Wall's Presses

Points on Graph	Price per unit	Quantity Demanded per unit	Total Revenue per year
A	$4,000	500	$2,000,000
B	3,200	____	____
C	2,400	____	____
D	1,600	____	____
E	800	____	____

b) Looking at Auto-Control's demand curve and demand schedule, would you describe the demand for the firm's presses as (a) elastic, (b) inelastic, (c) unitary elastic, or (d) both elastic and inelastic? Explain your answer.

---

c) As president of Auto-Control, you have called a meeting of top management to discuss the firm's pricing for the coming year. After explaining the purpose of the meeting, you have asked for comments and suggestions.

"If we want to increase our dollar sales revenue, then we must raise our selling price," suggests your finance manager.

"That may increase our sales revenue," replies your production manager, "but if we want to capture a larger share of the market, then the only answer is to increase our production to its maximum level--while maintaining our current price."

"Nonsense," yells your sales manager, "the obvious thing to do is cut our price down as low as possible."

Since you have to make the decision, explain how you would resolve the conflicting advice of your department managers. Then state what price Wall should charge to increase sales revenue on the presses *and* capture a larger share of the market by selling more units.

Question for Discussion

Consider the three market situations in Question 2. If a firm's demand curve is elastic, does the demand curve for the industry also have to be elastic? What if the firm's demand curve is inelastic?

Chapter 3

Finding target market opportunities with market segmentation

What This Chapter Is About

In this chapter you will learn how alert marketers find attractive market opportunities--ones that enable them to get a competitive advantage. Creatively defining a firm's markets (product-markets) can suggest many possibilities--and how to do this should be studied carefully. The focus is on how you can use market segmentation to identify possible target markets. Segmenting markets is vital to marketing strategy planning--but it is often difficult for beginners. So, a practical seven-step approach to segmenting markets is presented and illustrated. You will also see how more sophisticated approaches--like clustering and positioning--are used to make better market segmentation decisions.

To improve your understanding, try to apply the seven-step approach to a market in which you actually buy something. Then see how the dimensions in *your* own market segment affect the marketing mix which is offered to you. There is a logic to marketing strategy planning--marketing mixes flow directly from the characteristics of target markets. Try to get a feel for this interaction as you learn how to segment markets.

This chapter makes it clear why it is important to understand markets--and customers. In later chapters, you will build on this base--as you learn more about the demographic and behavioral dimensions of the consumer market and the buying behavior of intermediate customers.

This is a very important--if difficult--chapter, and deserves careful study. It is difficult because it requires *creative* thinking about markets--but this can also be a challenge, and help you learn how to find your own "breakthrough opportunity."

Important Terms

breakthrough opportunities, p. 65
competitive advantage, p. 65
market penetration, p. 65
market development, p. 66
product development, p. 66
diversification, p. 66
market, p. 67
generic market, p. 68
product-market, p. 68
market segmentation, p. 72
segmenting, p. 73

market segment, p. 73
single target market approach, p. 76
multiple target market approach, p. 76
combined target market approach, p. 76
combiners, p. 76
segmenters, p. 77
qualifying dimensions, p. 80
determining dimensions, p. 80
clustering techniques, p. 88
positioning, p. 90

True-False Questions

___ 1. Often, attractive opportunities are fairly close to markets the firm already knows.

___ 2. "Breakthrough opportunities" are ones which help innovators develop hard-to-copy marketing strategies that will be very profitable for a long time.

___ 3. A firm with a "competitive advantage" has a marketing mix that the target market sees as better than a competitor's mix.

___ 4. Marketing opportunities involving present markets and present products are called "market penetration" opportunities.

___ 5. A "market development" opportunity would involve a firm offering new or improved products to its present markets.

___ 6. When it comes to choosing among different types of opportunities, most firms tend to be production-oriented and usually think first of diversification.

___ 7. A market consists of a group of potential customers with similar needs.

___ 8. A generic market is a market with broadly similar needs and sellers offering various and often diverse ways of satisfying those needs.

___ 9. A product-market is a market with very similar needs and sellers offering various close substitute ways of satisfying those needs.

___ 10. A generic market description looks at markets narrowly--and from a producer's viewpoint.

___ 11. A firm's "relevant market for finding opportunities" should be bigger than its present product-market--but not so big that the firm couldn't expand and be an important competitor in this market.

___ 12. Just identifying the geographic boundaries of a firm's present market can suggest new marketing opportunities.

___ 13. A generic market description should include both customer-related and product-related terms.

___ 14. Effective market segmentation requires a two-step process: (1) naming broad product-markets and (2) segmenting these broad product-markets into more homogeneous sub-markets--also called product-markets--for the purpose of selecting target markets and developing suitable marketing mixes.

___ 15. Naming markets is a disaggregating process.

___ 16. Segmenting is an aggregating process.

___ 17. When segmenting markets, "good" market segments are ones which are heterogeneous within, homogeneous between, substantial, and operational.

___ 18. The multiple target market approach combines two or more homogeneous sub-markets into one larger target market as a basis for one strategy.

___ 19. A segmenter is usually attempting to satisfy a sub-market with its own unique demand curve--and therefore must settle for a smaller sales potential than a combiner.

___ 20. Customer-related segmenting dimensions are always more effective than situation-related dimensions.

___ 21. The determining dimensions may help identify the "core features" which will have to be offered to everyone in the broad product-market.

___ 22. The first step in segmenting consumer markets is to name the broad product-market area to be segmented.

___ 23. The "seven-step approach" cannot be used for industrial markets.

___ 24. The "seven-step approach" for consumer and industrial markets is similar except for the first step.

___ 25. Clustering techniques try to find similar patterns within sets of customer-related data.

___ 26. "Positioning" refers to a packaged goods manufacturer's efforts to obtain the best possible shelf or display location in retail stores.

___ 27. Positioning analysis is useful for combining but not for segmenting.

___ 28. The only way to "reposition" a product is to make some physical change in the product.

Answers to True-False Questions

1. T, p. 64	11. T, p. 70	21. F, p. 82
2. T, p. 65	12. T, p. 71	22. T, p. 83
3. T, p. 65	13. F, p. 71	23. F, p. 87
4. T, p. 65	14. T, p. 72	24. T, p. 88
5. F, p. 66	15. T, p. 72	25. T, p. 88
6. F, p. 67	16. T, p. 73	26. F, p. 88
7. F, p. 67	17. F, p. 75	27. F, p. 91
8. T, p. 68	18. F, p. 76	28. F, p. 92
9. T, p. 68	19. F, p. 78	
10. F, p. 69	20. F, p. 80	

Multiple-Choice Questions (Circle the correct response)

1. Breakthrough opportunities:
   a. are so rare that they should be pursued even when they do not match the firm's resources and objectives.
   b. seldom occur within or close to a firm's present markets.
   c. are especially important in our increasingly competitive markets.
   d. are those which a firm's competitors can copy quickly.
   e. are best achieved by trying to hold onto a firm's current market share.

2. When a firm tries to increase sales by selling its present products in new markets, this is called:
   a. market penetration.
   b. market development.
   c. product development.
   d. diversification.
   e. market integration.

3. A market consists of:
   a. a group of potential customers with similar needs.
   b. various kinds of products with similar characteristics.
   c. sellers offering substitute ways of satisfying needs.
   d. all the firms within a particular industry.
   e. both a and c.

4. A market in which sellers offer various close substitute ways of satisfying the market's needs is called a:
   a. generic market.
   b. relevant market.
   c. product-market.
   d. central market.
   e. homogeneous market.

5. Which of the following is the best example of a "generic market"?
   a. The expensive ten-speed bicycle market
   b. The U.S. college student creative expression market
   c. The photographic market
   d. The pet food market
   e. The teen-age market

6. A firm's "relevant market for finding opportunities":
   a. should be as large as possible.
   b. should have no geographic limits.
   c. should be no larger than its present product-market.
   d. should always be named in product-related terms.
   e. None of the above is a true statement.

7. Market segmentation:
   a. tries to find heterogeneous sub-markets within a market.
   b. means the same thing as marketing strategy planning.
   c. assumes that most sub-markets can be satisfied by the same marketing mix.
   d. assumes that any market is likely to consist of sub-markets.
   e. All of the above are true statements.

8. Naming broad product-markets is:
   a. an assorting process
   b. a disaggregating process
   c. a segmenting process
   d. an accumulating process
   e. an aggregating process

9. Segmenting:
   a. is essentially a disaggregating or "break it down" process.
   b. assumes that all customers can be grouped into homogeneous and profitable market segments.
   c. tries to aggregate together individuals who have similar needs and characteristics.
   d. usually results in firms aiming at smaller and less profitable markets.
   e. assumes that each individual should be treated as a separate target market.

10. "Good" market segments are those which are:
    a. heterogeneous within.
    b. operational.
    c. homogeneous between.
    d. substantial--meaning large enough to minimize operating costs.
    e. all of the above.

11. Having segmented its market, the Stuart Corp. has decided to treat each of two sub-markets as a separate target market requiring a different marketing mix. Apparently, Stuart is following the _____ target market approach.
    a. single
    b. combined
    c. multiple

12. Segmenting and combining are two alternate approaches to developing market-oriented strategies. Which of the following statements concerning these approaches is *true*?
    a. Combiners treat each sub-market as a separate target market.
    b. Segmenters try to develop a marketing mix that will have general appeal to several market segments.
    c. A combiner combines the demand curve in several markets into one demand curve.
    d. A segmenter assumes that the whole market consists of a fairly homogeneous group of customers.
    e. Both segmenters and combiners try to satisfy some people very well rather than a lot of people fairly well.

13. Customer-related (rather than situation-related) segmenting dimensions include:
    a. benefits offered.
    b. buying situation.
    c. brand familiarity.
    d. family life cycle.
    e. consumption or use patterns.

14. Which of the following types of dimensions would be the most important if one were particularly interested in why some target market was likely to buy a particular brand within a product-market?
    a. Primary dimensions
    b. Secondary dimensions
    c. Qualifying dimensions
    d. Determining dimensions
    e. Both a and c above.

15. The "seven-step approach" to segmenting markets:
    a. minimizes the need for management judgment and intuition.
    b. applies only to consumer markets.
    c. requires extensive market research and computer analysis.
    d. uses customer need dimensions, ignoring demographic and life-style dimensions.
    e. None of the above is a true statement.

16. Which of the following statements about clustering techniques is *true*?
    a. Clustering techniques try to find dissimilar patterns within sets of customer-related data.
    b. Computers are usually needed to search among all of the data for homogeneous groups of people.
    c. Computers identify the relevant dimensions and do the analysis.
    d. A cluster analysis of the toothpaste market indicated that most consumers seek the same benefits.
    e. All of the above are true.

17. "Positioning":
    a. involves a packaged-goods manufacturer's attempt to obtain the best possible shelf space for its products in retail outlets.
    b. is useful for segmenting but not combining.
    c. helps strategy planners see how customers view various brands or products in relation to each other.
    d. applies only to existing products, not new products.
    e. eliminates the need for subjective decision making in product planning.

Answers to Multiple-Choice Questions

1. c, p. 65
2. b, p. 66
3. e, p. 67
4. c, p. 68
5. b, p. 68
6. e, p. 70

7. d, p. 72
8. b, p. 72
9. c, p. 73
10. b, p. 75
11. c, p. 76
12. c, p. 78

13. d, p. 81
14. d, p. 82
15. e, p. 83-88
16. b, p. 88-89
17. c, p. 90-91

Exercise 3-1

Product-markets vs. generic markets

Introduction

A practical first step in searching for breakthrough opportunities is to define the firm's present (or potential) markets. Markets consist of potential customers with similar needs and sellers offering various ways of satisfying those needs.

Markets can be defined very broadly or very narrowly--with either extreme being a potential threat to effective strategy planning. For example, defining its market too broadly as "transportation" could result in General Motors seeing itself in direct competition with manufacturers of airplanes, ships, elevators, bicycles, little red wagons, and perhaps even spaceships! On the other hand, a definition such as "the market for six-passenger motor vehicles with gasoline-powered internal-combustion engines" would be too narrow--and doesn't even identify "potential customers."

While there is no simple and automatic way to define a firm's *relevant* market, marketers should start by defining the relevant generic market and product-market using the 3 and 4 part definitions discussed on pages 70-72 of the text and shown below:

$$\text{Generic Market Definition} \left\{ \begin{array}{c} \text{Product Type} \\ + \\ \text{Customer (User) Needs} \\ + \\ \text{Customer Types} \\ + \\ \text{Geographic Area} \end{array} \right\} \text{Product-Market Definition}$$

It often requires a lot of creativity to think in terms of generic markets and product-markets--but failure to do so can cause strategy planners to overlook breakthrough opportunities--and leave themselves exposed to new forms of competition. Just ask the manufacturers of kerosene lamps, buggy whips, and mathematical slide rules!

Assignment

This exercise will give you some practice in naming product-markets and generic markets. It will also require you to be creative and apply your marketing intuition.

Listed below are several generic markets and brand-name products. Using the 3 and 4 part definitions of generic markets and product-markets, suggest possible market names in the blanks. Note: There are no "right answers," but they should be logical and consistent. Generic markets should *not* include any product-related terms. A generic market can have several related product-markets. And a product is offered to a product-market which is a part of a larger generic market. Question 1 is answered to help you get started.

1. Generic market: Security for families in the world
   a) Product-market: Homeowner's insurance for financial security for home-owning families in the United States.
   b) Product-market: Guards for physical security for wealthy families in the world.
   c) Product-market: Smoke alarms for mental security for families in the developed countries.

2. Generic market: Family recreation by middle and upper income people in the United States

   a) Product-market: _____

   b) Product-market: _____

   c) Product-market: _____

3. Generic market: Idea recording by business executives in the United States

   a) Product-market: _____

   b) Product-market: _____

   c) Product-market: _____

4. Product: Sony Walkman (stereo AM/FM radio and cassette player)

   a) Product-market: _____

   b) Generic market: _____

5. Product: Michael Jackson (the singer) compact disc

   a) Product-market: _____

   b) Generic market: _____

6. Product: Keebler packaged animal crackers

   a) Product-market: _____

   b) Generic market: _____

Question for Discussion

How can a firm decide *which* and *how many* markets to enter?

Exercise 3-2

Seven-step approach to segmenting markets

Introduction

The development of successful marketing strategies depends to a large extent on the planner's ability to segment markets. Unfortunately, this is not a simple process. Segmenting usually requires considerable management judgment and skill. Those marketers who have the necessary judgment and skill will have a real advantage over their competitors in finding profitable opportunities.

Segmenting is basically a process of gathering individuals into homogeneous market segments on the basis of similar customer needs and characteristics. Although segmenting is often helped by the use of marketing research and computer techniques, such techniques are not always necessary--or economically practical. By using an organized approach, the strategy planner can sometimes rely on intuition and judgment to identify useful segments. One such approach is the "seven-step approach" discussed on pages 83-88 of the text. It is workable and has been used in the development of successful marketing strategies. It is especially useful when looking for new market opportunities.

This exercise is designed to illustrate the use of the seven-step approach to segmenting markets. Applying this approach, you will be asked to segment a market and then to think of what products might be most appropriate for each segment.

Assignment

Assume you have been asked to segment the following broad product-market: automotive vehicles for transporting families or small groups in the world. Think about the many product offerings in this market and the people who buy them. Then, answer the following questions.

1. In the space below, list all the needs you can think of that potential customers may have in this product-market area. Be sure to focus on *needs* rather than product features.

2. Using some scrap paper, work through steps 3-7 of the "seven-step approach" and identify *three to four* "good-sized" sub-markets of this product-market.

3. Summarize the work you did in Question 2 by using the following diagram to draw a picture of the product-market and the sub-product-markets you identified. Vary the size of the segments to show what you think might be their estimated market potential. Give each segment a name.

---

4. Now, for the product-markets that you identified in Question 2, show:
    a) the name of each segment.
    b) each segment's important needs.
    c) other customer characteristics for each segment--especially demographic or life-style dimensions.
    d) the type of products that would appeal to each segment.

    Product-Market 1

    a) Name: _____

    b) Needs: _____

        _____

    c) Characteristics: _____

        _____

        _____

    d) Products: _____

        _____

        _____

Product-Market 2

a)   Name: _____

b)   Needs: _____

_____

c)   Characteristics: _____

_____

_____

d)   Products: _____

_____

_____

Product-Market 3

a)   Name: _____

b)   Needs: _____

_____

c)   Characteristics: _____

_____

_____

d)   Products: _____

_____

_____

Product-Market 4

a)   Name: _____

b)   Needs: _____

_____

c)   Characteristics: _____

     _____

     _____

d)   Products: _____

     _____

     _____

Question for Discussion

If you were a marketing manager, what else would you like to know about possible product-markets before selecting a target market?

Exercise 3-3

Using positioning to evaluate marketing opportunities

Introduction

Finding target market opportunities is a continuing challenge for all marketers. Understanding how customers view current or proposed market offerings is often a crucial part of this challenge. And understanding customer perceptions is more difficult when different segments of the market have different needs and different views of how well current or proposed products meet those needs. Developing insights requires that you try to answer questions such as: Are there customer segments with needs which no existing products are satisfying very well? Could our existing product be modified to do a better job of satisfying the needs of some segment? Could promotion be used to communicate to consumers about aspects of the product--so that target customers would "see" it in a different way?

There are no easy answers to such questions, but *positioning* approaches can help. As explained in the text (pg. 90-92), positioning uses marketing research techniques which measure customer views of products or brands according to several product features (e.g., do consumers think of a brand of detergent as "gentle" or "strong" relative to other brands?). Usually, customers are also asked to decide the amount of each feature than would be "ideal" (e.g., how strong a detergent do you want?)

The results are plotted on a two- or three-dimensional diagram--called a "product space." Each dimension represents a product feature which the customers feel is important. The diagram shows how each product or brand was rated on each of the dimensions. In other words, it shows how the various products or brands are "positioned" relative to each other--and relative to the "ideal" products or brands of different segments of customers. Usually, circles are used to show segments of customers with similar "ideal points" along the dimensions.

The mechanics of how all this is done are beyond the scope of this course. But you should know that positioning research techniques produce a very useful graphic aid to help marketing managers do their job better. Looking at a product space for a market, a marketing planner may see opportunities to "reposition" existing products or brands through product and/or promotion changes. Or he may spot an empty space which calls for the introduction of a new product. Often, he may be quite surprised to see that customer views of market offerings differ a great deal from his own ideas.

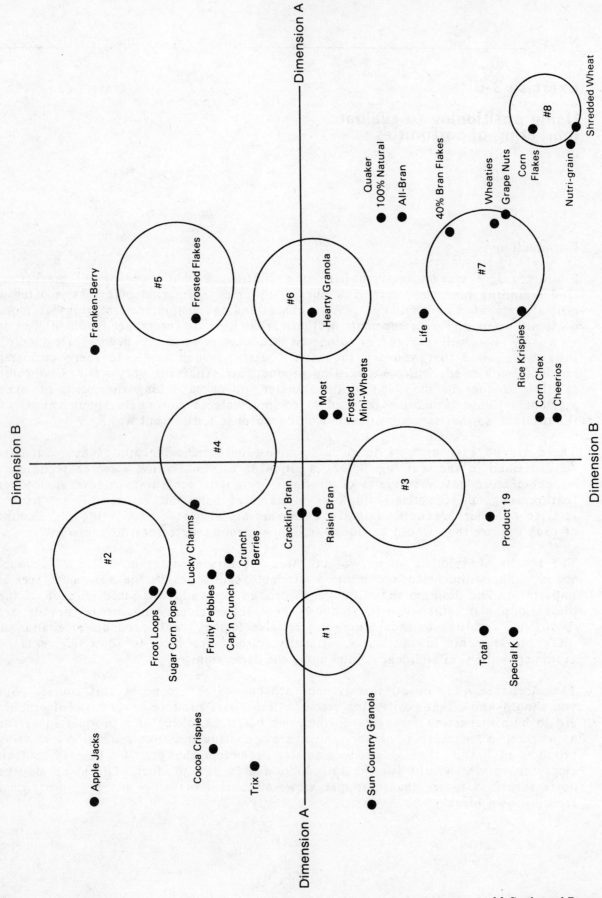

FIGURE 3-3
Product Space for Ready-to-Eat Breakfast Cereal

McCarthy and Perreault

Assignment

Figure 3-3 is a fictional "product space" diagram for ready-to-eat breakfast cereal. The diagram shows how target customers rated several brands of cereal along two product dimensions which have been identified only as Dimension A and Dimension B. The diagram also shows 8 segments of customers grouped together on the basis of similar "ideal points." For example, customers in segment #8 desire very little of attribute B and a lot of attribute A.

Study Figure 3-3 carefully and then answer the following questions.

1. a) Based on your interpretation of Figure 3-3, what product feature does Dimension A appear to represent?

    _____

    b) Based on your interpretation of Figure 3-3, what product feature does Dimension B appear to represent?

    _____

2. What opportunities for "repositioning" *existing* products do you see in Figure 3-3? Be specific, and indicate the segment(s) to which you want to target your appeal(s).

3. What opportunities for introducing *new* products do you see in Figure 3-3? Be specific, and indicate the segment(s) whose needs you would want to satisfy.

4.   If you were interested in targeting customers in segment #6, which existing brands would be your most direct competitors?

_____

_____

5.   If you were the marketing manager for Lucky Charms brand cereal and you were thinking about using the combined target market approach to appeal to two different segments, which segments would be the likely target for your marketing strategy? Briefly explain your choice.

_____

_____

_____

_____

6.   Are the two product dimensions shown in Figure 3-3 the two most important dimensions in choosing a brand of breakfast cereal? If not, what dimensions are most important?

7.   Do all potential customers agree as to which two dimensions are the most important dimensions in choosing a brand of breakfast cereal? If not, what are the implications for using "positioning" as an aid in evaluating market opportunities?

Question for Discussion

Is positioning an art or a science? Why?

Name: _____ Course & Section: _____

Exercise 3-4

Segmenting customers

This exercise is based on computer-aided problem number 3--Segmenting Customers. A complete description of the problem appears on page 17 of *Computer-Aided Problems to Accompany Basic Marketing*.

1. Micro Software's marketing manager is thinking about the possibility of combining two of the segments into a single target market. He is not certain which segments to combine. But he thinks he will be more successful if the two segments are as similar as possible.

    It occurred to him that the same spreadsheet he used to cluster customers could be used to compute a score showing how similar the segments are to each other. All that would be needed would be to enter the "summary" importance ratings for a segment in the spreadsheet, and then record how similar that segment is to each of the other segments. Complete this analysis for each of the segments and fill in the table below.

| Summary Importance Rating | | | | Overall Similarity Score | | |
No. of Features	Easy to Use	Easy to Learn	Segment	Fearful Typists	Power Users	Tech. Specialists
3	8	9	Fearful Typists	_____	_____	_____
9	2	2	Power Users	_____	_____	_____
7	5	6	Technical Specialists	_____	_____	_____

2. Based on this analysis, which pair of segments seem to be most similar (homogeneous) with respect to the importance of different software features?

    _____

3. Based on this analysis, which pair of segments seem to be least similar (homogeneous) with respect to the importance of different software features?

    _____

4. The marketing manager is thinking about developing a product that could be "positioned" to satisfy each of the two most similar segments "pretty well." He thinks that the summary importance ratings for each segment are a good indicator of what each segment's "ideal" product would be like. So, he decided to average the importance ratings for the *two most similar* segments and develop a product that matched that "average need." But, he wants to see how well such a product would meet the needs of the individual segments. To further evaluate this idea, complete the table below.

FOR the most similar segments:	Importance Rating for Each Factor		
	Features	Easy to Use	Easy to Learn
Importance ratings for one segment:	_____	_____	_____
Importance ratings for other segment:	_____	_____	_____
Sum of ratings for both segments:	_____	_____	_____
Average rating (sum divided by 2):	_____	_____	_____

5. If a product could be developed to match the average ratings above, how well do you think it would satisfy each of the segments? Briefly explain your answer. Hint: enter the "average" ratings (after rounding off to one decimal place) in the spreadsheet, and see how similar the needs met by this "average" product are with the needs of each of the different segments.

	Fearful Typists	Power Users	Technical Specialists
"Average" Product Similarity Score:	_____	_____	_____

Explanation: _____

_____

_____

6. A computer programmer at the company has suggested that they just try to produce a product that meets the average needs of all three segments. Use the same approach you used above to evaluate how similar a product based on the average would be to the needs of the different segments.

	Importance Rating for Each Factor			"Average" Product Similarity Score
	Features	Easy to Use	Easy to Learn	
Fearful typists:	_____	_____	_____	_____
Power users:	_____	_____	_____	_____
Specialists:	_____	_____	_____	_____
Sum:	_____	_____	_____	
Average:	_____	_____	_____	

7. Based on the "average product similarity scores" you computed in question 6 above, does it appear that the programmer's idea for a product would provide a good basis for using a combining approach to appeal to all three segments? Briefly explain your answer.

_____

_____

_____

_____

_____

_____

Chapter 4

Evaluating opportunities in uncontrollable environments

What This Chapter Is About

In the last chapter, you learned that finding opportunities takes a real understanding of customers. But marketing managers can not select target markets or plan strategies in a vacuum. Uncontrollable environments affect the attractiveness of possible opportunities. And opportunities need to be carefully evaluated and screened--to identify the really attractive ones.

A company's objectives can guide this process--and its resources may limit the search for opportunities, or alternatively give the firm a competitive advantage.

This chapter treats the competitive environment in some depth (building on the economic concepts reviewed in Appendix A, which follows Chapter 2). The marketing manager can't control competitors--but he can try to avoid head-on competition--or plan for it when it is inevitable.

The economic and technological environment can change rapidly. These shifts may require changes in marketing strategies.

The political and legal environment is given special attention because of its possible impact on the marketing manager. Further, the evolution of legislative thinking is outlined as a foundation for discussion in later chapters.

The cultural and social environment concerns the number of people and how they live and behave. A marketing manager must understand his markets--and cultural and social environments affect the way people buy.

Finding *attractive* opportunities requires screening and evaluation--and various approaches are presented towards the end of the chapter.

Important Terms

competitive environment, p. 101
pure competition, p. 101
equilibrium price, p. 102
oligopoly, p. 103
monopolistic competition, p. 105
economic and technological
  environment, p. 106

technological base, p. 107
consumerism, p. 108
nationalism, p. 108
cultural and social environment, p. 113
strategic business unit (SBU), p. 119
portfolio management, p. 119

True-False Questions

F 1. A business firm's only objective should be to earn enough profit to survive.

T 2. Trying to maximize short-run return on investment may not be good in the long run.

F 3. Winning a larger market share necessarily leads to greater profitability.

T 4. Company objectives should lead to a hierarchy of marketing objectives.

T 5. Attractive opportunities should make use of a firm's resources and its unique strengths.

F 6. A large producer with economies of scale always has a competitive advantage over smaller firms.

F 7. A patent owner has a 20-year monopoly to develop and use its new product, process, or material as it sees fit.

T 8. Although the marketing manager cannot control the competitive environment, he can choose strategies that will avoid head-on situations.

T 9. In pure competition, both the industry demand curve and the individual firm's demand curve are horizontal.

F 10. Except for oligopolies, most industries tend to become more competitive--that is, move toward pure competition.

T 11. Oligopoly situations develop when a market has a few sellers of essentially homogeneous products and a fairly elastic industry demand curve.

T 12. In oligopoly situations, individual firms are faced with a "kinked" demand curve.

F 13. In monopolistic competition, there is only one seller and that seller has complete control over the price of its unique product.

F 14. The inflation rate experienced by the United States in recent years was just about the highest in the world.

F 15. When the dollar is strong in international exchange, it is easier to sell U.S. products in overseas markets.

T 16. The technological base includes the technical skills and equipment which affect the way the resources of an economy are converted to output.

T 17. Changes in the technological environment could be rejected by the cultural and social environment--through the political and legal environment--even though such changes might help the economic environment.

F 18. Consumerism is a social movement seeking to give sellers as much power and legal rights as buyers and consumers.

T 19. Nationalism may affect marketing strategy planning by determining to whom and how much a firm may sell.

T 20. The political environment may either block or promote new marketing opportunities.

T 21. A marketing manager could be fined--or even sent to jail--for violating the Sherman Act.

T 22. The Clayton Act deals with tying contracts, exclusive dealing contracts, and price-fixing conspiracies.

F 23. Product warranties are regulated by the Magnuson-Moss Act.

T 24. Laws such as the Pure Food and Drug Act were passed because pro-competition legislation did not protect consumers very well in some areas.

F 25. The Consumer Product Safety Commission tries to encourage safe product design, but the commission has almost no power to deal with unsafe products.

T 26. Recent trends indicate a major shift in traditional thinking about buyer-seller relations from "let the seller beware" to "let the buyer beware."

F 27. Because the cultural and social environment tends to change slowly, firms should try to identify and work with cultural attitudes rather than trying to encourage big changes in the short run.

T 28. Product-market screening criteria should be mainly quantitative in nature, because qualitative criteria are too subjective.

T 29. Forecasts of the probable results of implementing whole strategic plans are needed to apply quantitative screening criteria.

F 30. The profit potentials of alternative strategic plans can be evaluated at the same time only if the plans are very similar.

T 31. The General Electric "strategic planning grid" forces company managers to make three-part judgments (high, medium, and low) about the business strengths and industry attractiveness of all proposed or existing products or businesses.

F 32. The G.E. "stop-light" evaluation method is a very objective approach because G.E. feels there are too many possible errors if it tries to use subjective criteria for judging "attractiveness" or "strength."

F 33. SBUs are small businesses which try to compete with major divisions of larger multi-product companies.

I 34. Portfolio management tends to emphasize current profitability and return on investment, often neglecting the long run.

Answers to True-False Questions

1.	F, p. 96	13.	F, p. 105	25.	F, p. 112
2.	T, p. 97	14.	F, p. 106	26.	F, p. 112
3.	F, p. 98	15.	F, p. 107	27.	T, p. 114
4.	T, p. 99	16.	T, p. 107	28.	F, p. 114
5.	T, p. 99	17.	T, p. 107	29.	T, p. 115
6.	F, p. 100	18.	F, p. 108	30.	F, p. 116
7.	F, p. 101	19.	T, p. 108	31.	T, p. 117
8.	T, p. 101	20.	T, p. 109	32.	F, p. 118
9.	F, p. 102	21.	T, p. 110	33.	F, p. 119
10.	T, p. 103	22.	F, p. 111	34.	T, p. 119
11.	F, p. 103	23.	T, p. 111		
12.	T, p. 103	24.	T, p. 112		

Multiple-Choice Questions (Circle the correct response)

1. Which of the following objectives of a business is the *most* important?
   a. To engage in some specific business activity which will perform a socially and economically useful function.
   b. To develop an organization to carry on the business and implement its strategies.
   c. To earn enough profit to survive.
   d. All three of the above are equally important, because a failure in any one could lead to a total failure of the business.

2. Of the following, the *last* objectives that a firm should specify are its:
   a. company objectives.
   b. marketing objectives.
   c. promotion objectives.
   d. advertising objectives.
   e. price objectives.

3. A first step in evaluating marketing opportunities is to:
   a. decide which markets the firm wishes to enter.
   b. consider the objectives and resources of the firm.
   c. hire a "futurist" as a marketing consultant.
   d. estimate market and sales potentials.
   e. find out if potential competitors are larger.

4. In which of the following situations would an individual firm be most likely to face a horizontal demand curve?
    a. Oligopoly
    b. Pure competition
    c. Monopoly
    d. Monopolistic competition
    e. None of the above--demand is always downward sloping.

5. Oligopoly situations are generally characterized by:
    a. essentially heterogeneous products.
    b. relatively few sellers, or a few large firms and perhaps many smaller firms.
    c. fairly elastic industry demand.
    d. a and b above--but not c.
    e. All of the above.

6. In an oligopoly situation:
    a. an individual firm's demand is inelastic above the "kink" and elastic below the kink.
    b. the market price is usually somewhere above the "kink."
    c. price wars usually increase profits for all competitors.
    d. price fluctuations may occur despite the kinked demand curve faced by each firm.
    e. All of the above are true statements.

7. A particular market is characterized by different (heterogeneous) products in the eyes of some customers and sellers who feel they do face some competition. This product-market is an example of:
    a. oligopoly.
    b. monopoly.
    c. monopolistic competition.
    d. pure competition.
    e. It could be any of the above.

8. Which of the following statements about the competitive environment is *true*?
    a. The industry demand curve in a pure competition situation is horizontal.
    b. Monopolistic competition is characterized by downsloping demand curves due to the lack of any substitute products.
    c. In a pure competition situation, an individual firm is faced with a very inelastic demand curve.
    d. Since a monopolistic competitor has a downsloping demand curve just like a pure monopolist, it has some control over its price.
    e. All of the above are true statements.

9. Which of the following is *not* an example of how the economic and technological environment may affect marketing strategy planning?
   a. The price of bicycles is rising because of inflation.
   b. Bicycle manufacturers are finding it difficult to keep up with the growing demand for bicycles because of raw material shortages.
   c. Because of exchange rates, imported bikes are cheaper than those made in the United States.
   d. Computer-controlled assembly lines can turn out a new bike every three and one-half seconds.
   e. The demand for bikes is increasing because consumers are becoming more health conscious.

10. President Kennedy's "Consumer Bill of Rights" did *not* include the right to:
    a. a clean and safe environment.
    b. safety.
    c. be informed.
    d. choose.
    e. be heard.

11. The Sherman Act now provides for:
    a. fines of up to $1,000,000 for corporations.
    b. fines of up to $100,000 for individuals.
    c. up to three years in jail for individuals.
    d. all of the above.
    e. only a and b above.

12. The Sherman Act is primarily designed to:
    a. prevent monopolies or conspiracies in restraint of trade.
    b. stop the flow of foreign products into the United States.
    c. prevent unfair or deceptive acts or practices in commerce.
    d. reduce price discrimination by manufacturers.
    e. eliminate deceptive selling practices.

13. The Federal Trade Commission Act of 1914 is primarily concerned with:
    a. deceptive warranties.
    b. price-fixing agreements.
    c. conspiracies in restraint of trade.
    d. mergers which might substantially lessen competition.
    e. unfair methods of competition.

14. The Clayton Act is *not* concerned with:
    a. product warranties.
    b. price discrimination by manufacturers.
    c. exclusive dealing contracts.
    d. tying contracts.
    e. encouraging competition.

15. A firm that discriminates in price on goods of "like grade and quality" may be in violation of the _____ Act.
    a. Sherman
    b. Robinson-Patman
    c. Wheeler-Lea
    d. Magnuson-Moss
    e. Antimerger

16. The Consumer Product Safety Commission is responsible for:
    a. developing and enforcing safety standards for bicycles.
    b. developing and enforcing environmental protection standards.
    c. preventing the distribution and sale of adulterated or misbranded foods, drugs, and cosmetics.
    d. All of the above.
    e. None of the above.

17. The recent interest in physical fitness has forced producers of food, clothing, and other products to reconsider their marketing strategies. Which of the following uncontrollable variables does this trend illustrate?
    a. economic and technological environment.
    b. cultural and social environment.
    c. existing business situation.
    d. political and legal environment.
    e. resources and objectives of the firm.

18. In the short run at least, which of the following is usually *beyond* the control of the marketing manager?
    a. political and legal environment.
    b. economic and technological environment.
    c. cultural and social environment.
    d. competitive environment.
    e. All of the above.

19. Product-market screening criteria should be:
    a. quantitative.
    b. qualitative.
    c. realistic and achievable.
    d. all of the above.
    e. all of the above *except* b.

20. Which of the following is a quantitative screening criteria?
    a. increase sales by $100,000.
    b. earn 25 percent return on investment.
    c. break even within one year.
    d. all of the above are quantitative criteria.

21. General Electric's "strategic planning grid":
    a. substitutes precise quantitative estimates for management judgment and intuition.
    b. places too much emphasis on industry attractiveness, almost ignoring the firm's own business strengths.
    c. emphasizes market share and market growth rate.
    d. is oversimplified in that it assumes all opportunities must be either "good" or "bad."
    e. None of the above is a true statement.

22. Organizational units within a larger company which focus their efforts on selected product-markets and are treated as separate profit centers are called:
    a. portfolios.
    b. strategic business units.
    c. BTUs.
    d. functional departments.
    e. basing points.

Answers to Multiple-Choice Questions

1. d, p. 96	9. e, p. 106-07	17. b, p. 113
2. d, p. 99	10. a, p. 108	18. e, p. 101-14
3. b, p. 99	11. d, p. 110	19. d, p. 114
4. b, p. 102	12. a, p. 111	20. d, p. 115
5. b, p. 103	13. e, p. 111	21. e, p. 117-18
6. d, p. 104	14. a, p. 111	22. b, p. 119
7. c, p. 105	15. b, p. 111	
8. d, p. 105	16. a, p. 112	

Exercise 4-1

How uncontrollable variables affect
marketing strategy planning

Introduction

Marketing managers are not free to choose *any* marketing strategy they please. On the contrary, their choice of strategies is usually affected by variables related to the:

1. Objectives and resources of the firm
2. Competitive environment
3. Economic and technological environment
4. Political and legal environment
5. Cultural and social environment

These variables are called "uncontrollable" because, in the short run, they are beyond the control of marketing managers--although in the long run, marketing managers may be able to influence some or all of these variables.

In the short run, at least, these uncontrollable variables may force marketing managers to change their present strategies--or even to choose less-than-ideal strategies. On the other hand, trends in the uncontrollable environments often create new opportunities for alert marketing strategy planners.

Assignment

This exercise is intended to stimulate your thinking about how the uncontrollable variables *might* affect marketing strategy planning. Read each of the following situations carefully and answer the questions that follow each situation.

1. The number of single-adult households in the United States continues to increase. This has had a big impact on some industries. How do you think a food manufacturer's marketing strategy might be influenced by this trend?

   _____

   _____

   _____

2. In 1987 scientists made major discoveries in the area of electrical "super-conductivity." The basic idea is that electrical wire and other electrical parts can be developed that will use electricity much more efficiently. These discoveries could have far reaching effects. But one of the earliest applications is likely to be in developing electric motors that are much smaller, more powerful, and require less electricity. Many think that it will finally mean that full-size, battery powered electric automobiles will be a practical possibility. If this technological advance develops as expected, how do you think it might affect (a) auto producers, (b) automobile service centers, and (c) consumers?

_____

_____

_____

3. In the early 1980s IBM introduced its very successful personal computer. But IBM's basic product was easy to copy, and within a few years many Japanese and Korean producers were competing for the business in this market with low-priced "clones" (imitations). Many retailers started carrying these computers because they were very popular with customers. IBM's profits fell dramatically as prices in the personal computer market fell and IBM faced a continuing decline in market share. In 1987, IBM introduced a new--and quite different--line of personal computers. How do you think the competition it faced earlier in the decade might have affected its marketing strategy for its new computers?

_____

_____

_____

4. In recent years, various federal agencies, schools, medical groups, and consumer advocates have been promoting greater concern for the nutritional value of food. Consequently, many people have reduced consumption of so-called "junk foods." Some consumers have begun to reemphasize the need for balanced meals, while others have become health-food addicts. What effect do you think these trends might have on the marketing efforts of a manufacturer of ready-to-eat cereals?

_____

_____

_____

Question for Discussion

How can marketers deal effectively with changing trends and developments in their uncontrollable environments?

Exercise 4-2

Analyzing the competitive environment

Introduction

Marketing managers do not always enjoy a full range of alternatives when planning a marketing mix. Their choices may be largely determined by the nature of the competitive environment.

For example, a firm might be able to use almost any marketing mix in a *pure monopoly* situation, while a firm's mix might be entirely determined by market forces in a *pure competition* situation. In an *oligopoly* situation, a firm would have some control over its marketing mix, but it might find it difficult to differentiate its product and any price-cutting could lead to a "price-war." Of course, most firms find themselves in a *monopolistic competition* situation where their control over their marketing mix can range from a lot to a little--depending on how competitive the monopolistic competition is.

It is not always easy to identify the nature of a firm's competitive environment. In general, one must consider many factors--besides just the number and size of competitors.

Perhaps the most important factor is how the target market is defined--an important topic discussed in Chapter 3. Other factors that should be considered include: (a) the similarity of competing products and marketing mixes--as seen by the target customers, (b) barriers to entry for new firms, and (c) seller concentration--(i.e., the extent to which a few large sellers control the bulk of industry sales).

Assignment

This exercise will give you some practice in analyzing the competitive environment. Read the following cases carefully and for each of them:

a)   Indicate the nature of the competitive environment, taking into consideration the probable target market.

Use the following terms to identify the nature of competition: pure competition, monopolistic competition, monopoly, and oligopoly.

Note: The term "monopolistic competition" can be used to describe situations ranging from near-monopoly to almost pure competition.

Try to distinguish between "moderately competitive monopolistic competition" situations and those which may be "extremely" or only "slightly" competitive--by labeling the latter as either "monopolistic competition approaching pure monopoly" or "monopolistic competition approaching pure competition."

b)   Briefly explain your answer, taking into account the various factors which were discussed above.

The first case has been answered for you as an example.

1.   Don's Truck Stop is a combination gasoline station-restaurant-motel which caters to long-distance truck drivers. It is located on the intersection of two major highways near a city of about 150,000 people. There are no other truck stops in the immediate area.

   a)   Nature of competition: <u>Monopolistic competition approaching pure monopoly.</u>

   b)   Explanation: <u>Although Don's Truck Stop probably gets a large share of the long-distance truckers' business, it does not have a pure monopoly because truckers can go into the city or on to the next truck stop. Further, there is nothing to prevent a potential competitor from locating nearby--which may very well happen if Don's is enjoying unusually high profits.</u>

2.   Mason City is supplied by five regional manufacturers of steel "I-beams." The I-beams are used in constructing large buildings. Three of these firms account for more than 80 percent of all the I-beams sold in the area. The I-beams are purchased either in standardized sizes or according to buyer specifications, and all five firms charge almost identical prices. When steel is in short supply, a few buyers have purchased some beams from other firms located outside the region, but high transportation costs make this an extremely expensive alternative. Two manufacturers have announced plans to boost their production capacity, and all five manufacturers have announced price increases of at least 12 percent for the coming year.

   a)   Nature of competition: _____

   b)   Explanation: _____

   _____

   _____

   _____

   _____

   _____

3. Jose Sanchez owns a chicken farm in southern California. Like thousands of other chicken farmers in the United States, Sanchez produces the eggs that end up on the breakfast tables of America, that are used by restaurants in preparing meals, and that are used in producing a variety of packaged foods. Jose's chicken flock has always been a very small portion of the 500,000,000 egg-laying hens in the United States. But like most other egg producers, he has decreased the size of his flock in recent years as the demand for eggs has declined. Now he plans to cut the size of his flock and production of eggs even further, since increasing consumer concern about the cholesterol in eggs is having a negative impact on demand.

    a) Nature of competition: _____

    b) Explanation: _____

        _____

        _____

        _____

        _____

        _____

4. Snow Castle, Inc. operates the only privately-owned ice rink in Midtown--a city of 250,000. It runs a full program of hockey, figure skating and public skating. It is also the "sponsor" of local "high school hockey"--trading practice ice for a share of the gate. Its only "ice time" competition is from the state university rink--which is only three miles away. The university rink management does not run competing programs--because its primary role is to serve the students and the hockey team. However, it does have a large amount of "extra time" and regularly sells blocks of time to groups--usually at prices which are below Snow Castle's prices (by 10-40 percent) and probably way below its variable costs for fuel and cleanup--given the size (6,000 seat) arena.

    a) Nature of competition: _____

    b) Explanation: _____

        _____

        _____

        _____

        _____

        _____

5.   Quality Cleaners specializes in dry cleaning of clothing and other household items--as well as operating a shirt laundry. It operates a central processing plant and 10 conveniently located branches where dry cleaning can be dropped off and picked up a day or two later. This company is located in a city of 250,000 where there are about 70 other dry cleaners (some of whom also have multiple-outlet operations). All these cleaners charge approximately the same "low" prices for basically the same services--because a steady influx of new dry cleaners has tended to keep prices at a fairly low level. Further, some firms have not been able to attract enough business to cover their rising labor costs and have been forced out of business.

a)   Nature of competition: _____

b)   Explanation: _____

_____

_____

_____

_____

_____

Question for Discussion

Have the firms described in the above cases achieved any "competitive advantage" over their competitors? If not, what steps might they take in the future to achieve some competitive advantage?

McCarthy and Perreault

Exercise 4-3

How the legal environment affects marketing strategy planning

Introduction

Even in the "free enterprise" economy of the United States, a marketing strategy planner faces many legal constraints. These laws are often confusing--and may even appear contradictory. Further, the laws are frequently written vaguely by legislators--to allow the courts to interpret and apply them. But the interpretation may vary depending on the current political environment. In spite of these problems, it is critical that marketing managers make every effort to understand the political-legal environments--because business must operate and develop its marketing strategies within these environments.

Assignment

The following cases describe marketing activities which might be judged illegal. Study each case carefully--and determine the law (or laws) which appear to be *most relevant* to each situation. Then state why you answered as you did. You should refer to the following list of laws in completing this exercise:

Sherman Antitrust Act	Wheeler-Lea Act
Clayton Act	Antimerger Act
Federal Trade Commission Act	Consumer Product Safety Act
Robinson-Patman Act	Magnuson-Moss Act

Note: Most of these laws are discussed in this chapter and summarized in Exhibit 4-7 on page 111 of the text--and this is the depth of understanding expected here. Most are discussed later--see subject index--but here we want to get a "big picture" feel for the likely impact of legislation.

The first case is answered for you as an example--but try to answer it yourself before looking at the suggested answer! [Note: You do not have to decide on legality, but merely indicate what law(s) *might* be involved or be most relevant in the situation.]

1. The Makin Corporation--a large manufacturer of industrial drill presses with an estimated 45 percent share of the U.S. market--wanted to diversify its product line. After investigating several possibilities, Makin decided to enter the rapidly growing market for industrial band saws--which are used to cut metal bars and tubes. The company felt it would take too long to develop its own

manufacturing and distribution facilities, and therefore chose to diversify by buying firms already in the band-saw business.

Over a two-year period, Makin bought out three leading producers of band saws. Some observers have predicted that Makin will dominate the market for industrial band saws within another three years.

a) Federal legislation: <u>Antimerger Act</u>

b) Reason: <u>The firm is engaged in mergers which may tend to substantially lessen competition in the band-saw industry.</u>

2. Acme Wholesale has been selling automobile wax, upholstery cleaner and other items used to clean cars through car parts retailers. Recently the company decided to sell its products through drugstore chains. To encourage the drugstore chains to purchase in large quantities, Acme offered them a special 15 percent quantity discount. Acme does not plan to offer the quantity discounts to its car parts retailers. Several drugstore chains have already agreed to carry the products, but one large national chain--whose business Acme really wants--has refused to stock the products unless Acme agrees to give the chain an additional 5 percent "advertising allowance."

a) Federal legislation: _____

b) Reason: _____

_____

_____

_____

3. A college student in Florida recently read a magazine ad for "an amazing new isometric exercise device" being sold by a firm in California. According to the ad, "individual results vary, but through only 5 minutes a day of 'effortless exercise' you can expect to add up to 2 inches to your biceps and up to 3 inches to your chest while losing up to 4 inches from your waistline and up to 10 pounds from your present weight during an average 14-day period." The ad stated that the body shaper could be purchased by mail for only $9.95 and added that "your money will be promptly refunded if not satisfactory."

The student ordered the exerciser--enclosing a money order for the specified amount. About a month later, he received a package containing a hard rubber cable about 2 feet long, and a small pamphlet describing various diet plans. Believing he had been cheated, he demanded that his money be refunded as advertised. Shortly afterwards, he received a form letter from the firm stating that his request for a refund had been denied on the grounds that "your money is entirely satisfactory to us."

a) Federal legislation: _____

b) Reason: _____

_____

_____

_____

4. Anne Martin purchased a new Japanese color television set at a discount house in New York. When the set broke down four months later and Anne brought it in for service, the salesperson who sold Anne the set suggested that she read the written warranty issued by the manufacturer. To her surprise, the manufacturer's "full one-year warranty" read as follows:

The manufacturer warranties this television set against all possible defects for a period of one full year, except for the picture tube, which is covered for 90 days, and except for all plastic parts, which are not covered at all. Should this set fail to operate during this period, it should be shipped at the purchaser's expense in the original carton to the manufacturer's official service representative, Ajax TV Repair, 4470 Alamo Drive, Los Angeles, California. The sum of $49.95 should be enclosed to cover handling charges. This is the only warranty provided by the manufacturer, and all other express or implied warranties are hereby excluded. This warranty does not cover damage caused by improper handling or abuse. The manufacturer shall be the sole judge of whether any parts are defective or whether they were damaged through improper handling or abuse.

a) Federal legislation: _____

b) Reason: _____

_____

_____

_____

5. The retail food market in Cay West is dominated by three national and three regional food chains. About a year ago, one of the regional chains started discount pricing. This action set off a chain reaction among the other major food retailers--who responded with discount plans of their own. A severe price war followed, forcing several small independent supermarkets out of business--but having little effect on the relative market shares of the six chains.

The price war did have a big impact on the chains' already low profit margins and now the national chains seem to have decided to declare a truce. Recently, executives from the three national chains met and decided not to compete with each other on a price basis in the future. Further, they discussed ways of increasing their collective market share at the expense of the three regional chains.

a) Federal legislation: _____

b) Reason: _____

_____

_____

_____

6. TRM, Inc. has just discovered that some of its ten-speed racing bicycles were manufactured with an improperly welded joint which could cause the entire frame to collapse under stress--such as being ridden into a curb. Company officials estimate that no more than 5 percent of the 10,000 racers manufactured and sold during the past year were defective. Rather than engage in an expensive recall, TRM, Inc. has notified its retailers to repair the bicycles at no cost to the owner whenever a defective model is discovered.

a) Federal legislation: _____

b) Reason: _____

_____

_____

_____

Question for Discussion

Marketing-related legislation has often had different objectives and varying degrees of interpretation and enforcement. Why? What is the current trend? In which direction does the political and legal environment appear to be moving?

Exercise 4-4

Company resources

This exercise is based on computer-aided problem number 4--Company Resources.
A complete description of the problem appears on page 18 of *Computer-Aided Problems to Accompany Basic Marketing*.

1. Mediquip has focused on lowering costs because the market appears to be price-sensitive. But Mediquip sees that there may be other ways to take advantage of its company strengths. Laser Tech already has parts it could use in producing the laser scalpel, but that may reduce its flexibility. Mediquip product designers think they can develop a product that better meets a doctor's needs if Mediquip spends $50,000 for front-end design costs, but they wonder if a profit can still be earned with a product that costs $7,400 to produce. Mediquip's marketing manager thinks that the firm could get a 70 percent share of the market--leaving only a 30 percent share for Laser Tech-- if it could develop this product and still set a price to meet what Laser Tech will have to charge. Based on this situation, what would Mediquip's average cost per machine be, and what price would it have to charge to earn a $1,000 profit per machine? Based on these estimates, would you recommend that Mediquip move ahead with the idea of improving the product? Why?

    Average cost per machine: $_____ Price: $_____

    _____

    _____

    _____

    _____

    _____

2. Mediquip can keep its product development plans secret until it enters the market. But Mediquip is wondering about what Laser Tech might do if Mediquip does keep its plans secret. For example, Laser Tech might think that it would be able to capture 70 percent share of the market and set its price to cover its costs based on that quantity. In this case, what would Laser Tech estimate as its likely average cost per machine? What price would it set if it expected each unit to contribute $1,000 to profit?

    Average cost per machine: $_____ Price: $_____

3. If these events occur, each firm would enter the market with a price that had been set assuming that it would win 70 percent of the market. Clearly, it's not possible for each firm to have 70 percent share of the market. If Mediquip developed the improved product but it turned out that Mediquip only captured 40 percent of the market, its sales, costs, and profits might look quite different than it had planned. For this case, fill in the information requested below.

Quantity Mediquip would sell with 40% of the market: _____ units

Average cost per unit: $_____
(assuming it spent the extra money on product design and unit product costs, but then only won 40% of the market)

Total design, producing and selling costs for this situation: $_____

4. In the space provided below, calculate what profit (or loss) Mediquip would earn in this situation:

Actual total revenue =   quantity actually sold x price set assuming 70 percent share

Actual total revenue = $_____

Actual total costs = $_____

Profit (loss) = $_____
(total revenue minus total costs)

5. Drawing on this analysis, briefly explain several important reasons why a marketing manager should understand the competitive environment when planning a marketing strategy.

Reason number 1: _____

Explanation: _____

_____

_____

Reason number 2: _____

Explanation: _____

_____

_____

Chapter 5

Getting information for marketing decisions

What This Chapter Is About

Marketing managers need information to plan effective marketing strategies. Chapter 5 stresses that getting good information for marketing decisions involves much more than just surveys.

Many managers now rely on marketing information systems to help meet their recurring information needs. But marketing managers must also deal with ever-changing needs in dynamic markets. So you should understand how marketing research can help marketing managers solve problems--and make better decisions.

A scientific approach to marketing research is explained and illustrated. This approach can help marketing managers solve problems--not just collect data.

This chapter also shows that the text's strategy planning framework is especially helpful in identifying marketing problems. This framework, along with a "scientific approach," can be very helpful in solving real problems. Often, small bits of information available *now* are far more valuable than an extensive research report which cannot be available for several months.

Try to understand how to go about a scientific approach to problem solving--just finding the right problem is sometimes half the job. This is something you should be able to do by the end of the text--even though you do not have all the tools and skills needed to do a formal research project. Specialists can be hired to do that part of the job if you--as the marketing manager--have correctly identified what information is needed to make the marketing strategy decisions.

Important Terms

marketing information system (MIS), p. 124
decision support system (DSS), p. 126
marketing model, p. 126
marketing research, p. 127
scientific method, p. 128
hypotheses, p. 128
marketing research process, p. 129
situation analysis, p. 131
secondary data, p. 132
primary data, p. 132
research proposal, p. 134

qualitative research, p. 135
focus group interview, p. 135
quantitative research, p. 136
response rate, p. 136
experimental method, p. 139
statistical packages, p. 140
population, p. 141
sample, p. 141
random sampling, p. 141
confidence interval, p. 141
validity, p. 142

True-False Questions

___ 1. A marketing information system is an organized way of using "one-shot" research projects to gather and analyze information that will help marketing managers make better decisions.

___ 2. The key advantage in using an MIS is that it makes available information accessible.

___ 3. A decision support system (DSS) is a computer program that makes it easy for a marketing manager to get and use information as he is making decisions.

___ 4. Decision support systems that include marketing models allow the manager to see how answers to questions might change in various situations.

___ 5. Marketing research is best defined as a set of techniques applied by specialists in survey design or statistical methods.

___ 6. Marketing research details may be handled by staff or outside specialists, but the marketing manager must know how to plan and evaluate research projects.

___ 7. The scientific method is a decision-making approach that focuses on being objective and orderly in testing ideas before accepting them.

___ 8. Hypotheses are statements of fact about relationships between things or what will happen in the future.

___ 9. The marketing research process is a five-step application of the scientific method that includes: defining the problem, analyzing the situation, getting problem-specific data, interpreting the data, and solving the problem.

___ 10. Defining the problem--although usually the easiest job of the marketing researcher--is also the most important job.

___ 11. Developing a list that includes all possible problem areas is a sensible start to the situation analysis step.

___ 12. Gathering primary data about the problem area is part of analyzing the situation.

___ 13. Secondary data is information which is already collected or published.

___ 14. The *Statistical Abstract of the United States* is a good source of primary data.

___ 15. A written research proposal is a plan that specifies what marketing research information will be obtained and how.

___ 16. The two basic methods for obtaining information about customers are questioning and observing.

___ 17. Qualitative research seeks in-depth, open-ended responses.

___ 18. A focus group interview involves interviewing 6 to 10 people in an informal group setting.

___ 19. It is typical to use quantitative research in preparation for doing qualitative research.

___ 20. Quantitative research seeks structured responses that can be summarized in numbers--like percentages, averages, or other statistics.

___ 21. A common quantitative research approach to summarize consumers' opinions and preferences is to have respondents indicate how much they agree or disagree with a questionnaire statement.

___ 22. The response rate is the percent of people contacted who complete a questionnaire.

___ 23. Mail surveys are economical per questionnaire--if a large number of people respond.

___ 24. A mail survey is the best research approach if you want respondents to expand on particular points and give in-depth information.

___ 25. With the observation method, the researcher avoids talking to the subject.

___ 26. The use of computer scanners to observe what customers actually do is changing research methods for many firms.

___ 27. With the experimental method, the responses of groups which are similar, except on the characteristic being tested, are compared.

___ 28. The experimental method is the most widely used marketing research method because managers want and need quantitative information to make better decisions.

___ 29. Statistical packages are easy-to-use computer programs that help analyze data.

___ 30. In regard to marketing research, *population* means the total group that responds to a survey.

___ 31. In most marketing research studies, only a sample--a part of the relevant population--is surveyed.

___ 32. Random sampling is sampling in which each member of the population does not have the same chance of being included in the sample.

___ 33. With random samples, researchers can narrow confidence intervals by increasing sample sizes.

___ 34. Validity concerns the extent to which data measures what it is intended to measure.

___ 35. Conducting and interpreting a marketing research project should be left entirely to the researcher because most marketing managers have no training in this area.

___ 36. One should always seek to obtain as much marketing information as possible before making a decision.

Answers to True-False Questions

1. F, p. 124	13. T, p. 132	25. T, p. 138
2. T, p. 124	14. F, p. 133	26. T, p. 139
3. T, p. 126	15. T, p. 134	27. T, p. 139
4. T, p. 126	16. T, p. 135	28. F, p. 140
5. F, p. 127	17. T, p. 135	29. T, p. 140
6. T, p. 128	18. T, p. 135	30. F, p. 141
7. T, p. 128	19. F, p. 135	31. T, p. 141
8. F, p. 128	20. T, p. 136	32. F, p. 141
9. T, p. 129	21. T, p. 136	33. T, p. 141
10. F, p. 130	22. T, p. 136	34. T, p. 142
11. T, p. 131	23. T, p. 136	35. F, p. 142
12. F, p. 132	24. F, p. 138	36. F, p. 144

Multiple-Choice Questions (Circle the correct response)

1. Which of the following statements about marketing information systems is *true*?
   a. Marketing information systems are used to gather and analyze data from intracompany sources, while marketing research deals with external sources.
   b. Most firms can or could generate more market-related data than they could possibly use.
   c. Computerized marketing information systems tend to increase the quantity of information available for decision making but not without some corresponding decrease in quality.
   d. The value of decision support systems is limited because the manager can't use them while he is actually making his decisions.
   e. All of the above are true statements.

2. Marketing research:
   a. requires a market research department in the company.
   b. consists mainly of survey design and statistical techniques.
   c. should be planned by research specialists.
   d. is needed to keep isolated marketing planners in touch with their markets.
   e. All of the above are true.

3. In small companies,
   a. there is no need for marketing research.
   b. there should be a marketing research department--or there will be no one to do marketing research.
   c. the emphasis of marketing research should be on customer surveys.
   d. salespeople often do what marketing research gets done.

4. The scientific method is important in marketing research because it:
   a. forces the researcher to follow certain procedures, thereby reducing the need to rely on intuition.
   b. develops hypotheses and then tests them.
   c. specifies a marketing strategy which is almost bound to succeed.
   d. Both a and b are correct.
   e. All of the above are correct.

5. The most important--and often the most difficult step--of the marketing research process is:
   a. analyzing the situation.
   b. collecting data.
   c. observation.
   d. defining the problem.
   e. interpreting the data.

6. When analyzing the situation, the marketing analyst:
   a. sizes up the situation by talking with executives in competitive companies.
   b. seeks information that is already available in the problem area.
   c. begins to talk informally to a random sample of customers.
   d. talks to experts in data analysis at trade association meetings.
   e. All of the above.

7. A small manufacturing firm has just experienced a rapid drop in sales. The marketing manager thinks that he knows what the problem is and has been carefully analyzing secondary data to check his thinking. His next step should be to:
   a. conduct an experiment.
   b. develop a formal research project to gather primary data.
   c. conduct informal discussion with outsiders, including middlemen, to see if he has correctly defined the problem.
   d. develop a hypothesis and predict the future behavior of sales.
   e. initiate corrective action before sales drop any further.

8. Which of the following is a good source for locating secondary data:
   a. a focus group interview.
   b. personal interviews with customers.
   c. the *Statistical Abstract of the United States.*
   d. a marketing research survey.
   e. none of the above.

9. A marketing analyst would *not* use which of the following research methods when gathering primary data?
   a. Observation
   b. Experiment
   c. Mail survey
   d. Library search
   e. Personal interviews

10. With regard to getting problem-specific data:
    a. the observation method involves asking consumers direct questions about their observations.
    b. telephone surveys are declining in popularity.
    c. focus group interviews are usually more representative than a set of personal interviews.
    d. mail surveys are limited to short, simple questions--extensive questioning cannot be done.
    e. None of the above is a true statement.

11. To be effective, marketing research should be:
    a. quantitative.
    b. qualitative.
    c. either or both--depending on the situation.

12. Experimental method research:
    a. is often hard to use in "real world" markets.
    b. always uses observing rather than questioning.
    c. is more popular than focus group interviews.
    d. is used to compare groups for differences.
    e. all of the above.

13. A statistical package is most likely to be used for a marketing research project that:
    a. used focus group interviews.
    b. relied on secondary data.
    c. included a mail survey.
    d. consisted of open-ended questions in a personal interview.
    e. was based on qualitative research.

14. Using random samples:
    a. guarantees that the findings will be valid.
    b. is stressed by theoretical statisticians--but usually is unnecessary in marketing research.
    c. guarantees that the sample will have the same characteristics as the population.
    d. allows the researcher to use confidence intervals to evaluate estimates from the sample data.
    e. All of the above are true statements.

15. At the step when data are interpreted, a marketing manager should:
   a. leave it to the technical specialists to draw the correct conclusions.
   b. realize that statistical summaries from a sample may not be precise for the whole population.
   c. know that quantitative survey responses are valid, but qualitative research may not be valid.
   d. be satisfied with the sample used as long as it is large.
   e. All of the above are correct.

16. Which of the following statements about marketing research is *false*?
   a. A low response rate may affect the accuracy of results.
   b. You never can get all of the information which might be useful.
   c. Getting more or better information is not always worth the cost.
   d. Because of the risks involved, marketing managers should never base their decision on incomplete information.
   e. A marketing manager should evaluate *beforehand* whether research findings will be relevant.

Answers to Multiple-Choice Questions

1. b, p. 124-27	7. c, p. 131	13. c, p. 140
2. d, p. 127	8. c, p. 133	14. d, p. 141
3. d, p. 127	9. d, p. 135	15. b, p. 141-43
4. d, p. 128	10. e, p. 135-37	16. d, p. 144
5. d, p. 130	11. c, p. 135-36	
6. b, p. 131	12. e, p. 139-40	

Exercise 5-1

Locating sources of secondary data

Introduction

Marketing managers often fail to take full advantage of all the information that is available to help them make effective decisions. While time and cost factors usually prevent one from obtaining perfect information, there is often much more information--already published and readily available--than managers actually use.

On the other hand, too many marketers tend to be "survey researchers" who feel they must always rush out to gather original data--i.e., *primary data*--whenever some problem arises. They tend to overlook the large amount of *secondary data* that is already in the firm's internal records or in various published sources. This data is often available for free--or for a fee that is usually far less than the cost of obtaining primary data.

Because secondary data can be very helpful when doing a situation analysis or when evaluating alternative solutions to marketing problems, marketers should know what kinds of data are available. This exercise will show you what kinds of data are usually available--free--and where to find it. We can't make you an "instant expert" on how to use the business library. But we do want you to become familiar with some of the most used sources of marketing data. Other sources of data will be introduced in later exercises.

Assignment

In this exercise you are asked to find data relating to a specified product-- sporting goods--and to a specified market area--San Diego, California. Note that you could use the same information sources for almost *any* product or geographic area. List your answers in the space provided.

Note: Some of the sources mentioned may not be available in your school library. If so, just state "Not available."

1. Go to *Thomas' Register of American Manufacturers.* Under <u>Products and Services,</u> look up the list of manufacturers of sporting goods. Choose one of the largest of these manufacturers--according to the classification system used by the *Register.* Then, go to the <u>Company Profiles</u> section and in the space below copy the information provided by the *Register* for that company.

2. Go to the most recent edition of *Moody's Industrial Manual* and list the following information about the manufacturer you chose above:

    a) The name of the company's president: _____

    b) Net sales for the past year: _____

    c) Net income for the past year in both dollars and as a percentage of sales:

        $_____   _____%

3. a) Go to the most recent edition of the *Wall Street Journal Index* and look up the above manufacturer in the Corporate News section. List one item concerning the manufacturer, indicating the month, day, page, and column in which the item appeared.

    b) Then look up sporting goods in the General News section. List one item concerning the product, indicating the month, day, page, and column in which each item appeared.

4. Go to the most recent edition of the *Monthly Catalog of U.S. Government Publications* and list one publication dealing with sporting goods or the industry.

5. Go to the *Standard Industrial Classification Manual* and find the industry titles and codes that would include manufacturers, wholesalers, and retailers of sporting goods.

   a) SIC code for manufacturers: _____

      Industry title: _____

   b) SIC code for wholesalers: _____

      Industry title: _____

   c) SIC code for retailers: _____

      Industry title: _____

6. Using the appropriate SIC code, go to the *1982 Census of Retail Trade*. For the San Diego Metropolitan Statistical Area (MSA), list the total number of sporting goods establishments and also the total dollar sales of these outlets.

   Number _____ Sales _____

7. Using the appropriate SIC code, go to the *1982 Census of Wholesale Trade*. For the San Diego MSA, list the total number of wholesale establishments for sporting goods, and also the total dollar sales of these establishments.

   Number _____ Sales _____

8. Using the appropriate SIC code, go to the *1982 Census of Manufacturers*. For the San Diego MSA, list the total number of manufacturers of sporting goods and also the value of their shipments.

   Number _____ Shipments _____

9. Go to the *1980 Census of Population* and find the following data:

   a) The population of California _____

   b) The county and the population of the county in which San Diego is located:

      County _____ Population _____

   c) The population of the San Diego MSA and what counties are included in this MSA:

      Population _____ Counties _____

   d) The population of the city of San Diego: _____

   e) The median income of families (married couples with children under 18) living in the San Diego MSA: _____

10. Go to the most recent edition of *Sales & Marketing Management's Survey of Buying Power* and find the Buying Power Index (BPI) for the San Diego MSA.

Buying Power Index: _____

11. Go to the most recent edition of *The Statistical Abstract of the United States.* For "sporting goods," list the total dollars spent in television for retail and local advertising.

Retail and local television _____

12. Go to Standard Rate & Data Service's *Consumer Magazine* and *Farm Publication Rates and Data* or *Business Publications Rates and Data.* Choose a publication in which your company (from question 1 above) might advertise and list the following information:

Name of publication _____

Total circulation _____

Cost for a one time, full page, black and white ad _____

Question for Discussion

With so much *secondary* data readily available, why is there ever a need for a marketing manager to gather *primary* data?

Exercise 5-2

Evaluating marketing research

Introduction

Marketing managers need good information to develop effective marketing strategies. They need to know about the uncontrollable environment, about possible target customers, and about the marketing mix decisions they can make.

Sometimes the only way to get needed information is with marketing research. When this is the case, the manager can sometimes get help--perhaps from marketing research specialists in the firm or from outside specialists. But, marketing managers must be able to explain what their problems are--and what kinds of information they need. They should also know about some of the basic decisions made during the research process--so they know the limitations of the research. They need to be able to see if the results of a research project will really solve the problem!

It is true that marketing research can involve many technical details--that is why specialists are often involved. But, often a marketing manager can use "common sense"--and knowledge of marketing strategy planning--to improve marketing research.

Assignment

In this exercise you are presented with short cases that involve marketing research. You are asked to identify and comment about the possible limitations of the research. The cases are accompanied by questions that will help to get your thinking started.

You will need to know about the marketing research ideas discussed in Chapter 5 to evaluate the cases. But, remember that the idea here is *not* just to memorize the points from the text. Rather, you should really think about the *problem*, and use common sense along with the information from the book to evaluate the case situation.

A sample answer is provided to the first case--to give you an example of the type of thinking that might be helpful. But--before you read the answer--think about how you would answer the question yourself.

1. A marketing manager for a big industrial equipment company wanted to get ideas about new products he should develop. A salesman suggested that they conduct a few focus group interviews with a few "friendly" customers--to get

some ideas. This seemed like a good idea, so an outside marketing specialist was hired to set up and videotape two focus group sessions.

After the sessions, the specialist presented a short summary report. His main conclusion was that 40 percent of the participants wanted a certain type of machine, and urged the company to develop one quickly "since the market will be large." He also said that from watching the tapes he was certain that the customers were unhappy with the products they had been getting from the firm. This left the marketing manager quite concerned and wondering what to do.

a)   Is a focus group interview a good basis for drawing the type of conclusions offered by the outside researcher? Why or why not?

Sample Answer

The conclusion probably is not justified. A focus group interview includes relatively few customers, and they may not be representative. Also, trying to provide quantitative summaries of the qualitative results might be really misleading. The new product might be a good idea, but just because a few people in a focus group mentioned it does not mean that there will be a large market. That will require more study.

b)   Should the manager hire the marketing research firm to do a large survey to see if customers are really unhappy, as he suggests based on the focus groups? Why or why not?

Sample Answer

It is too early to be thinking about rushing out to do a big expensive survey. After all, conclusions reached by watching a focus group interview can vary a lot depending on who watches it. As a start, the marketing manager might watch the tapes of the focus groups and see if he draws the same conclusions. Other views might be sought as well. Even if the conclusion seems correct, it would be best to define the problem more specifically, and do a situation analysis to get a better idea about what research is needed.

2.   A marketing manager for a bank wants to survey potential customers to see if they know about the bank's new drive-in window services. An outside marketing research specialist tells the manager that for $5,000 the research firm can send out a mail survey to 500 people, tabulate the results, and present a report. He explains that the bank will need to provide a computer mailing list of people who have accounts at the bank--to save costs in developing the sample. He concludes by pointing out that the research will be quite inexpensive: "We will give you results from a representative sample of 500 people, at only $10 per respondent. And you can be confident with a sample of 500 that the statistics are accurate."

a)   Is the proposed sample well-suited to the manager's problem? Why or why not?

b)   Is the researcher's concluding statement misleading? (*Hint:* Think about the response rate issue.) Why or why not?

3.   A marketing manager for a Mercedes dealership is trying to decide how many cars to order during the coming year--to be sure to have enough on hand to meet demand. He decides that it would be useful to do a survey of customers to whom he has sold Mercedes in the last year. He wants to know how satisfied they are with their current car, and he wants to know how many want to buy another Mercedes from him in the coming year. He would also like to know if they could afford another expensive car so soon. He decides to have salesmen call the customers and ask the following questions:

(1)   How do you feel about the car you bought from us? Are you very satisfied, or only moderately satisfied?

(2)   Do you plan to buy another Mercedes from us during the coming year? Yes, you plan to buy; or no, you don't plan to buy.

(3)   I have one final question, and your response will be strictly confidential and used only in statistical summaries with answers from other respondents. Would you please tell us your annual income? $ _____

a)   Do you think that customers will give a valid response to the second question? Why or why not?

b)   Do you think that customers will give a valid response to the last question? Why or why not?

c)   What is there about the way that the first question is worded that might keep the manager from getting valid information about how satisfied a customer really is? (*Hint:* Read the whole question several times carefully from the point-of-view of different customers.)

4.   A marketing manager for an expensive men's clothing store is concerned that profits have dropped, and he has noticed that many customers who once were "regulars" are not coming back anymore. He decides to send out a questionnaire to a sample of old customers, using addresses from his mailing list. He wrote a letter asking customers to respond to his questionnaire. He also provided a postage paid envelope for return of the completed forms. The instructions on the short questionnaire were:

(1)   Please discuss the things you liked most about this store the last time you purchased clothing here?

(2)   Please explain what you like least about this store. Please discuss anything that bothers you.

(3)   Please tell us what other men's clothing stores you shop at, and what is it about each store that you like?

a)   Is a mail survey useful for questions like these? Why or why not?

b)   What would you recommend if the manager asked you for ideas on how to get better information about his problem?

Question for Discussion

How do the limitations of qualitative research differ from the limitations of quantitative research?

Name: _____ Course & Section: _____

Exercise 5-3

Marketing research

This exercise is based on computer-aided problem number 5--Marketing Research. A complete description of the problem appears on pages 19-20 of *Computer-Aided Problems to Accompany Basic Marketing.*

1. Texmac asked firms that had the old machine if they would replace it with their new product if it were priced at $10,000. Forty percent said that they would buy the new equipment. Texmac asked another question of the respondents who said that they would not buy the new equipment at $10,000. Specifically it asked if they would buy the new machine if it were priced at $9,750. Another 25 firms said that they would buy the new machine at the lower price. Texmac figures that those who said that they would buy the machine at the higher price would also buy it at the lower price.

    Based on this information and information from the spreadsheet for the problem (assuming that there are 5,000 firms), calculate what percent of the sample would buy the machine at the lower price:

    _____ percent who would buy only at the $9,750 price.

    plus _____ percent who would buy at either price.

    equals _____ total percent who would buy at lower price.

2. Now, use the spreadsheet to compute what results the firm would expect based on the lower price ($9,750) and the total percent who would buy at the lower price. Fill in the table below to compare these results with the results that would be expected at the higher price ($10,000).

	Price=$10,000	Price=$9,750
Expected quantity of replacements:	_____	_____
Total expected revenue:	_____	_____
Expected contribution to profit:	_____	_____

    Based on your analysis, would you recommend that Texmac set the price at $10,000 or $9,750?

    Price: $_____

3. The marketing manager at Texmac wants more detail about what might happen at the price you are recommending. He knows that the number of "old machines" reported by the 500 sample firms may not be exactly representative of the total population. But, marketing research specialists at the firm say that he can be 95 percent confident that the estimate of the number of old machines per 500 firms is probably accurate within a confidence interval of plus or minus 20 machines. Thus, the marketing manager wants to know how your estimate of contribution to profit might change if the actual number of old machines per 500 in the market varies over the range of the confidence interval. To provide this information, do a "What If" analysis and complete the table below. (Note: use the price and percent who would buy based on your recommendation from the previous page).

Estimated Number of Old Machines	Expected Profit
200 (minimum)	_____
204	_____
208	_____
212	_____
216	_____
220	_____
224	_____
228	_____
232	_____
236	_____
240 (maximum)	_____

4. Texmac's marketing manager says that the market opportunity will be less attractive than it looks if the actual number of textile producers in the population is smaller than the company thinks. Indicate if you agree or disagree with his statement. Briefly discuss why.

_____

_____

_____

Chapter 6

Demographic dimensions of the U.S. consumer market

What This Chapter Is About

Marketing-oriented managers must understand their customers--and Chapter 6 is the first of a group of three chapters about customers and their buying behavior. Actually, we know a great deal about potential customers. Therefore, there is no reason to rely on erroneous stereotypes or vague generalizations.

In this chapter you will see why demographic dimensions are important in selecting target markets. You will see how the U.S. population is changing--and why these changes are vital to marketing strategy planning. You will see how the age distribution is shifting--and how consumer spending patterns vary considerably by age, stage in family life cycle, and other dimensions.

Really understanding the material in this chapter will help you to deepen your skills in segmenting markets and evaluating market opportunities. So don't just memorize a lot of "facts." Instead, try to get a "feel" for relationships. Demographic relationships are enduring--and a good understanding of these relationships will help you avoid mistakes when decisions about the size or attractiveness of potential markets must be made quickly.

Important Terms

birth rate, p. 151
Metropolitan Statistical Area (MSA), p. 155
gross national product (GNP), p. 156
disposable income, p. 159

discretionary income, p. 160
empty nesters, p. 164
senior citizens, p. 164

True-False Questions

____ 1. Consumers who are 50 or older make up about half of the population, but they only have about 25 percent of the disposable income.

____ 2. Based on population alone, the Northeast United States looks like a more attractive market than the West Coast.

____ 3. Several of the Western states have experienced over 35 percent increase in population in the 1980s while some of the Northeastern states are actually declining in population.

___ 4. In spite of declining birth rates, it seems certain that the U.S. population will continue to grow--at least for sixty years or more.

___ 5. The birth rate--the number of babies per 1,000 people--has continued to decline for the last fifty years.

___ 6. Despite a declining birth rate, the average age of the population will continue to decrease for some time due to the effects of the post-World War II baby boom.

___ 7. During the 1980s, there have been big increases in the 25-44 age group and that growth will carry over to the 45-64 age group in the 1990s.

___ 8. About 80 percent of all households consist of married couples with children under 18.

___ 9. Single-adult households account for about 20 percent of all households in the United States.

___ 10. About 15 percent of all Americans live and work on farms in rural areas.

___ 11. A Metropolitan Statistical Area (MSA) is an integrated economic and social unit having a population nucleus of at least one million people.

___ 12. Consolidated Metropolitan Statistical Areas, the largest MSAs, have 1 million or more in population.

___ 13. Over 15 percent of all Americans move each year.

___ 14. The gross national product is a limited measure of the output of the economy since it considers the total market value of goods, but not services, produced in a year.

___ 15. The distribution of income in the United States has been changing drastically since 1930, moving a greater proportion of the families into the middle and upper income levels.

___ 16. More than 40 percent of the total U.S. income goes to the well-to-do households with incomes over $73,000--the top 5 percent.

___ 17. Disposable income is the income remaining after taxes and savings have been subtracted.

___ 18. Most discretionary income is spent on necessities.

___ 19. While income has a direct bearing on spending patterns, other demographic dimensions--such as age and stage in family life cycle--may be just as important to marketers.

___ 20. "Empty nesters" are an important group of highly mobile individuals who do not maintain a regular place of residence and thus are a very difficult group to track.

___ 21. Many firms cater to the senior citizen market--although about half of these older people are below the poverty level.

___ 22. More than 1 out of 10 families speaks a language other than English at home.

___ 23. More than 55 percent of married women now work outside the home.

Answers to True-False Questions

1. F, p. 148	9. T, p. 154	17. F, p. 159
2. T, p. 148	10. F, p. 154	18. F, p. 160
3. T, p. 150	11. F, p. 155	19. T, p. 162
4. T, p. 151	12. T, p. 155	20. F, p. 164
5. F, p. 151	13. T, p. 156	21. F, p. 164
6. F, p. 152	14. F, p. 156	22. T, p. 165
7. T, p. 153	15. T, p. 157	23. T, p. 166
8. F, p. 154	16. F, p. 158	

Multiple-Choice Questions (Circle the correct response)

1. Which of the following statements about the U.S. population is *true*?
   a. Between 1930 and 1987, the population doubled in every state in the nation.
   b. The U.S. population will stop growing by the year 2000.
   c. Our population is getting younger despite decreasing birth rates.
   d. Less than 5 percent of the population now live and work on farms.
   e. All of the above are true statements.

2. The state with the largest percentage increase in population between 1980 and 1990 is:
   a. New York
   b. Nevada
   c. Illinois
   d. Ohio
   e. Michigan

3. Which of the following is *not* an accurate statement about consumer markets in the United States?
   a. There are already over 225 million people in the United States.
   b. The average age of the U.S. population is rising.
   c. The number of people in the 25-44 age group will decline very substantially by 1990.
   d. Single-adult households account for about 20 percent of all households.
   e. About half of the people who move are moving to a new city.

4. Which of the following statements is *true*?
   a. A Metropolitan Statistical Area generally centers on one urbanized area of 50,000 or more in population and includes bordering "urban" areas.
   b. Some national marketers sell only in the largest Metropolitan Statistical Areas.
   c. Metropolitan Statistical Areas are a more useful classification method for marketers than political boundaries.
   d. All of the above are true statements.
   e. None of the above are true statements.

5. Mobility has an important bearing on marketing planning. Approximately what percent of Americans move each year?
   a. 7 percent
   b. 17 percent
   c. 27 percent
   d. 37 percent
   e. 50 percent

6. The income distribution in the United States
   a. makes little difference to marketing decisions, since it can't be controlled by the marketing manager.
   b. has stayed about the same for 50 years.
   c. now has a larger percent of people at the lower levels.
   d. shows that higher income people still receive a very large share of the total income.
   e. none of the above are true.

7. With respect to income, government data indicate that:
   a. the U.S. gross national product now exceeds $5 trillion.
   b. most Americans are still at the bottom of the income pyramid.
   c. middle-income families are enjoying huge increases in real income.
   d. there are only a few families in the United States with incomes over $45,000.
   e. None of the above is a true statement.

8. Disposable income is defined as:
   a. total market value of goods and services produced.
   b. gross national product per capita.
   c. income available after taxes.
   d. income available before taxes.
   e. income available after taxes and "necessities."

9. Which of the following statements is true?
   a. Most senior citizens have income below the poverty level.
   b. Singles and young couples are more willing to try new products.
   c. Empty nesters are frequently big spenders.
   d. b and c are true statements, but not a.
   e. All of the above are true statements.

10. Which of the following stages in the family life cycle can be described as follows: Financially even better off as husband earns more and more wives work. May replace durables and furniture, and buy cars, boats, dental services, and more expensive recreation and travel. May buy bigger houses.
    a. Newly married couples with no children
    b. Empty nest
    c. Full nest III--older couples with dependent children
    d. Senior citizen I--older married couple, no children living with them, head retired
    e. Full nest I--youngest child under 6

Answers to Multiple-Choice Questions

1. d, p. 150-54   5. b, p. 156   9. d, p. 161-66
2. b, p. 150   6. d, p. 158   10. c, p. 163
3. c, p. 153   7. e, p. 156-59
4. d, p. 155   8. c, p. 159

Exercise 6-1

How demographic trends affect marketing strategy planning

Introduction

A common approach to identifying markets uses "demographic" characteristics of customers--such as age, sex, race, education, occupation, geographical location, income, marital status, and family size. The popularity of demographics is due to the fact that such characteristics are easily measured, easily understood, and readily available in published form. Demographic characteristics are very useful for identifying market segments, planning appropriate marketing mixes and estimating market potential.

This exercise will stress another major use of demographics--to monitor changes and trends in the uncontrollable cultural and social environments to help find new marketing opportunities.

We will focus on four major demographic trends:

1. The maturing of the post-World War II "baby boom" generation
2. The increasing number and age of elderly people
3. The increasing number of women in the labor force
4. The trend toward smaller family units

You will be asked to evaluate the likely positive or negative effects of these four trends on three major industries.

Assignment

Listed below are three major industries in the United States. In the space provided, discuss the likely positive and/or negative effects of the above-mentioned demographic trends on *each* of the three industries. Base your answers on the text discussion and your general knowledge--DO NOT DO ANY LIBRARY OR FIELD RESEARCH. Use your head instead--to apply what you already know!

Industries

Apparel   Home Furnishings   Restaurants

1. Industry: Apparel

    a) Effects of baby boom generation maturing:

    b) Effects of more elderly persons:

    c) Effects of more working women:

    d) Effects of smaller family units:

2. Industry: Home Furnishings

a) Effects of baby boom generation maturing:

b) Effects of more elderly persons:

c) Effects of more working women:

d) Effects of smaller family units:

3.   Industry: Restaurants

    a)   Effects of baby boom generation maturing:

    b)   Effects of more elderly persons:

    c)   Effects of more working women:

    d)   Effects of smaller family units:

Question for Discussion

Name some other important demographic trends. How might these trends affect the three industries discussed in the exercise?

Exercise 6-2

Marketers must know their markets

Introduction

The "golden rule" of marketing is: "Know thy market!" Firms that live by this rule are generally more successful than those that do not. And the fact that *most* new businesses and products fail is ample proof that many firms do *not* know their markets.

Some marketers pay close attention to government statistics--anxious to take advantage of any new opportunities such data may reveal. Surprisingly, however, many marketers seem to be almost totally unaware of how much valuable demographic data is already available.

This exercise has a twofold purpose. First, it will help you see what you know about the U.S. market. If you are like most people, some of your views will be grossly inaccurate. That explains our other purpose--to familiarize you with the kinds of demographic data that are usually available in published form.

Every marketer should be an expert on sources of marketing information. In Exercise 5-1, you learned about several valuable sources. Now, we will look in depth at just one source--the *Statistical Abstract of the United States*. Issued annually by the U.S. Department of Commerce, the *Abstract* contains over 1,000 summary tables of statistics describing social, political, and economic trends in the United States and world markets. Each issue also contains a "Bibliography of Sources and Statistics" which--together with detailed footnotes--can guide you to more specific sources of information. The *Abstract* is probably the best starting point for locating statistical data--and an invaluable reference book for any marketer who wishes to keep informed of demographic trends.

Assignment

The following list of questions is designed to check your knowledge of the U.S. market. For each question, make your best guess as to what the correct answer is and write your "guesstimate" in column A. *Do not try to look up the correct answer in any reference source until you have completed column A!* There is no penalty for being wrong!

After you have completed column A, go to a library and obtain the *most recent* available edition of the *Statistical Abstract of the United States*. Use the *Abstract* to look up the correct answers to each question and write the answers in column B.

When data are given for several different years, always use the most recent year shown. Note that every question *can* be answered from the *Abstract*. (And while you're digging through the *Abstract* for the answers, take a look at all the other kinds of information it provides!)

(Show date of *Abstract* used _____)

		(A) Your Guesstimates	(B) Answers from *Abstract*

1. What is the total U.S. population?

2. How many households are there in the United States and what percentage have less than 3 persons?

3. What is the U.S. birth rate per 1,000 population?

4. What percentage of the total U.S. population live in each of the following regions?
   a) Northeast
   b) North Central
   c) South
   d) West

5. Which three states in the United States have the highest per capita income?

6. What is the median age of the U.S. population?

7. What percentage of all persons 25 years and over in the United States:
   a) are *not* high school graduates?
   b) have completed at least 4 years of college?

8. What is the annual U.S. per capita consumption of:
   a) eggs?
   b) coffee?
   c) beer?

9. What percentage of the total U.S. labor force is the female labor force?

10. What percentage of all families in the United States have incomes of:
    a) less than $5,000?
    b) more than $25,000?

11. What percentage of total personal consumption
    expenditures are made for the following products?
    a) Food, beverages, and tobacco
    b) Clothing, accessories, and jewelry
    c) Transportation

12. What percentage of all U.S. households own:
    a)   a color TV set?
    b)   a dishwasher?

Question for Discussion

How do your "guesstimates" compare with the answers found in the *Statistical Abstract of the United States?* What does this mean regarding marketing strategy planning?

Name: _____ Course & Section: _____

Exercise 6-3

Demographic analysis

This exercise is based on computer-aided problem number 6--Demographic Analysis. A complete description of the problem appears on pages 20-21 of *Computer-Aided Problems to Accompany Basic Marketing.*

1. Stylco's marketing manager had not given a lot of thought to how market growth might affect the firm. The amount people were spending on clothes had not been increasing in the past, and he had become accustomed to a "steady state" business. The current situation has made him think about this in more detail. In fact, he is wondering how much the growth rate of the adult customer group will influence Stylco's profits. To provide some insight, do a What If analysis to show how profit from the adult line in the year 2000 might change by varying the growth rate between a minimum of 4 percent and 44 percent.

growth rate %	profit
4	$_____
8	$_____
12	$_____
16	$_____
20	$_____
24	$_____
28	$_____
32	$_____
36	$_____
40	$_____
44	$_____

2. Stylco's marketing manager does not really expect the growth rate for this age group to drop as low as 4 percent, or to be as high as 44 percent. But this analysis does show that the profitability of a marketing strategy over time might be influenced a lot by changes in demographic trends. Briefly contrast the disadvantages of a market that is declining in size with the advantages of selecting a growing market.

_____

_____

_____

_____

3. Stylco's marketing manager has read that the number of people in the 45 to 64 age range is not only increasing rapidly, but that people in this age group are likely to become less homogeneous over time. There will be even greater differences in characteristics like income and education. Stylco's marketing manager thinks that this may open an opportunity to target really wealthy consumers in this age group with a more expensive (and profitable) product line. He estimates that this wealthy segment of the 45-64 age group will include 9,290,600 people in 1990, and that this segment will grow at a 35 percent rate between 1990 and 2000. The marketing mix changes he has in mind would result in a profit of $15 per unit. The other segment of his market, which accounts for the rest of the people, will only grow at a 29.8 percent rate.

Answer the following questions. (Hint: do a separate analysis on the spreadsheet for each of the two segments, and then calculate the summary results.)

If, by targeting the wealthy consumers he could increase his ratio of unit sales to population to .002, what profit could he expect to earn from a marketing mix aimed at this subgroup.

profit: $_____

4. If he also continued to offer a marketing mix for the remainder of the adult customers--and maintained his ratio of unit sales to population at .001--what profit (in the year 2000) could he expect to earn from a marketing mix aimed at this subgroup?

(Hint: First, determine how large this segment is likely to be, and then change the spreadsheet to analyze a segment of that size--assuming that the profit per unit for that segment remains at $8.00 a unit.)

size of "remainder" segment: _____
(total size minus size of wealthy segment)

profit from this segment: $_____

5. If he followed this approach of developing different strategies for the two different segments, what would his total profit be (in the year 2000) from the two segments of the 45 to 64 year old customers? (Sum of profit estimates on previous page.)

total profit from 45 to 64 age customers: $_____

6. Briefly discuss how this compares with the profits he might expect from the adult customers based on the current approach. Would it make sense to develop a different marketing mix for each segment of the 45 to 64 age customers? Why or why not?

_____

_____

_____

_____

Chapter 7

Behavioral dimensions of the consumer market

What This Chapter Is About

Chapter 7 focuses on the contribution of the behavioral sciences to our understanding of consumer behavior. As we saw in Chapter 6, demographic analysis does not fully explain *why* people buy or *what* they buy.

The importance of considering several behavioral dimensions at the same time is stressed. This is not easy because there are many psychological and sociological theories. Nevertheless, marketing managers must make decisions based on their knowledge of potential target markets. They must do their best to integrate the various theories and findings. This chapter is intended to get you started on this task.

Several buyer behavior models are presented to help organize your thinking. Then their interrelation is suggested in a "big" model of the consumer's problem solving process. Try to find a way of integrating these models together for yourself. Behavioral science findings can be a great help, but you still must add your own judgment to apply the various findings in particular markets. These findings coupled with "market sense" can take you a long way in marketing strategy planning.

Important Terms

stimulus-response model, p. 171
economic men, p. 171
needs, p. 172
wants, p. 172
drive, p. 172
physiological needs, p. 172
safety needs, p. 172
social needs, p. 172
personal needs, p. 172
economic needs, p. 174
selective exposure, p. 175
selective perception, p. 175
selective retention, p. 175
learning, p. 176
cues, p. 176
response, p. 176
reinforcement, p. 176
attitude, p. 177

belief, p. 177
psychographics, p. 178
life-style analysis, p. 178
social class, p. 180
upper class, p. 181
upper-middle class, p. 182
lower-middle class, p. 182
upper-lower class, p. 182
lower-lower class, p. 182
reference group, p. 183
opinion leader, p. 184
culture, p. 184
extensive problem solving, p. 187
limited problem solving, p. 188
routinized response behavior, p. 188
low involvement purchases, p. 188
adoption process, p. 188
dissonance, p. 189

True-False Questions

T 1. Because demographic analysis isn't of much value in predicting which products and brands will be purchased, many marketers have turned to the behavioral sciences for insight and help.

F 2. The "black box" model of buyer behavior is based on the stimulus-response model--and explains why consumers behave the way they do.

T 3. Behavioral scientists suggest that the "black box" works in a more complicated way than the "economic-man" model.

T ~~4.~~ A drive is a strong need that is learned during a person's life.

T 5. Motivation theory suggests that people have hierarchies of needs, and that they never reach a state of complete satisfaction.

F 6. The PSSP needs are power, security, social acceptance, and prestige.

F ~~7.~~ The basic needs (PSSP) can help explain what we buy--but the economic needs can help explain why we buy specific product features.

T 8. Economic needs include things such as convenience, efficiency in operation or use, dependability in use, and economy of purchase or use.

T 9. Selective perception refers to a person's ability to screen out or modify ideas, messages, or information that conflict with previously learned attitudes and beliefs.

T 10. Learning is a change in a person's thought processes caused by prior experience.

F 11. Reinforcement of the learning process occurs when a cue follows a response and leads to a reduction in the drive tension.

T 12. An attitude is a person's point of view towards something.

F 13. Advertising is so powerful that changing consumers' negative attitudes is usually the easiest part of the marketing manager's job.

T ~~14.~~ Personality traits have been very useful to marketers in predicting which products or brands target customers will choose.

T ~~F~~ 15. Life-style analysis refers to the analysis of a person's day-to-day pattern of living--as expressed in his activities, interests, and opinions.

T 16. Social influences are concerned with how an individual interacts with family, social class, and other groups who may have influence on the buying process.

T 17. Buying responsibility and influence within a family vary greatly--depending on the product and the family.

F 18. The social class system in the United States is usually measured in terms of income, race, and occupation.

T F 19. More than half of our society is *not* middle class.

T 20. Middle-class consumers tend to be more future-oriented and self-confident than lower-class consumers.

T 21. A person normally has several reference groups.

F 22. "Opinion leaders" are generally higher income people and better educated.

T 23. The attitudes and beliefs that we usually associate with culture tend to change slowly.

T 24. Different purchase situations may require different marketing mixes--even when the same target market is involved.

T 25. A grid of evaluative criteria can be used to help managers think about how customers evaluate a marketing mix.

T 26. A homemaker doing weekly grocery shopping is more likely to use extensive problem-solving than limited problem-solving or routinized response behavior.

F 27. Low involvement products are products which are seldom purchased by the target market.

T 28. In the adoption process, the evaluation step usually comes before the trial step.

T 29. Dissonance might cause a consumer to pay more attention to automobile advertisements after a new car is purchased than before the purchase.

T 30. Knowing how a target market handles the problem-solving process, the adoption process, and learning can aid marketing strategy planning.

Answers to True-False Questions

1. T, p. 170	11. F, p. 176	21. T, p. 183
2. F, p. 171	12. T, p. 177	22. F, p. 184
3. T, p. 171	13. F, p. 178	23. T, p. 184
4. F, p. 172	14. F, p. 178	24. T, p. 184
5. T, p. 172-74	15. T, p. 178	25. F, p. 185
6. F, p. 172	16. T, p. 180	26. F, p. 188
7. T, p. 174	17. T, p. 180	27. F, p. 188
8. T, p. 174	18. F, p. 181	28. T, p. 188
9. T, p. 175	19. T, p. 182	29. T, p. 189
10. T, p. 176	20. T, p. 183	30. T, p. 189

Multiple-Choice Questions (Circle the correct response)

 1. According to the text, the consumer "black box" model:
   a. is controlled by social influences.
   b. is a stimulus-response model.
   c. reveals that we all behave like "economic men."
   d. is controlled by psychological variables.
   e. explains why people behave the way they do.

2. Which of the following is *not* a psychological variable?
   a. Social class
   b. Motivation
   c. Perception
   d. Attitudes
   e. Learning

 3. According to motivation theory, the *last* needs a family would usually seek to satisfy would be:
   a. safety needs.
   b. personal needs.
   c. physiological needs.
   d. social needs.

4. Motivation theory suggests that:
   a. lower-level needs must be completely satisfied before higher-level needs become important.
   b. a particular good or service might satisfy different levels of needs at the same time.
   c. all consumers satisfy needs in the same order.
   d. self-esteem is an example of a social need.
   e. All of the above are true statements.

 5. Why customers select specific product features may be best explained by:
   a. physiological needs.
   b. safety needs.
   c. personal needs.
   d. economic needs.
   e. social needs.

6. When consumers screen out or modify ideas, messages, and information that conflict with previously learned attitudes and beliefs, this is called:
   a. selective retention.
   b. selective exposure.
   c. selective perception.
   d. selective dissonance.
   e. selective cognition.

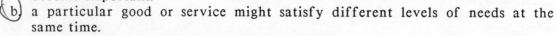

7. A change in a person's thought processes caused by prior experience is called:
   a. learning
   b. attitude change
   c. belief change
   d. response
   e. reinforcement

8. Which of the following is not a major element in the learning process?
   a. Drive
   b. Cues
   c. Dissonance
   d. Reinforcement
   e. Response

9. An attitude:
   a. is easily changed.
   b. is a person's point of view toward something.
   c. is the same as opinion and belief.
   d. is a reliable indication of intention to buy.
   e. All of the above are true statements.

10. The AIO items used in life-style analysis include:
    a. activities, interests, and opinions.
    b. attitudes, interests, and opinions.
    c. activities, intentions, and opinions.
    d. attitudes, intentions, and opinions.
    e. attitudes, income, and opinions.

11. Which of the following is *not* a social influence?
    a. Culture
    b. Social class
    c. Family
    d. Reference group
    e. Personality

12. According to the text, social class is usually measured in terms of:
    a. income.
    b. occupation, education, and housing arrangements.
    c. income, occupation, and education.
    d. race, religion, and occupation.
    e. income, occupation, and religion.

13. Jack Simmons, now an account representative responsible for selling computer systems to some of ABC Corporation's major accounts--has been with ABC since graduating from Southern University in 1965. Jack's father was a plumber, but Jack is a professional--one of ABC's top five salespeople--and earns about $70,000 a year in salary and commissions. Jack is a member of the _____ social class.
    a. upper
    b. upper-middle
    c. lower-middle
    d. upper-lower
    e. lower-lower

14. For which of the following products would reference group influence probably be *least important*?
    a. Clothing
    b. Cigarettes
    c. Furniture
    d. Canned peaches
    e. Wine

15. Opinion leaders are:
    a. usually better educated.
    b. usually reference group leaders.
    c. not necessarily opinion leaders on all subjects.
    d. usually wealthy, middle- or upper-class people.
    e. All of the above are true statements.

16. Behavioral scientists recognize different *levels* of consumer problem solving. Which of the following is *not* one of these levels?
    a. Routinized response behavior
    b. Limited problem solving
    c. Rational problem solving
    d. Extensive problem solving
    e. All of the above are recognized levels of problem solving.

17. Which of the following gives the proper *ordering* of the stages in the "adoption process"?
    a. Awareness, interest, trial, evaluation, decision, dissonance
    b. Awareness, interest, trial, decision, evaluation, confirmation
    c. Awareness, interest, evaluation, trial, decision, confirmation
    d. Interest, awareness, trial, decision, evaluation, dissonance
    e. Awareness, interest, evaluation, decision, trial, confirmation

18. Dissonance is:
    a. a type of cue.
    b. a form of laziness commonly observed among low-income consumers.
    c. a type of positive reinforcement.
    d. tension caused by uncertainty about the rightness of a decision.
    e. none of the above.

19. The present state of our knowledge about consumer behavior is such that:
    a. the behavioral sciences provide the marketing manager with a complete explanation of the "whys" of consumer behavior.
    b. we still must rely heavily on intuition and judgment to explain and predict consumer behavior.
    c. relevant market dimensions can be easily identified and measured using "psychographics."
    d. marketing research can't tell us much more about specific aspects of consumer behavior.
    e. All of the above are true statements.

Answers to Multiple-Choice Questions

1. b, p. 171	8. c, p. 176	15. c, p. 184
2. a, p. 172	9. b, p. 177	16. c, p. 187
3. b, p. 172	10. a, p. 178	17. c, p. 188
4. b, p. 172-74	11. e, p. 180	18. d, p. 189
5. d, p. 174	12. b, p. 181	19. b, p. 190
6. c, p. 175	13. b, p. 182	
7. a, p. 176	14. d, p. 183	

Exercise 7-1

Psychological variables and social influences affect consumer buying behavior

Introduction

To plan good marketing strategies, marketing managers must try to improve their understanding of buying behavior. Ideally, marketers would like to know *how* and *why* individual consumers buy the way they do. Then it might be possible to group individual consumers with similar needs and buying behavior into homogeneous market segments for which suitable marketing mixes could be developed.

This is easier said than done, however, because human behavior is very complex. Traditional demographic analysis, for example, can be used to study basic trends in consumer spending patterns, but it is of little use in explaining *why* people like, choose, buy, and use the products and brands they do.

For this reason, many marketers have turned to the behavioral sciences for help in understanding how and why consumers behave as they do. However, there is no "grand theory" available right now which ties together all the behavioral theories and concepts in a way which will explain and predict all aspects of human behavior. Therefore, marketers must try to understand the various behavioral theories and concepts. Then they can put them together into a model of consumer behavior which works in their own particular situation.

Hopefully, the complex decision-making processes which take place within the consumer's "black box" are clearer to you after reading Chapter 7 of the text. Although the simplified model of buyer behavior presented in the text can't explain or predict consumer behavior, it does provide a useful framework which identifies the major variables which influence consumer behavior.

This exercise should improve your understanding of various psychological variables and social influences which may affect a consumer's behavior. You will recall from Chapter 7 that psychological variables focus on the individual while social influences involve relations with others.

Assignment

In the short cases which follow, a variety of psychological variables and social influences are operating to influence a consumer's response. For each case, identify the relevant psychological variables and social influences and briefly explain how that item is illustrated in the case. The first case has been completed for you as an example.

1.   Joan and Paul Davis and their two children are considering the purchase of a recreational vehicle. Paul is enthusiastic because, he argues, the RV would be perfect for family camping trips, as well as fishing trips with his friends. Joan is less in favor of the purchase. She is nervous about camping in remote locations--and wonders how they would get help in emergencies. She also remembers a report that RVs get low gas mileage and are, therefore, expensive to run. Paul is quick to point out that the same report described the large potential savings of a week-long vacation in an RV compared to staying at a hotel or motel.

   a.   Psychological variables

        1)   PSSP hierarchy   Explanation: Joan is afraid of being isolated-- safety needs.

        2)   Selective Processes   Explanation: Joan only remembers the part of the report that supports her viewpoint.

   b.   Social influences

        1)   Family   Explanation: Paul wants to take family camping vacations, but Joan is concerned about the family's safety.

        2)   Reference Group   Explanation: Paul wants to take his friends on a fishing trip in "his" RV.

2.   Bill Ebner has a busy life, and he has lots of activities in the evening. Because of this, he decided to buy a videocassette recorder (VCR)--so he wouldn't miss his favorite TV shows. He also liked the idea of "skipping" past the ads on shows he taped. There are two types of recorders, but he knew he wanted one like his friends own--so he could trade tapes. In fact, a friend who recommended the RCA brand TV he bought also suggested that he buy an RCA recorder. Bill has enjoyed his TV, so he bought what the friend suggested, even though he thought it was probably more expensive than some of the other brands.

   a.   Psychological variables

        1) _____   Explanation: _____

        _____

        2) _____   Explanation: _____

        _____

3) _____ Explanation: _____

_____

b.   Social influences

1) _____ Explanation: _____

_____

2) _____ Explanation: _____

_____

2.   Mindy Petrucci is planning a vacation, but is unsure where she wants to go or
     what she wants to do. She has asked her "well traveled" boss for his advice,
     and has started noticing magazine articles about the various possibilities. She
     is most interested in a Club Med package to the Caribbean. It offers an "all-
     inclusive package of food, drink, organized activities and instruction, and free
     use of all facilities--including swimming, tennis, wind-surfing, sailing, water-
     skiing, snorkeling, scuba-diving, ping-pong, crafts, games--as well as nightly
     entertainment." All this is available in one, informal, self-contained place.
     Mindy is an outdoors-type who enjoys sports and excitement. She hates
     getting dressed up and is very interested in meeting new people. She
     remembers that two of her friends went last year and had a great time.

     a.   Psychological variables

     1) _____ Explanation: _____

     _____

     2) _____ Explanation: _____

     b.   Social influences

     1) _____ Explanation: _____

     _____

3.   Robert Ezzell just returned from a year in France as an exchange student. To
     see his old friends, he is planning a dinner party with a French menu. As he
     is shopping for the necessary supplies, he recalls his first experience with
     escargot--a delicacy of broiled snails he plans to serve at his party. When
     Robert was told by his host family what he had been served, he was not sure
     he would be able to eat it. Nothing in his American upbringing had prepared
     him to eat snails. However, he did not want to offend his hosts, so he smiled
     bravely and downed the escargot. To his amazement it was delicious, and he
     now enjoys escargot frequently. He is sure he will have to be very persuasive
     to overcome his friends' initial reactions.

a.   Psychological variables

   1) _____   Explanation: _____

   _____

   2) _____   Explanation: _____

   _____

   3) _____   Explanation: _____

   _____

b.   Social influences

   1) _____   Explanation: _____

   _____

Question for Discussion

Which items--psychological variables or social influences--have the most influence over consumer behavior and thus are more important for the marketing strategy planner?

Exercise 7-2

Consumer behavior is a problem-solving process

Introduction

While consumer behavior may often appear to be quite irrational to the casual observer, most behavioral scientists agree that consumers are *problem solvers* seeking to relieve tension caused by their unsatisfied needs. How an individual consumer goes about solving problems depends on the intra-personal and inter-personal variables that affect that individual. In general, however, most consumers tend to follow the following five-step problem-solving process:

1. Becoming aware of--or interested in--the problem.
2. Gathering information about possible solutions.
3. Evaluating alternative solutions--perhaps trying some out.
4. Deciding on the appropriate solution.
5. Evaluating the decision.

The length of time it takes to complete the problem-solving process and how much attention is given to each of the five steps depends, of course, on the nature of the problem and how much experience an individual has had in trying to solve this particular kind of problem. To understand the process better, it helps to recognize three levels of problem solving: *extensive problem solving, limited problem solving*, and *routinized response behavior.*

The purpose of this exercise is to illustrate the three levels of consumer problem solving by relating the problem-solving process to *your* problem-solving experiences in the marketplace.

Assignment

Think of *three* recent purchases that *you* made that involved extensive problem solving, limited problem solving, and routinized response behavior. For each of these purchases, outline the problem-solving process that you used. You may wish to follow the five-step process listed above, indicating how you went about performing each of the five steps.

1. Routinized response behavior: Product _____

   Explanation:

2.   Limited problem-solving: Product _____

     Explanation:

3.   Extensive problem-solving: Product _____

     Explanation:

Question for Discussion

Which of the three levels of problem solving offers marketers the most opportunity?
The least opportunity? Why?

Exercise 7-3

Selective processes

This exercise is based on computer-aided problem number 7--Selective Processes. A complete description of the problem appears on pages 21-22 of *Computer-Aided Problems to Accompany Basic Marketing*.

1. Submag's marketing manager analyzed the response of a previous mailing to customers on the *first* mailing list. He found that 3,105 subscriptions were received from a total mailing of 25,000 promotion pieces.

    What percent of the people who received the initial mailing subscribed? _____

2. By analyzing subscription orders from the first list by zip code area, he found that the orders from people who lived in large cities averaged $4.00, substantially higher than their "country cousins." He concluded that city residents were more interested in his magazines. The company that provided the first mailing list said that it could use a computer to sort future lists so that Submag only got names and addresses of people who live in large cities. This service would cost an extra $.02 per name (mailing). Would it make sense for Submag to target its promotion at people who live in large cities and spend more (i.e., by using the sorted mailing list)? Explain your answer.

    _____

    _____

    _____

3. Submag's marketing manager thinks that people who live in large cities are also less likely to miss the point of the ads. This would result in losing fewer potential customers due to selective exposure. Assuming 25,000 mailings, do an analysis that shows how the number of subscribers and expected profit change as the percent of consumers lost due to selective perception varies between 50 percent to 70 percent, and then answer the questions below. (Note: remember that city dwellers are likely to spend an average of $4.00 per subscription, and that it will cost $.34 per mailing).

    In this situation, how many subscribers would be required to earn a profit of $8,060?

    _____ number of subscribers

At a profit of $8,060, what percent of potential customers would be lost due to selective perception?

_____ percent

If the percentage of customers lost due to selective perception were reduced from the above percent to 52 percent, what would the difference in expected profits be?

$_____.00 profit at 52 percent lost due to selective perception

-_____8,060.00

$_____ difference in profit if selective perception is reduced

4. The supplier of the first list has told Submag's marketing manager that other direct mail marketers have found that people in large cities are more likely to open the envelope and read a mailing if the name is printed directly on the envelope (instead of on an adhesive mailing label) or if the name and address is printed on the letter itself. It would cost Submag an extra 2 cents per mailing to add this personalizing. This would probably reduce the number of people who threw out the mailings without opening them. If using the sorted mailing list and personalizing the letters reduced the percentage of potential customers lost due to selective exposure to 4 percent, would it make sense for Submag to go to the extra expense of personalizing the letters? Explain your answer.

_____

_____

_____

_____

_____

_____

Chapter 8

Industrial and intermediate customers and their buying behavior

What This Chapter Is About

Chapter 8 discusses the buying behavior of the important industrial and intermediate customers who buy for resale or for use in their own businesses. They buy more goods and services than final customers!

Intermediate customers tend to be much more economic in their buying behavior than final consumers. Further, some must follow pre-set bidding and bargaining processes. Yet, they too have emotional needs. And sometimes a number of different people may influence the final purchase decision. Keep in mind that intermediate customers are problem solvers too. Many of the ideas in Chapter 7 carry over--but with some adaptation.

This chapter deserves careful study because your past experience as a consumer is not as helpful here as it was in the last few chapters. Intermediate customers are much less numerous. In some cases it is possible to create a separate marketing mix for each individual intermediate customer. Understanding these customers is necessary to plan marketing strategies for them. Try to see how they are both similar and different from final customers.

Important Terms

intermediate customers, p. 194
standard industrial classification
  (SIC) codes, p. 196
new-task buying, p. 198
straight rebuy, p. 198
modified rebuy, p. 199
purchasing agents, p. 199
vendor analysis, p. 200
multiple buying influence, p. 201
buying center, p. 202

inspection buying, p. 203
sampling buying, p. 203
description (specification) buying, p. 203
negotiated contract buying, p. 204
requisition, p. 205
just-in-time delivery, p. 206
reciprocity, p. 206
open to buy, p. 210
resident buyers, p. 211

True-False Questions

_____ 1. Intermediate customers are wholesalers or retailers, but not buyers who buy to produce other goods and services.

___ 2. Since sellers usually approach each intermediate customer directly through a sales representative, it is possible that there can be a special marketing strategy for each individual customer.

___ 3. Retailers are the largest group of intermediate customers.

___ 4. Manufacturers tend to be concentrated by geographic location and industry, and the majority of them are quite small.

___ 5. Two-digit SIC code breakdowns start with broad industry categories, but more detailed data may be available for three-digit and four-digit industries.

___ 6. When the majority of a company's purchases involve straight rebuy buying, these purchases occupy most of an effective buyer's time.

___ 7. A salesperson usually must see the industrial buyer or purchasing agent first, before any other employee in the firm is contacted.

___ 8. "Vendor analysis" involves formal rating of suppliers on all relevant areas of performance.

___ 9. Emotional needs are often quite relevant for the typical purchasing agent, and therefore a marketing mix should seek to satisfy both the buyer's company needs and the buyer's individual needs.

___ 10. Strong multiple-buying influence is most likely to be involved when there is new-task buying.

___ 11. Multiple-buying influence makes the promotion job easier.

___ 12. A buying center consists of all the people who participate in or influence a purchase.

___ 13. Buying by inspection would probably be necessary for a firm that wanted to purchase a large supply of nuts and bolts.

___ 14. As products become more standardized, perhaps because of more careful grading and better quality control, sampling buying becomes possible.

___ 15. Services are usually purchased by description.

___ 16. Negotiated contracts commonly are used for products which can be described sufficiently well that suppliers know what is wanted and can submit definite prices or bids.

___ 17. Even if a firm has developed the best marketing mix possible, it probably will not get all of the business of its industrial customers.

___ 18. A requisition is a request to buy something.

___ 19. Industrial buyers typically do not even see a sales rep for straight rebuys.

___ 20. Buyers who delegate routine buying to a computer might be more favorably impressed by a new company's offer of an attractive marketing mix, perhaps for a whole line of products, rather than just a lower price for a particular order.

___ 21. "Just-in-time" delivery means reliably getting products there before or very soon after they are needed.

___ 22. Purchasing agents tend to resist reciprocity, but it may be forced on them by their sales departments.

___ 23. Compared to manufacturers, services firms are more numerous, smaller, and more spread out.

___ 24. Most retail and wholesale buyers see themselves as selling agents for manufacturers.

___ 25. The large number of items bought and stocked by wholesalers and retailers makes it imperative that inventories be watched carefully.

___ 26. The retail buyer is "open-to-buy" whenever his cost of merchandise is less than his forecasted sales.

___ 27. Resident buyers are employees of retail stores whose job it is to reach the many small manufacturers in central markets who cannot afford large sales departments.

___ 28. Committee buying by retailers will probably force better strategy planning by wholesalers and manufacturers, instead of relying just on persuasive salespeople.

___ 29. The government market is the largest customer group in the United States--accounting for about 21 percent of the U.S. gross national product.

___ 30. All government customers are required by law to use a mandatory bidding procedure which is open to public review.

___ 31. Government buyers avoid the use of negotiated contracts whenever there are a lot of intangible factors.

1. F, p. 195	12. T, p. 202	23. T, p. 207
2. T, p. 195	13. F, p. 203	24. F, p. 208
3. F, p. 195	14. T, p. 203	25. T, p. 209
4. T, p. 195	15. T, p. 204	26. F, p. 210
5. T, p. 196	16. F, p. 204	27. F, p. 211
6. F, p. 198	17. T, p. 205	28. T, p. 211
7. T, p. 199	18. T, p. 205	29. T, p. 211
8. T, p. 200	19. T, p. 205	30. F, p. 212
9. T, p. 200	20. T, p. 205	31. F, p. 213
10. T, p. 201	21. F, p. 206	
11. F, p. 202	22. T, p. 206	

Multiple-Choice Questions (Circle the correct response)

1. The bulk of all buying done in the United States is not by final consumers--but rather by intermediate customers. Which of the following is an intermediate customer?
   a. a manufacturer.
   b. a retailer.
   c. a wholesaler.
   d. a government agency.
   e. All of the above are intermediate customers.

2. Which of the following SIC codes would provide the most specific information about a sub-category of an industry?
   a. 3
   b. 31
   c. 314
   d. 3142
   e. Cannot be determined without additional information.

3. A large manufacturer is about to purchase a large supply of an unfamiliar chemical that will be used in the production of an important new product. What kind of buying would the company be most likely to do?
   a. New-task buying
   b. Straight rebuy buying
   c. Modified rebuy buying

4. In comparison to the buying of final consumers, the purchasing of industrial buyers:
   a. is strictly economic and not at all emotional.
   b. is always based on bids from multiple suppliers.
   c. leans basically toward economy, quality, and dependability.
   d. is even less predictable.
   e. Both a and c are true statements.

5. Today, many agricultural commodities and manufactured items are subject to rigid control or grading. As a result, the buying and selling of these goods can be done at a low cost by:
   a. inspection.
   b. sampling.
   c. description.
   d. negotiated contracts.

6. An automobile manufacturer's practice of buying some of its raw materials from other manufacturers who in turn buy from it is an example of:
   a. tying contracts.
   b. vendor analysis.
   c. buying by description.
   d. being "open to buy."
   e. reciprocity.

7. As contrasted with manufacturers, producers of services are:
   a. more geographically spread out.
   b. more numerous.
   c. less well represented by SIC data.
   d. All of the above.
   e. None of the above.

8. Which of the following statements about retail buying is *false*?
   a. In most retail operations, a "resident buyer" runs his own department--and his decision is final.
   b. Retail buyers may be responsible for supervising the salesclerks who sell the merchandise they buy.
   c. Retail buyers make most purchases as straight rebuys.
   d. A retail buyer is usually "open to buy" only when he has not spent all of his budgeted funds.
   e. In large retail stores, buyers tend to specialize in certain lines.

9. Which of the following statements about bidding for government business is *true*?
   a. Government buying needs are hard to identify--and their primary concern is with finding the lowest price.
   b. Government buyers avoid using negotiated contracts since they must purchase at a pre-set price.
   c. A government buyer may be forced to accept the lowest bid whether he wants the goods or not.
   d. The biggest job of the government buyer is to locate enough potential suppliers so the bidding procedure works effectively.
   e. All of the above are true statements.

Answers to Multiple-Choice Questions

1. e, p. 195   4. c, p. 199   7. d, p. 207
2. d, p. 197   5. c, p. 203   8. a, p. 211
3. a, p. 198   6. e, p. 206   9. c, p. 212-13

Name: _____ Course & Section: _____

Exercise 8-1

Analyzing industrial buying behavior

Introduction

Some people see industrial buying and consumer buying as two very different processes. Industrial buying is thought of as "economic," while consumer buying is seen as "emotional." In fact, closer study of buying processes suggests that industrial and consumer buying may be quite similar in many ways. For example, like consumers, industrial buyers are *problem solvers*. And while their problems may be very different, both consumer and industrial buyers seem to use three levels of problem solving. In Chapter 7, we saw that consumer buyers do extended, limited, and routinized problem solving. Similarly, industrial buyers do *new-task, straight rebuy, and modified rebuy buying*.

Recognition of the three levels of problem solving by industrial buyers *and* the different problem solving steps they pass through has important implications for market analysis. It suggests that industrial markets can be segmented not only in terms of product-related needs, industry categories, and geographic location--but also in terms of similarities and differences in buying behavior. *Each level of problem solving may require a different marketing mix*--especially in regard to the promotion variable--even when identical goods or services are involved. Knowing the nature of buying behavior at each level helps to determine the proper ingredients for a marketing mix.

This exercise shows how knowledge of industrial buying behavior can improve marketing strategy planning--in three "case" situations. You will be asked to identify the problem solving level for an industrial product. Then you will discuss likely buying behavior and how this might affect a firm's marketing strategy planning.

Assignment

Assume the role of marketing manager for a large firm that produces stain-resistant fabrics that are used by furniture companies to upholster chairs, sofas, and love seats. Similar fabrics are typically available to the furniture producers from several competing suppliers, including some larger and some smaller firms. While some slight differences in patterns and colors may exist, all of the suppliers produce fashionable fabrics that meet the quality and style standards set by the customers' production and marketing departments. In fact, most of the competing suppliers use the exact same method to treat fabrics so that they will resist stains. And, with few exceptions, the prices charged by all suppliers tend to be almost identical.

Recently, you learned--from your sales force--of three potential customers whose needs might be satisfied by the fabric you sell. Read each of the three buying situations described below, and then:

a) Determine which level of problem solving--new-task buying, straight rebuy, or modified rebuy--applies to each situation.

b) Discuss in detail the probable nature of the firm's buying behavior in each situation. Which of the five problem solving steps in Chapter 7 (page 185) would be most important in each situation? Why? Which is the next most important? Why? How important would multiple buying influence be in each situation?

c) Explain how your firm might vary its marketing mix to satisfy the potential customer's needs in each situation.

Situation 1:

The potential customer has been selling a very successful line of upholstered furniture for a number of years. The company has not been using a stain-resistant fabric. But, furniture retailers have recently been complaining that the furniture gets soiled very easily. The potential customer thinks that your stain-resistant fabric could possibly be used instead of the fabric it gets from its current supplier.

a) Level of problem solving: _____

b) Nature of buying behavior:

c) Marketing mix:

Situation 2:

The customer has been purchasing a similar fabric from one of your firm's competitors for several years, but is dissatisfied with its present supplier's delivery service and technical support.

a)   Level of problem solving: _____

b)   Nature of buying behavior:

c)   Marketing mix:

Situation 3:

The customer has been purchasing all of its fabric from one of your competitors on a regular basis for several years. No change in this procedure is expected.

a) Level of problem solving: _____

b) Nature of buying behavior:

c) Marketing mix:

Question for Discussion

In which of the three buying situations would emotional needs be most important? Least important? To what extent does this depend on the overlap between individual buyer needs and company needs?

Exercise 8-2

Using SIC codes to analyze industrial markets

Introduction

Compared to the final consumer market, industrial markets have a smaller number of customers and much of the buying potential is concentrated among a relatively few large firms. Further, firms within the same industry tend to cluster together by geographic location. For these reasons, it may be less difficult to analyze industrial markets than consumer markets.

Much published data is available to help the marketing manager analyze industrial markets. The most important source of information is the federal government-- which regularly collects data on the number of establishments, their sales volumes, and number of employees for a large number of industry groups. The data is reported for Standard Industrial Classification (SIC) code industries--broken down by region, state, county, and Standard Metropolitan Statistical Area. As explained in Chapter 8 of the text, the SIC system combines and classifies industrial firms on the basis of product produced--or operation performed. Almost 100 major industry groups are identified by two-digit codes. Code 20, for example, identifies the "food and kindred products" industry. Each major industry is then subdivided into three-digit industries (e.g., code 202, "dairy products") which in turn are subdivided further into four-digit industries (e.g., code 2021, "creamery butter"). However, four-digit detail is not available for all industries in every geographic area because the Census Bureau will not disclose an individual firm's data.

Assignment

Eaton Manufacturing Company produces a line of electrical products for industrial markets. Eaton's recently-appointed marketing manager is currently in the process of reevaluating the firm's marketing strategy for an important product, "electric widgets," which he suspects may not be realizing its full sales potential. In particular, he feels that Eaton has been following a "mass-marketing" approach for this product and has neglected to identify which markets the product appeals to and their relative importance.

The marketing manager began his analysis by attempting to determine which four-digit SIC industries may have some need for electric widgets. First, he analyzed past sales records for the product and assigned SIC codes to previous and present customers. Next, he asked his sales manager to go through the SIC manual and check off the four-digit industries which he believed would be relevant for the product. Finally, to make sure that other potential customers were not being overlooked, he conducted a survey of companies falling under other SIC categories to find out whether they might have any possible use for the product. As a result of this analysis, a total of 12 industries were identified as potential target markets for electric widgets. These industries are listed in columns 1 and 2 of Table 8-1.

TABLE 8-1
Calculation of Market Potential for "Electric Widgets" Using Market Survey
Approach for National and Illinois Markets

SIC Code (1)	Potential "Industry" Target Markets (2)	Market Survey Results			National Market Number of Production Workers (1,000) (6)	Estimated National Market Potential ($1,000) (7)	Illinois Market Number of Production Workers (1,000) (8)	Estimated Illinois Market Potential ($1,000) (9)
		Product Purchases (3)	Number of Production Workers (4)	Average Purchases per Worker (5)				
3611	Electric measuring instruments	$ 11,250	3,750	$_____	45.1	$_____	3.1	$_____
3612	Transformers..............	50,150	4,616	10.86	37.6	408.3	3.8	41.3
3621	Motors and generators	28,400	10,896	2.61	78.3	204.4	3.0	7.8
3622	Industrial controls	40,100	4,678	8.57	30.8	264.0	3.2	27.4
3631	Household cooking equipment	2,600	2,104	1.24	16.9	21.0	3.9	4.8
3632	Household refrigerators and freezers...................	149,600	5,215	28.69	40.2	1,153.3	—	—
3633	Household laundry equipment	35,200	3,497	10.07	17.8	179.2	—	—
3634	Electric housewares and fans	1,200	3,208	0.37	40.3	14.9	3.7	1.4
3635	Household vacuum cleaners	1,875	402	4.66	7.5	35.0	—	—
3636	Sewing machines	600	912	0.66	4.9	3.2	—	—
3661	Telephone and telegraph apparatus.................	65,500	6,451	10.15	101.6	1,031.2	—	—
3662	Radio and TV communication equipment	132,100	6,889	19.18	185.7	3,561.7	7.5	143.8
	Total.................	$518,575				$7,247.3		$235.8

Column:
(1),(2) Four-digit SIC industries making up the industrial market for "electric widgets."
(3)   Dollar value, classified by industries, of purchases of "electric widgets" as reported by those firms included in the survey.
(4)   Number of production workers as reported by those firms included in the survey.
(5)   Average dollar value of "electric widget" purchases per production worker for each SIC industry. Computed by dividing column 3 by column 4.
(6)   Number of production workers for the entire U.S. market for the given SIC industries. Source: U.S. Bureau of Census. *Annual Survey of Manufactures.*
(7)   The resultant estimated national market potential for the total market. Computed by multiplying column 6 by column 5.
(8)   Number of production workers for Illinois trading area for the given SIC industries. Note: Blanks in column 8 indicate either that there are no firms in Illinois for a particular SIC industry, or that there are only a few firms and the Census Bureau has deleted the information to avoid disclosure.
(9)   The resultant estimated Illinois area market potential. Computed by multiplying column 8 by column 5.

McCarthy and Perreault

Having identified 12 potential target markets for electric widgets, the marketing manager then conducted another survey of a sample of firms belonging to each industry to determine the market potential for each industry. Included in the data he collected were the amount of each firm's annual dollar purchases for the product and the number of production workers employed. This data is summarized in columns 3 and 4 of Table 8-1. From the sample data for each SIC industry, the marketing manager then calculated the average dollar purchases per production worker. The results are shown in column 5.

1.   Complete column 5 of Table 8-1 by calculating the average dollar purchases per worker for SIC industry #3611--electric measuring instruments. Show your calculations below.

In order to project the sample data to the entire U.S. market, Eaton's marketing manager turned to the *Annual Survey of Manufacturers* to find the national total of production workers employed by each industry. From this data, shown in column 6, he was then able to estimate the national market potential for each SIC industry by multiplying column 6 by column 5. These estimates are shown in column 7.

2.   Complete column 7 of Table 8-1 by calculating the national market potential for SIC industry #3611. Show your calculations below.

Finally, because Eaton's sales territories were aligned according to states, the marketing manager proceeded to estimate the market potential for each industry in each state. For example, he again turned to the *Annual Survey of Manufactures* to determine the number of production workers employed in the state of Illinois for those industries that operated in Illinois. From this data, shown in column 8, he was then able to estimate the market potential for each SIC industry within Illinois. The results, computed by multiplying column 8 by column 5, are shown in column 9.

3.   Complete column 9 of Table 8-1 by calculating the market potential in Illinois for SIC industry #3611. Show your calculations below.

4.   a)   *For all industries combined*, what percentage of the total national market potential for electric widgets is represented by the state of Illinois? Show your work below.

b)   *For SIC industry #3611 only*, what percentage of the national market potential for electric widgets is represented by the state of Illinois? Show your work below.

5.   Suppose Eaton's marketing manager learned that his firm's electric widget sales to SIC industry #3622 amounted to about 15 percent of its national market potential for that industry--while sales to the other 11 industries ranged from 5-10 percent. Suppose further that he then decided that the firm should aim at achieving 15 percent of its national market potential in *each* of the 12 SIC industries--and set his sales quotas accordingly. Is it likely that Eaton could achieve these sales quotas? Why or why not? Comment on this approach to marketing strategy planning.

6.   Which of the 12 SIC industries would you select as your target market(s) for the electric widgets if you were Eaton's marketing manager? Why?

a)   For the national market:

b)   For the Illinois market:

Question for Discussion

After selecting its target market(s), how could Eaton then go about identifying and reaching those firms which make up the target market(s)? What other information would be needed and how could the information be obtained?

Exercise 8-3

Vendor analysis

This exercise is based on computer-aided problem number 8--Vendor Analysis. A complete description of the problem appears on pages 22-23 of *Computer-Aided Problems to Accompany Basic Marketing*.

1. Supplier 2 is thinking about adding U.S. wholesalers to its channel of distribution. The supplier would ship in large, economical quantities to the wholesaler and the wholesaler would keep a stock of chips on hand. The wholesaler would charge CompuTech a higher price--$1.90 a chip. But with the chips available from a reliable wholesaler CompuTech's inventory cost as a percent of its total order would only be 2 percent. In addition, the cost of transportation would only be $.01 per chip. Assuming CompuTech planned to buy 84,500 chips, what would its total costs be with and without the wholesaler? Should CompuTech encourage the supplier to add a wholesaler to the channel?

    $_____ CompuTech's total cost buying direct from Supplier 2

    $_____ CompuTech's total cost buying through the wholesaler

    _____

    _____

    _____

2. Supplier 2 has explored the idea of adding wholesalers to the channel, but has found that it will take at least another year to find suitable wholesalers and develop relationships. As a result, if CompuTech deals with supplier 2 its inventory cost as a percent of the total order would remain at 5.4 percent, and transportation cost would remain at $.03 per chip. But the supplier is still interested in improving its marketing mix now--so it can develop a strong relationship with CompuTech. Based on an analysis of CompuTech's needs, supplier 2 has developed a new design for the electronic memory chips.

    The redesigned chips would have a built-in connector, so CompuTech would not have to buy separate connectors. In addition, the new design would make it faster and easier to replace a defective chip. The supplier estimates that with the new design it would cost CompuTech only $1.00 to replace a bad chip.

    The supplier has not yet priced the new chip, but it would cost the supplier an additional $.06 to produce each chip. If the supplier set the price of the chip at $1.93 each (the old price of $1.87 plus the additional $.06), how much would the new design cost CompuTech on an order of 84,500 chips. (Hint: compute CompuTech's total cost for the current design based on an order quantity of 84,500 chips, and then compute the total cost assuming the new price, the reduced cost of replacing a defective chip, and no cost for a connector.)

$_____ CompuTech's total cost for 84,500 chips, old design

-_____ CompuTech's total cost for 84,500 chips, new design

$_____ amount CompuTech would save with new chips at $1.93 each

3. The supplier is thinking about pricing the new design at a price higher than $1.93--so it can make more profit than it would have made with the old design. But the supplier also wants CompuTech's total cost to be lower than it would have been with the old design. What price would you recommend? Explain the reason for your recommendation. (Hint: set the values on the spreadsheet to correspond to CompuTech's costs if it buys the new design, but vary its cost--the supplier's price--for the chips and display CompuTech's total vendor cost.)

$_____ = Supplier 2's price for the new chips

Explanation: _____

_____

_____

_____

_____

_____

Chapter 9

Elements of product planning

What This Chapter Is About

Chapter 9 introduces the idea of a "product"--which may be a physical good or a service or (often) a blend of both.

Then, the need for product classes--to relate products to marketing mix planning is explained. Two sets of product classes--for consumer products and industrial products--are introduced. Notice that the same product might be classified in two or more ways at the same time--depending on the attitudes of potential customers.

These product classes should be studied carefully. They are an important thread linking our discussion of marketing strategy planning. In fact, these product classes can be a shorthand way of describing how customers look at Products--and this has a direct bearing on Place (how the Product will get to them) and Promotion (what the seller should tell them).

Chapter 9 also discusses other important aspects of Product--branding, packaging and warranties.

Branding is concerned with identifying the product. A good brand can help improve the product's image and reinforce the firm's effort to increase the product's degree of brand familiarity.

The advantages and disadvantages of both dealer and manufacturer branding should be studied carefully. They will help you understand the "battle of the brands"--and why some markets are so competitive.

Packaging can actually improve a product--perhaps making it more appealing and/or protecting it from damage. Packaging can also complement promotion efforts by making the whole product more attractive or carrying a promotion message.

By the end of the chapter you should see that wise decisions on packaging and branding can improve any marketing mix--and may help a firm avoid extremely competitive--or even pure competition--situations.

Important Terms

product, p. 218
product assortment, p. 221
product line, p. 221
individual product, p. 221
consumer products, p. 221
industrial products, p. 221
convenience products, p. 223
staples, p. 224
impulse products, p. 224
emergency products, p. 224
shopping products, p. 224
homogeneous shopping products, p. 224
heterogeneous shopping products, p. 225
specialty products, p. 225
unsought products, p. 226
new unsought products, p. 226
regularly unsought products, p. 226
derived demand, p. 227
capital item, p. 227
expense item, p. 227
installations, p. 228
accessories, p. 230
raw materials, p. 230
farm products, p. 230
natural products, p. 230
components, p. 231

supplies, p. 233
professional services, p. 234
branding, p. 235
brand name, p. 235
trademark, p. 235
brand familiarity, p. 238
brand rejection, p. 238
brand non-recognition, p. 238
brand recognition, p. 238
brand preference, p. 239
brand insistence, p. 239
family brand, p. 240
licensed brand, p. 240
individual brands, p. 241
generic products, p. 241
manufacturer brands, p. 241
dealer brands, p. 241
battle of the brands, p. 243
packaging, p. 243
Federal Fair Packaging and Labeling
. Act, p. 245
unit-pricing, p. 245
universal product code (UPC), p. 245
Magnuson-Moss Act, p. 246
warranty, p. 246

True-False Questions

__T__ 1. A "product" may not include a physical good at all.

__F__ 2. It is usually easier to achieve economies of scale when the product emphasis is on a service rather than a good.

__T__ 3. It's usually harder to balance supply and demand for services than for physical goods.

__F__ 4. A product line should be thought of as a firm's product assortment.

__T__ 5. An individual product is a particular product within a product line and is usually differentiated by brand, level of service, size, price, or some other characteristic.

__T__ 6. Consumer product classes are based on how consumers think about and shop for a product.

__T__ 7. Convenience products are products a consumer needs but isn't willing to spend much time or effort to shop for.

_F_ 8. Because customers are not willing to spend much time or effort shopping for staples, branding is of little importance.

_T_ 9. Impulse products are items that the customer decides to purchase on sight, may have bought the same way many times before, and wants "right now."

_F_ 10. The distinctive aspect of emergency products is that they are only purchased when the consumer is in danger.

_T_ 11. Shopping products are those products that a customer feels are worth the time and effort to compare with competing products.

_T_ 12. If customers see a product as a homogeneous shopping product, they will base their purchase decisions on the one variable they feel is or can be different--price.

_F_ 13. Price is considered irrelevant for products that the customer sees as heterogeneous shopping products.

_F_ 14. Specialty products are expensive and unusual products that customers insist upon having and generally have to travel far to find.

_F_ 15. Unsought products are those products that have no potential value for customers.

_F_ 16. A consumer product must be either a convenience product, a shopping product, or a specialty product--it cannot be all three.

_F_ 17. In times of recession, a good marketing mix aimed at intermediate customers may not be very effective unless it has some impact on final consumer demand, because the demand for final consumer products is derived from the demand for industrial products.

_F_ 18. The fact that the demand for most industrial products is derived means that industry demand will be fairly elastic, although the demand facing individual firms may be extremely inelastic.

_F_ 19. For tax purposes, the cost of an industrial expense item is spread over a number of years.

_T_ 20. Since industrial products buyers do relatively little shopping compared to consumer products buyers, the industrial products classification system is determined by how buyers think about the products and how they will be used.

_F_ 21. Installations include only buildings and land rights--such as factories, farms, stores, office buildings, mining deposits, and timber rights.
+ MAJOR EQUIPMENT

_T_ 22. If a customer purchases an installation, it is a capital item, but if it is leased the lease payments are an expense item.

_T_ 23. Although accessory equipment are capital items, purchasing agents usually have more say in buying accessories than in buying installations.

_T_ 24. Raw materials become part of a physical good--and they are expense items.

_F_ 25. In contrast to farm products, natural products are produced by fewer and larger companies that are quite responsive to market demands and inclined to limit supply to maintain stable prices.

_F_ 26. Component parts and materials are capital items which have had more processing than raw materials.

_T_ 27. Although the industry demand for components may be fairly inelastic, there often are many suppliers--so buyers operate in a fairly competitive market.

_T_ 28. A product originally considered a component part when it was sold in the OEM market might become a consumer product for the replacement market--and probably would require a different marketing mix.

_F_ 29. Supplies are commonly described as MRO items, meaning that "More Rational Ordering" procedures are normally followed for them.

_T_ 30. High-level executives may negotiate contracts for some important operating supplies that are needed regularly and cost a lot.

_T_ 31. Maintenance supplies are similar to consumers' convenience products--and branding may become important for such products.

_F_ 32. Demand for repair items is quite inelastic--and the market is never very competitive.

_T_ 33. Professional services are expense items, and often the cost of buying them outside the firm is compared with the cost of having company personnel do them.

_F_ 34. The terms branding, brand name, and trademark all mean about the same thing--and can be used interchangeably.

_F_ 35. Branding is advantageous to producers--but not to customers.

_T_ 36. Despite the many advantages of branding, a marketing manager would probably be wise to avoid spending large amounts on branding unless the quality can be easily maintained.

_T_ 37. A firm whose products have reached the brand insistence stage will enjoy a more inelastic demand curve than a firm whose products have achieved brand preference.

_T_ 38. The Lanham Act specifies what types of trademarks can be protected by law and makes provisions for registration records--but it does not force registration.

_T_ 39. A licensed brand is a well-known brand that different sellers pay a fee to use.

_T_ 40. Generic products are products which have no brand at all other than identification of their contents and the manufacturer or middleman.

_T_ 41. The major disadvantage of manufacturers' brands is that manufacturers normally offer lower gross margins than the middleman might be able to earn with his own brands.

_T_ 42. Eventually, dealer-branded products may win the "battle of the brands," perhaps because dealers are closer to customers and they can control shelf space.

_F_ 43. While packing is concerned with protecting the product, packaging refers only to promotion.

_F_ 44. Packaging plays no role when the product emphasis is on service.

_F_ 45. Better protective packaging is more important to final consumers than to manufacturers and middlemen.

_T_ 46. A firm should adopt a more expensive package only when the overall effect will be to reduce the total distribution cost for its product.

_F_ 47. If enforced, the Federal Fair Packaging and Labeling Act of 1966 would all but eliminate a manufacturer's control over the packaging of its products.

_T_ 48. Unit-pricing involves placing the price per ounce (or some other standard measure) on or near a product.

_T_ 49. Large supermarket chains have been eager to use the universal product code system--to speed the checkout process and eliminate the need for marking the price on every item.

_F_ 50. The Magnuson-Moss Act requires all manufacturers to offer consumers written warranties for all products.

_T_ 51. A warranty explains what a seller promises about its product.

1. T, p. 219	18. F, p. 227	35. F, p. 237
2. F, p. 220	19. F, p. 227	36. T, p. 237
3. T, p. 220	20. T, p. 228	37. T, p. 239
4. F, p. 221	21. F, p. 228	38. T, p. 239
5. T, p. 221	22. T, p. 229	39. T, p. 240
6. T, p. 222	23. T, p. 230	40. T, p. 241
7. T, p. 223	24. T, p. 231	41. T, p. 242
8. F, p. 224	25. T, p. 231	42. T, p. 243
9. T, p. 224	26. F, p. 231	43. F, p. 243
10. F, p. 224	27. T, p. 232	44. F, p. 243
11. T, p. 224	28. T, p. 232	45. F, p. 243
12. T, p. 225	29. F, p. 233	46. F, p. 244
13. F, p. 225	30. T, p. 233	47. F, p. 245
14. F, p. 225	31. T, p. 234	48. T, p. 245
15. F, p. 226	32. F, p. 234	49. T, p. 245
16. F, p. 226	33. T, p. 234	50. F, p. 246
17. F, p. 227	34. F, p. 235	51. T, p. 246

Multiple-Choice Questions (Circle the correct response)

1. According to the text, the term "product" means:
    a. any tangible item that satisfies needs.
    b. goods but not services.
    c. the need-satisfying offering of a firm.
    d. any item that is mass produced by a firm.
    e. all of the above.

2. The set of all products a firm sells is called its:
    a. product line.
    b. individual products.
    c. product assortment.
    d. tangible products.

3. The text's consumer product classes are based upon:
    a. methods of distribution.
    b. SIC codes.
    c. the nature of the products.
    d. the way people think about and buy products.
    e. the way firms view their products.

4. Which of the following is *not* included as a product class in the classification system for consumer products given in the text?
    a. Convenience products
    b. Staple products
    c. Specialty products
    d. Shopping products
    e. Durable products

5. While doing her weekly food shopping, Doris Brown walked over to the frozen food display case in search of some family dessert items. She was just about to select a half gallon of ice cream, when she noticed some frozen yogurt in the case. Since her family enjoyed regular yogurt, she decided to serve the frozen yogurt to them as dessert that evening. In this case, the frozen yogurt should be classified as:
   a. a staple product.
   b. an emergency product.
   c. a specialty product.
   d. an impulse product.
   e. a shopping product.

6. You are stranded in your automobile during a snowstorm. You decide to walk to the closest service station for tire chains. In this case you would consider the tire chains as:
   a. emergency products.
   b. staple products.
   c. impulse products.
   d. shopping products.
   e. specialty products.

7. Mr. Collins feels that most people are too emotional and status-minded concerning their automobile purchases. "An automobile's only function is transportation," he says, "and those high-priced 'chrome-wagons' can't do anything that most lower priced cars won't do." Collins only considers Fords, Chevrolets, and Plymouths when he looks around for a new car and he feels all these cars are alike. For him automobiles are:
   a. a specialty product.
   b. a homogeneous shopping product.
   c. a convenience staple product.
   d. a heterogeneous shopping product.
   e. a staple product.

8. Specialty products would be best described as having:
   a. brand insistence and inelastic demand.
   b. brand preference and inelastic demand.
   c. brand insistence and elastic demand.
   d. brand preference and elastic demand.
   e. a relatively high price and durability.

9. Which of the following statements about consumer products is *true*?
   a. Convenience products are those that customers want to buy at the lowest possible price.
   b. Shopping products are those products for which customers usually want to use routinized buying behavior.
   c. Specialty products are those that customers usually are least willing to search for.
   d. Unsought products are not shopped for at all.
   e. None of the above statements are true.

10. Motels are a good example of:
    a. convenience products.
    b. shopping products.
    c. specialty products.
    d. unsought products.
    e. Could be any of the above.

11. Which of the following is *not* a general characteristic of most industrial products?
    a. Buyers tend to buy from only one supplier.
    b. Their demand is derived from the demand for final consumer products.
    c. Industry demand may be inelastic while each company's demand may be elastic.
    d. Buying is basically concerned with economic factors.
    e. All of the above are characteristics for most industrial products.

12. Tax regulations affect industrial buying decisions because:
    a. expense items are depreciated.
    b. capital items are written off over several years.
    c. installations are expensed in one year.
    d. capital items are expensed in one year.

13. The industrial product classes discussed in the text are based on:
    a. the shopping behavior of the buyer.
    b. how sellers think about products.
    c. how the products are to be used.
    d. all of the above.
    e. both b and c.

14. Which of the following is *not* one of the industrial product classes discussed in the text?
    a. Professional services
    b. Farm products
    c. Component parts
    d. Accessory equipment
    e. Fabrications

15. Which of the following industrial products to be purchased by a firm is *most* likely to involve top management in the buying decision?
    a. Raw materials
    b. Accessory equipment
    c. Operating supplies
    d. Installations
    e. Component parts

16. Which of the following would *not* be classified as accessory equipment?
    a. Office typewriters
    b. Filing cases
    c. Portable drills
    d. All of the above might be accessory equipment.
    e. None of the above is likely to be accessory equipment.

17. Raw materials are usually broken down into two broad categories which are:
    a. domestic animals and crops.
    b. farm products and natural products.
    c. forest products and mineral products.
    d. maintenance materials and operating materials.
    e. farm products and chemicals.

18. A marketing manager for a firm which produces component parts should keep in mind that:
    a. most component buyers prefer to rely on one reliable source of supply.
    b. the replacement market for component parts generally requires the same marketing mix as the one used to serve the original equipment market.
    c. any product originally sold as a component part becomes a consumer product when sold in the replacement market.
    d. the original equipment market and the replacement market for component parts should be viewed as separate target markets.
    e. All of the above are true statements.

19. Which of the following would *not* be considered as a component part by an auto manufacturer?
    a. Automobile batteries
    b. Steel sheets
    c. Automobile jacks
    d. Tires
    e. All of the above can be considered component parts, except when they are sold in the replacement market.

20. Supplies may be divided into three main categories. Lubricating oils and greases for machines on the production line would be classified as:
    a. maintenance items.
    b. production items.
    c. operating supplies.
    d. repair supplies.
    e. accessories.

21. A "brand name" is:
    a. any means of product identification.
    b. a word used to identify a seller's products.
    c. the same thing as "branding."
    d. the same thing as a "trademark."
    e. All of the above.

22. Which of the following conditions would *not* be favorable to branding?
    a. Dependable and widespread availability is possible
    b. Economies of scale in production
    c. Fluctuations in product quality due to inevitable variations in raw materials
    d. Product easy to identify by brand name or trademark
    e. Large market with a variety of needs and preferences

23. What degree of brand familiarity has a manufacturer achieved when the firm's particular brand is chosen out of habit or past experience, even though various "name" brands are available?
    a. Brand rejection
    b. Brand preference
    c. Brand recognition
    d. Brand insistence
    e. Nonrecognition of brand

24. Which of the following statements about the Lanham Act is *true*?
    a. It spells out what kinds of brand names can be protected.
    b. Registration under the Lanham Act only applies to licensed brands.
    c. The Lanham Act makes registration of a brand name mandatory.
    d. Registering under the Lanham Act does not help protect a trademark to be used in foreign markets.
    e. All of the above are true statements.

25. A firm that has decided to brand all its products under one label is following a policy of:
    a. dealer branding.
    b. generic branding.
    c. family branding.
    d. generic branding.
    e. None of the above.

26. Which of the following statements about manufacturer or dealer brands is *true*?
    a. Dealer brands are distributed only by chain-store retailers.
    b. Dealer brands may be distributed as widely or more widely than many manufacturers' brands.
    c. Dealer brands are the same as "licensed brands."
    d. Manufacturer brands are sometimes called private brands.
    e. All of the above are true.

27. Which of the following statements regarding the "battle of the brands" is *true*?
    a. It is pretty well over as the dealers now control the marketplace.
    b. Middlemen have no real advantages in the battle of the brands.
    c. If the present trend continues, manufacturers will control all middlemen.
    d. Manufacturer brands may be losing ground to dealer brands.
    e. The battle of the brands has increased the differences in price between manufacturer brands and dealer brands.

28. Which of the following statements about the strategic importance of packaging is *false*?
    a. A package may have more promotional impact than a firm's advertising efforts.
    b. A new package can become the major factor in a new marketing strategy by significantly improving the product.
    c. Packaging is concerned with both protection and promotion.
    d. Better packaging always raises total distribution costs.
    e. A package should satisfy not only the needs of consumers but also those of intermediate customers.

29. The Federal Fair Packaging and Labeling Act:
    a. suggests voluntary informative labeling of food products with respect to their nutrients, weight, and volume.
    b. made unit pricing mandatory.
    c. encouraged each firm to use a different size package, so consumers would have more choice.
    d. prohibits the use of universal product codes as a substitute for marking prices on retail products.
    e. basically requires that consumer products be clearly labeled in understandable terms.

30. The Magnuson-Moss Act requires that:
    a. all firms provide written warranties for all products.
    b. a warranty must be clearly written, if one is offered.
    c. all warranties be strong warranties.
    d. all warranties be for at least one year.
    e. all of the above.

Answers to Multiple-Choice Questions

1. c, p. 218-19	11. a, p. 227	21. b, p. 235
2. c, p. 221	12. b, p. 227	22. c, p. 237
3. d, p. 223	13. e, p. 228	23. b, p. 239
4. e, p. 223	14. e, p. 228	24. a, p. 239
5. a, p. 224	15. d, p. 229	25. c, p. 240
6. a, p. 224	16. d, p. 230	26. b, p. 241-42
7. b, p. 225	17. b, p. 230	27. d, p. 243
8. a, p. 225	18. d, p. 232	28. d, p. 243
9. d, p. 226	19. b, p. 232	29. e, p. 245
10. e, p. 226	20. c, p. 233	30. b, p. 246

Exercise 9-1

Classifying consumer products

Introduction

Consumer product classes are based on *the way people think about and buy products*. However, different groups of potential customers may have different needs and buying behavior for the same product. Thus, the same product could be placed in two or more product classes--depending on the needs and behavior of target customers. Therefore, product planners should focus on specific groups of customers (i.e., market segments) whose needs and buying behavior are relatively homogeneous.

This exercise will give you some practice in using consumer product classes. As you do the exercise, you will see that the product classes have very little meaning unless they are related to specific target markets.

Assignment

The buying behavior of several customers or potential customers is described below for Kodak Disc cameras.* Assume in each situation that the customer being described is representative of a particular group of customers--all possessing the same needs and exhibiting similar buying behavior. Then: (a) indicate in which consumer product class the product should be placed based on the characteristics of each group of customers and (b) state *why* you placed the product in this class. Use the following classes, which are described on pages 223-26 in the text.

Staple convenience product   Heterogeneous shopping product
Impulse convenience product   Specialty product
Emergency convenience product   New unsought product
Homogeneous convenience product Regularly unsought product

The first situation has been answered for you as an example.

Situation 1.   Mary Wang, a college student, wished to purchase a camera as a birthday gift for her boyfriend. Although Mary could only afford to spend about $70, she wanted a camera of reasonably good quality-- but also one which would be easy to operate. Knowing very little about cameras, Mary asked a salesperson at the Campus Camera Shop for his advice. He recommended that she buy a Kodak Disc camera because of its low price and many convenient features.

Product class: <u>Heterogeneous shopping product.</u>

Reason: <u>Customer spends time and effort to compare quality and features, has little concern for brand, and is not too concerned about price as long as it's within her budget.</u>

Situation 2.   Gene Fisk teaches high school science courses. He spends most of his leisure time with amateur photography. In fact, he enjoys photography so much that for several years he has volunteered to teach the advanced photography workshop offered by the city recreation department. He has won several awards for his photographs of desert landscapes. Gene has even earned extra cash by selling some of his photos to companies that print postcards. Several of his friends have encouraged him to turn professional, but he prefers using his talents mainly as a hobby.

Product class: _____

Reason: _____

_____

_____

_____

_____

_____

_____

_____

Situation 3.   Bob Goff was at a friend's house and saw some photographs that the friend had taken with a Kodak Disc camera. He was so impressed by the quality of the pictures that he decided to purchase the same camera. The next day he went to a nearby camera store and found that the store did not have the camera in stock--although it did have other "pocket cameras" in stock in the same price range. The salesperson in the store assured him that the others were just as good. But Goff ignored this advice and tried two other stores that were also out of stock. Getting frustrated, Gene was ready to drive downtown to a large camera store when he came upon a display of Kodak Disc cameras in a nearby drugstore. He quickly bought one-- even though he felt the price would probably be lower at the camera store.

Product class: _____

Reason: _____

_____

_____

_____

_____

_____

_____

_____

Situation 4.   While Mrs. Peckham was shopping in her local supermarket, she came upon a special display of Kodak Disc cameras. At first, she doubted the product quality because they were priced quite low compared to her friend's Nikon camera. But remembering all the Kodak advertisements she had seen on television and in magazines, she decided to buy one to take photographs of her grandchildren who were visiting for the week.

Product class: _____

Reason: _____

_____

_____

_____

_____

_____

_____

Situation 5.   Ellen Pierce walked into a K mart store and told the clerk at the camera counter that she wanted to buy a pocket camera with a built-in flash. The clerk said the store carried several such cameras, including the Kodak Disc. "I'll take the one with the lowest price," Ellen told the clerk.

Product class: _____

Reason: _____

_____

_____

_____

_____

_____

_____

_____

Situation 6. While deep-sea fishing off the coast of California, Vicky Shaw caught a large swordfish. She decided that her friends back home would never believe her "fish story" if she didn't have pictures. But she did not have a camera. As soon as the boat got back to the dock, Vicky went to a nearby tourist shop. She was pleased to see a display of Kodak Disc cameras, but was sorry to see a much higher price than the same camera sold for in her home town. She bought one anyway, because she wanted to take some pictures right away before the fish was taken away to the fish market.

Product class: _____

Reason: _____

_____

_____

_____

_____

_____

_____

Question for Discussion

What implications do your answers to the above exercises have for Kodak when planning its marketing strategies? Be specific?

Exercise 9-2

Classifying industrial products

Introduction

Compared to consumer products buyers, industrial products buyers do relatively little shopping. The accepted practice is for the seller to come to the buyer. This means that industrial product classes based on shopping behavior are *not* useful. The industrial product classes are determined by *how buyers think about products* and *how the products are to be used*.

The industrial product classes may be easier to use than consumer product classes, because industrial buyers tend to have similar views of the same products. Another reason is that the way a purchase is treated for tax purposes affects its classification. The treatment is determined by the Internal Revenue Service rather than the buyer--so little variation is possible.

However, it is possible that a product may be placed in different classes by two buyers because of how they view the purchase. A "small" truck might be classified as an "accessory" by a large manufacturer, while a small manufacturer would view the same truck as an important "installation." Thus, how the customer sees the product is the determining factor--and it will affect marketing mix planning!

Assignment

This exercise focuses on the essential differences between industrial product classes. After carefully reading the following cases, indicate which type of industrial product each case is *primarily* concerned with. Use the following classes:

installations	component materials
accessories	supplies
raw materials	professional services
component parts	

Then explain your answers, taking into consideration the various characteristics of each type of product as explained in the text on pages 228-35. The first case is answered for you as an example.

1. The Perry Company produces a wide variety of metal coil and flat springs for use by many types of industrial customers--including manufacturers of watches, toys, ballpoint pens, weighing scales, office equipment, garage doors, and

automobiles. The springs are generally shipped finished and ready for assembly, although minor processing is sometimes required later. Perry faces stiff competition for most of its products, which are mass-produced and processed to commonly accepted standards. Since price and quality often vary only slightly between Perry and its competitors, the company stresses availability and prompt delivery in its selling appeals. Recently, Perry started an aggressive promotion campaign to find new customers for custom-made springs--in an effort to increase profits through the sale of higher-margin products.

a) Product Class: <u>Component parts</u>

b) Reason: <u>Springs become a part of the finished product--with little or no further processing required--and are treated as expense items. Since they go into the final product, a replacement market could develop. As repair items, the springs would then be "supplies" or some kind(s) of consumer products.</u>

2. Andy Claxton works for Atlantis Steel Company. It's his job to be certain that all of the equipment in the steel mill keeps running--and to be certain that broken machines are quickly fixed. One of his duties is to maintain an adequate inventory of repair parts and equipment, such as bearings, gears, and circuit breakers. His parts inventory is very large--because there are so many different types of equipment in the mill. Thus, Claxton must order a large variety of parts from many suppliers--along with large quantities of lubricating oils and grease.

a) Product Class: _____

b) Reason: _____

_____

_____

_____

_____

3. Fresno Raisin Company buys raisins from hundreds of small raisin growers in the central valley of California. The raisins are accumulated, sorted, and stored until they are sold to candy companies, cereal manufacturers, and other food processing firms.

a) Product Class: _____

b) Reason: _____

_____

_____

_____

_____

4. Sue Traykus has worked for XYZ Co. as a purchasing agent for nearly ten years and reacts rather strongly when people refer to purchasing as dull, routine work. "Purchasing is an extremely demanding field," she argues. "A purchasing agent can have a tremendous effect on corporate profits." She recently purchased several new IBM typewriters to be used by the accounting office. Ordinarily she would order something like the typewriters as soon as a requisition slip was submitted to her through proper channels. Due to the company's current cost-cutting program, however, she was required to pass the requisition along to a special top-level budget committee for further approval. Almost a month passed before the order was finally sent to a supplier. "An amazing amount of attention for such a standardized product," said Sue Traykus.

    a) Product Class: _____

    b) Reason: _____

    _____

    _____

    _____

    _____

5. Advanced Micro Devices, Inc. (AMD) distributes disk drives that are used in producing microcomputers. Producing a microcomputer is now a simple assembly operation--since most of the key parts are standardized and readily available. As a result, hundreds of small companies make similar computers--and they all use the same type "industry-standard" disk drive. AMD faces stiff competition for the business of these firms. There are about a dozen other distributors that sell disk drives, and several Korean and Japanese disk drive producers have their own sales forces to sell direct to the microcomputer firms. In fact, AMD often gets only part of a customer's business--since many of the purchasing agents want several suppliers to ensure availability of the needed disk drives.

    a) Product Class: _____

    b) Reason: _____

    _____

    _____

    _____

    _____

6. Market Facts is a marketing research company that helps clients improve their management and marketing decision making--through data collection and evaluation. The firm employs specialists in consumer, industrial, transportation, medical, and government research. It offers clients national field surveys, consumer mail panels, test marketing facilities, shopping center interviews, group interviewing facilities, and a telephone interviewing center-- in addition to sophisticated computer and data analysis programs.

a) Product Class: _____

b) Reason: _____

_____

_____

_____

_____

7. Bobby Cox owns Cox Cabinet Company. Cox Cabinet is one of only four firms that produce kitchen and bathroom cabinets used by local home-builders in the Raleigh, North Carolina area. Two years ago Cox retired and made George Kline, his shop supervisor, the manager of the company, Kline has done a fine job, and sales have climbed steadily ever since--despite a downturn in construction of new houses. Although the company is doing well, Kline thinks that it is not meeting its full potential because the equipment it uses to make laminated countertops is inadequate. He would like to purchase a new heavy-duty laminating machine to improve productivity. However, Bobby Cox wants to postpone the $10,000 purchase until the business cycle takes an upswing.

a) Product Class: _____

b) Reason: _____

_____

_____

_____

_____

Question for Discussion

Which types of products would most likely be associated with the following kinds of buying: (a) new-task buying, (b) straight rebuy, (c) modified rebuy? Why? Illustrate with examples from Exercise 9-2.

McCarthy and Perreault

Name: _____ Course & Section: _____

Exercise 9-3

Achieving brand familiarity

Introduction

In hopes of developing a strong "customer franchise, " American firms spend billions of dollars annually to promote brands for their products. Nevertheless, many brands are, for practical purposes, valueless because of their *nonrecognition* among potential customers. And while obtaining *brand recognition* may be a significant achievement--given the many nondescript brands on the market--this level of brand familiarity does not guarantee sales for the firm. To win a favorable position in monopolistic competition, a firm may need to develop *brand preference* or even *brand insistence* for its products.

Why are some firms more successful than others in their branding efforts? The reasons are not always clear. Unfortunately, brand loyalty, like many aspects of buying behavior, remains a rather mysterious phenomenon. In general, a firm probably must produce a good product and continually promote it, but this alone may not ensure a high level of brand familiarity--particularly if the firm does not direct its efforts toward some specific target market.

This exercise gets at some important problems in branding--such as conditions favorable to branding--and the difficulty of achieving brand familiarity for certain types of products. As you do the exercise, you may begin to wonder if brands are really relevant for some product classes. You may also wish to speculate about how much effort is spent promoting brands to consumers who have no use for the product in question--or for whom brand names are meaningless.

Assignment

1. List *from memory* (DO NOT DO ANY "RESEARCH") up to five brand names for each of the following product types. List the first brands that come to mind. If you cannot think of *any* brands for a particular product type, write "none" on the first line.

   a) Jams: _____   d) Upholstered _____
      _____   furniture: _____
      _____   _____
      _____   _____
      _____   _____

b)   Shampoo: _____   e)   Crayons: _____
                _____   _____
                _____   _____
                _____   _____
                                                       _____
c)   Glue: _____   f)   Dishwashers: _____
                _____   _____
                _____   _____
                _____   _____
                _____   _____

2.   What level of brand familiarity do you think exists among the majority of consumers for each of the following products?

     Product Types   *Level of Brand Familiarity*

     a)   Jams: _____

     b)   Shampoo: _____

     c)   Glue: _____

     d)   Upholstered furniture: _____

     e)   Crayons: _____

     f)   Dishwashers: _____

3.   From the product types listed in questions 1 and 2, indicate for which one branding would be *most appropriate* and explain what conditions make branding so favorable for that product type.

     Product type: _____

     Conditions:

4.   From the product types listed in questions 1 and 2, indicate for which one branding would be *least appropriate* and explain what conditions make branding so unfavorable for that product type.

     Product type: _____

     Conditions:

Question for Discussion

Does a firm have a right to use any brand name it chooses?

Exercise 9-4

Comparing branded product offerings

Introduction

Most manufacturers of consumer products use *manufacturers' brands* (often called "national brands") to try to develop a loyal group of customers for their products. At the same time, more and more wholesalers and retailers are offering consumers *dealer brands* (sometimes called "private brands") to try to develop channel and store loyalty. As a result, millions of dollars are spent each year for promotion in a "battle of the brands."

The "battle of the brands" takes many forms--and attitudes toward brands vary a lot both among consumers and marketers. Some retailers tend to stock mainly manufacturers' brands. Meanwhile, some manufacturers--particularly in the shoe industry--have opened up their own retail outlets to promote their own brands.

To add to the "battle of the brands," many food retailers are now carrying *generic products*--unbranded products in plain packages (or unpackaged!)--to appeal to price-conscious consumers. This gives consumers even more products to choose from--but may make it more difficult and confusing to determine the "best buy."

This exercise is designed to give you additional insight into the "battle of the brands." You are asked to make price comparisons between manufacturers' brands, dealer brands, and generic products--and then decide which is the "better buy."

Assignment

1. Visit a large chain supermarket and record the prices of the items listed on the next page. For each item, select one manufacturer brand, one dealer brand, and one generic product. If no generic product is available, write the price of the dealer brand in the generic column. If the store carries neither a dealer brand nor a generic product, write the price of the manufacturer brand in all three columns. Each column must be completely filled out so that you can compare the totals for all three columns.

2. Which do you think is the "better buy"--manufacturer brands, dealer brands, or generic products? Why? What factors did you take into consideration in deciding which is the better buy?

PRICE COMPARISON CHART

Name and Location of store: _____

Date visited: _____

Item and Approximate Size	Manufacturer Brand	Dealer Brand	Generic Product
Ketchup (14-oz. bottle)			
Instant coffee (8-oz. jar)			
Corn flakes (12-oz. box)			
Peanut butter (1-lb. 2-oz. jar)			
White vinegar (1 qt.)			
Tomato soup (10-oz. can)			
Bathroom tissue (4-pack)			
Cream style corn (17-oz. can)			
Sliced yellow ciing peaches (29-oz. can)			
Tomato juice (46-oz. can)			
Bar soap (bath size)			
Shortening (3-lb. can)			
White flour (5-lb. bag)			
Chocolate cake mix (1-lb. 3-oz. package)			
Liquid detergent for dishes (32-oz. container)			
Facial tissue (box of 400 or 200 double)			
Mouthwash (12-oz. bottle)			
Liquid bleach (1 gal.)			
Powdered detergent (3-lb. box)			
Total cost of a basket of goods			

Question for Discussion

For what reason(s) would a supermarket want to stock dealer brands or generic products when heavily-advertised manufacturer brands are available?

Exercise 9-5

Branding decision

This exercise is based on computer-aided problem number 9--Branding Decision. A complete description of the problem appears on pages 23-24 of *Computer-Aided Problems to Accompany Basic Marketing*.

1. After some thought, Farm Fresh's marketing manager has concluded that there might be a side effect of the FoodWorld proposal which he had not considered earlier. Specifically, he had not planned on reducing his promotion spending if he accepted the FoodWorld proposal. Yet, FoodWorld would be doing some of its own promotion for the FoodWorld brand. As a result, Farm Fresh could reallocate some of its promotion money to attract new customers in areas where it had not been doing promotion. He is interested in evaluating this idea more closely, and would like to know how much sales (in cases) of the Farm Fresh brand would have to increase (beyond the 90,000 cases he was expecting from the proposed arrangement) to make the same profit the firm makes at present. (Hint: use the What If analysis to vary the total number of cases of the Farm Fresh brand in the right hand column and display the total profit for the current situation and the proposed situation. Repeat the process with new minimum and maximum quantity values until you find a quantity that produces about the same profit.)

    _____ number of cases to make about the same profit

    - ___90,000___ number of cases expected under the original proposal

    _____ needed increase in number of cases to earn current profit

2. Even if Farm Fresh were able to attract some new customers, the marketing manager knows that it might take awhile. In the meantime, he is worried about profits. One idea he has is to make a counterproposal of his own. He is thinking about accepting the proposal if FoodWorld is willing to pay a higher price for the cases produced under the FoodWorld brand. He would like to set a price for those cases so that his firm's total profits would stay about the same as now. What price per case for the FoodWorld brand would result in about the same profits as at present? (Hint: use the What If analysis to vary the price per case for the FoodWorld brand and display the total profit for the current situation and the proposed situation. Repeat the process with new minimum and maximum price values until you find a price that produces about the same profit.)

    $_____ price you would recommend

Chapter 10

Product management and new–product development

What This Chapter Is About

Chapter 10 introduces product life cycles--and shows the need for managing products and developing new products.

Modern markets are dynamic--and the concepts introduced in this chapter should deepen your understanding of how and why markets evolve. Product life cycles should be studied carefully--to see how marketing strategies must be adjusted over time. In later chapters you will get more detail about how the marketing mix typically changes at different stages of the life cycle. So now is the time to build a good base for what is to come.

This chapter is one of the most important in the text, because new products are vital for the continued success of a business. Yet, a large share of new products fail. Such failures can be avoided by using the new-product development process discussed in the text. Think about this process carefully, and try to see how you could help develop more satisfying and profitable products. Creativity in product planning--perhaps seeing unsatisfied market needs--could lead to breakthrough opportunities!

Important Terms

product life cycle, p. 252
market introduction, p. 252
market growth, p. 252
market maturity, p. 253
sales decline, p. 254
fashion, p. 255
fashion cycle, p. 255
distinctiveness stage, p. 255
emulation stage, p. 255

economic emulation stage, p. 255
fad, p. 256
new product, p. 263
Federal Trade Commission (FTC), p. 264
Consumer Product Safety Act, p. 267
product liability, p. 267
concept testing, p. 268
product managers, p. 273
brand managers, p. 273

True-False Questions

___ 1. The product life cycle is divided into four major stages: market introduction, market growth, market maturity, and market saturation.

___ 2. A firm's marketing mix usually must change--and different target markets may be appealed to--as a product moves through the different stages of its life cycle.

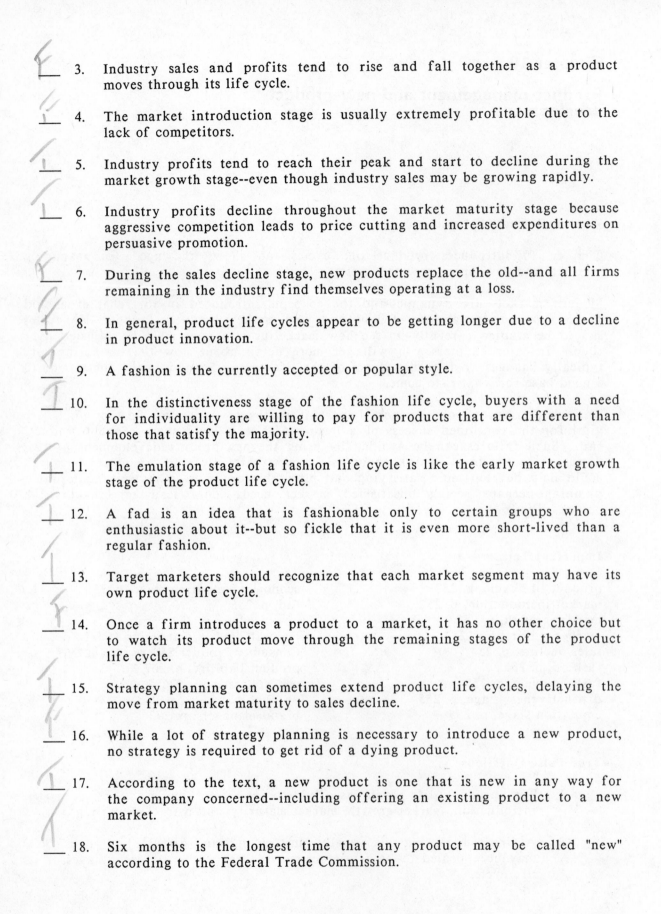

_F_   3. Industry sales and profits tend to rise and fall together as a product moves through its life cycle.

_F_   4. The market introduction stage is usually extremely profitable due to the lack of competitors.

_T_   5. Industry profits tend to reach their peak and start to decline during the market growth stage--even though industry sales may be growing rapidly.

_T_   6. Industry profits decline throughout the market maturity stage because aggressive competition leads to price cutting and increased expenditures on persuasive promotion.

_F_   7. During the sales decline stage, new products replace the old--and all firms remaining in the industry find themselves operating at a loss.

_F_   8. In general, product life cycles appear to be getting longer due to a decline in product innovation.

___   9. A fashion is the currently accepted or popular style.

_T_   10. In the distinctiveness stage of the fashion life cycle, buyers with a need for individuality are willing to pay for products that are different than those that satisfy the majority.

_T_   11. The emulation stage of a fashion life cycle is like the early market growth stage of the product life cycle.

_T_   12. A fad is an idea that is fashionable only to certain groups who are enthusiastic about it--but so fickle that it is even more short-lived than a regular fashion.

_T_   13. Target marketers should recognize that each market segment may have its own product life cycle.

_F_   14. Once a firm introduces a product to a market, it has no other choice but to watch its product move through the remaining stages of the product life cycle.

_T_   15. Strategy planning can sometimes extend product life cycles, delaying the move from market maturity to sales decline.

_F_   16. While a lot of strategy planning is necessary to introduce a new product, no strategy is required to get rid of a dying product.

_T_   17. According to the text, a new product is one that is new in any way for the company concerned--including offering an existing product to a new market.

___   18. Six months is the longest time that any product may be called "new" according to the Federal Trade Commission.

       McCarthy and Perreault

_F_ 19. Since new products are vital to the survival of most firms, the objective of the new-product development process should be to approve as many new-product ideas as possible.

_F_ 20. Product planners should consider long-term welfare in addition to immediate satisfaction--and therefore should offer "pleasing products" instead of "desirable products."

_F_ 21. The Consumer Product Safety Commission tries to encourage firms to design safe products--but it has no real power to effectively deal with unsafe products.

_T_ 22. Product liability means the legal obligation of sellers to pay damages to individuals who are injured by defective or unsafe products.

_T_ 23. Concept testing is done before any tangible product has been developed--and involves marketing research to determine potential customers' attitudes towards the new-product idea.

_F_ 24. The development step (in new-product development) involves the testing of physical products as well as test marketing--something that must be done for all products prior to commercialization.

_T_ 25. The specific organization arrangement for new-product development may not be too important--as long as there is top-level support.

_T_ 26. Product managers sometimes have profit responsibilities and much power, but often they are "product champions" who are mainly involved in planning and getting promotion done.

Answers to True-False Questions

1. F, p. 252	10. T, p. 255	19. F, p. 264
2. T, p. 252	11. T, p. 255	20. F, p. 267
3. F, p. 252	12. T, p. 256	21. F, p. 267
4. F, p. 252	13. T, p. 258	22. T, p. 267
5. T, p. 253	14. F, p. 259	23. T, p. 268
6. T, p. 253	15. T, p. 261	24. F, p. 270
7. F, p. 254	16. F, p. 262	25. T, p. 272
8. F, p. 254	17. T, p. 263	26. T, p. 273
9. T, p. 255	18. T, p. 264	

Multiple-Choice Questions (Circle the correct response)

1. The product life cycle has four stages. Which of the following is *not* one of these?
    a. Market introduction
    b. Market growth
    c. Market maturity
    d. Economic competition
    e. Sales decline

2. During the *market introduction* stage of the product life cycle:
    a. considerable money is spent on promotion while place development is left until later stages.
    b. products usually show large profits if marketers have successfully carved out new markets.
    c. most potential customers are quite anxious to try out the new-product concept.
    d. funds are being invested in marketing with the expectation of *future* profits.
    e. product and promotion are more important than place and price.

3. Which of the following statements regarding the *market growth* stage of the product life cycle is *false*?
    a. Innovators still earn profits--but this stage is less profitable for them than the previous stage.
    b. This is the time of peak profitability for the industry.
    c. The sales of the total industry are rising fairly rapidly as more and more customers buy.
    d. Monopolistic competition is common during this stage.

4. In planning for different stages of the product life cycle, strategy planners must be aware that:
    a. losses can be expected during the market introduction stage.
    b. the life cycles of mature product-markets can be extended through strategic product adjustments.
    c. offering the product to a new market segment may start a whole new life cycle.
    d. products can be withdrawn from the market before the sales decline stage-- but even here a phase-out strategy is usually required.
    e. All of the above are true statements.

5. A particular industry is experiencing no real sales growth and declining profits in the face of oligopolistic competition. Demand has become quite elastic--as consumers see competing products as almost homogeneous. Several firms have dropped out of the industry, and there has been only one recent new entry. Firms in the industry are attempting to avoid price-cutting by budgeting huge amounts for persuasive advertising. In which stage of the product life cycle are firms in this industry competing?
    a. Market maturity
    b. Sales decline
    c. Market growth
    d. Market introduction

6. Marketing managers should recognize that:
    a. product life cycles appear to be getting longer.
    b. every segment within a market has the same product life cycle.
    c. the product life cycle describes the sales and profits of individual products, not industry sales and profits.
    d. firms that enter mature markets have to compete with established firms for declining industry profits.
    e. None of the above is a true statement.

7. Which of the following statements about fashions and fads is *false*?
    a. A fad is an idea that is fashionable only to certain enthusiastic but perhaps fickle groups.
    b. A fashion refers to the currently accepted or popular style.
    c. In the economic emulation stage, many consumers want the currently popular fashion--but at a lower price.
    d. Fashion cycles usually lead the relevant product life cycle.
    e. How a particular fashion gets started is not well understood.

8. Which of the following statements about "new products" is *false*?
    a. In order for it to be considered new, there should be a functionally significant change in the product--according to the FTC.
    b. A product should be considered "new" by a particular firm if it is new in any way for that company.
    c. The FTC considers six months as the maximum time that a product should be called "new."
    d. A product may be called "new" any time a package change or modification is made, according to the FTC.
    e. A product should be considered "new" by a firm if it is aimed at new markets.

9. With regard to the new-product development process:
    a. the objective should be to "kill" all ideas that probably will not be profitable.
    b. screening criteria should be entirely quantitative--as qualitative criteria tend to allow for too much subjectivity and bias.
    c. the idea evaluation step involves product-usage tests by potential customers to determine if the concept is appealing.
    d. market tests are essential for all products prior to commercialization.
    e. concept testing is usually done as soon as a product has been developed and can be put into consumers' hands.

10. Which of the following types of products provides low immediate satisfaction but high long-run consumer welfare?
    a. Salutary products
    b. Pleasing products
    c. Desirable products
    d. Deficient products

11. The Consumer Product Safety Commission can:
    a. order costly repairs of "unsafe products."
    b. back up its orders with fines.
    c. order returns of "unsafe products."
    d. back up its orders with jail sentences.
    e. All of the above are true.

12. Product or brand managers are commonly used when a firm:
    a. has several different kinds of products or brands.
    b. wants to eliminate the job of the advertising manager.
    c. has one or a few products--all of which are important to its success.
    d. wants to eliminate the job of sales manager.
    e. wants one person to have authority over all the functional areas that affect the profitability of a particular product.

Answers to Multiple-Choice Questions

1. d, p. 252	5. a, p. 253	9. a, p. 264-65
2. d, p. 252	6. d, p. 253	10. a, p. 267
3. a, p. 252-53	7. d, p. 255-57	11. e, p. 267
4. e, p. 252-54	8. d, p. 263-64	12. a, p. 273

Exercise 10-1

Identifying a product's stage in the product life cycle

Introduction

This exercise is designed to improve your understanding of the product life cycle--a valuable model for marketing strategy planning. For example, the product life cycle can help decide if and when it will be to a company's advantage to add, change, or drop a given product. Further, where a product is along its life cycle suggests a workable blend of the "four Ps."

Assignment

Read the following five cases carefully and for each one:

a) Decide which stage of the product life cycle best describes the situation in the case--considering the relevant product-market.

b) Briefly explain your answer, including such factors as profitability, number of competitors, place, promotion, and pricing.

1. Black & Decker recently announced its move into the home appliance business with a new line of coffee makers, can openers, knife sharpeners, and electric knives. Although other established firms have dropped their appliance lines because of poor profits, Black and Decker says it expects to earn good profits from its growing share of the market. Citing the trend toward smaller kitchens, Black and Decker says that its appliances are new and improved compared to those on the market from dozens of other companies--because its space-saver design allows the appliances to be attached under kitchen cabinets rather than taking counter space. B&D plans to spend millions of dollars on TV advertising to increase consumer awareness of the advantages of the B&D brand. B&D has been able to obtain distribution through a wide array of mass-merchandisers, department stores, drugstores, hardware stores, and kitchen stores.

   a) Stage of product life cycle: _____

   b) Explanation: _____

   _____

2. Altos Stereo Systems is just entering the fast-growing, but increasingly competitive compact disc player market. The Altos marketing manager is confident that he can capture a profitable share of the market because his firm's player has--as a standard feature--a remote control unit that is an extra cost option on players from well-known competitors like Pioneer and Sony. To attract support from traditional retailers of home electronics products, Altos is offering a very low wholesale price. Even at the very low suggested retail price, this will make the Altos player very profitable for the retailers. Altos' marketing manager says that this very aggressive pricing will pay off. He predicts that in the next decade compact discs will replace long-play stereo records--and that already prices of the discs are dropping rapidly. He says that this will stimulate even faster growth in the disc player market.

    a) Stage of product life cycle: _____

    b) Explanation: _____

        _____

3. General Electric recently announced that it was pulling out of the portable phonograph business, citing the trend toward sophisticated stereo systems and taped music. Despite sales of about a million units a year (about 50 percent of the market), GE was not able to maintain an adequate profit margin on the portable phonographs due to increasing costs, heavy price competition and a steady 10-year decline in industry sales. Those firms still making portables were not planning to increase production despite GE's announcement.

    a) Stage of product life cycle: _____

    b) Explanation: _____

        _____

4. Beauty Care, Inc., one of the nation's largest producers of personal care products, has just announced plans to sell a new shampoo called Gentle-Care. The company is spending heavily on magazine and TV ads that will promote Gentle-Care as "The shampoo that everyone can use daily. No other shampoo is as gentle on your hair or provides as clean and natural a scent." Free samples of Gentle-Care will be attached to packages of other Beauty Care products, and magazine ads will include cents-off coupons. Despite intense competition, Beauty Care expects its new product to capture a 5 percent share of the slowly growing shampoo market.

    a) Stage of product life cycle: _____

    b) Explanation: _____

        _____

McCarthy and Perreault

5. One of the largest food manufacturers is testing a new product for the large soft-drink market--a patented paper cup coated with a secret formula. All the consumer has to do is add water and it becomes a carbonated beverage! It is no longer necessary to carry home six-packs or eight-packs. There are no empty bottles or cans to return, and less storage space is needed. The product can also be distributed through normal wholesale channels rather than requiring the special distribution networks now used by the bottling industry. Therefore, the product offers economy as well as convenience.

    a) Stage of product life cycle: _____

    b) Explanation: _____

        _____

Question for Discussion

What alternatives should a firm consider when it finds some or all of its products in the market maturity stage of the product life cycle?

Exercise 10-2

New-product development process

Introduction

The product life cycle shows us that markets and competition are dynamic. Over time old products are replaced with new ones. And as markets mature, firms usually face increasing price competition and erosion of their profit margins. To succeed in spite of these pressures, firms must constantly look for new market opportunities--and that often means identifying and developing new product ideas-- and effective strategies to go with them.

While the new-product development process is crucial to the survival and success of most firms, it is also a challenge. Even the best-run companies sometimes "miss" opportunities that--after the fact--seem obvious. And too often companies go ahead and introduce new products that turn out to be costly failures. Marketing managers can increase the odds of success in this area by really understanding the steps of the new-product development process--and what it takes to generate and screen new product ideas.

This exercise is intended to help develop your skills in this area.

Assignment

The short descriptions that follow provide information about different companies. In each case, there is at least one major problem with the way the company is currently approaching the new-product development process. Read and evaluate each statement carefully, and then explain:

a)   your diagnosis of the problem, and
b)   your recommendation for what the company should do as a substitute for what is described in the case situation.

1.   Wind Riders, Inc. has been successful producing and marketing wind-surfing boards. In searching for new product opportunities, the company became interested in hang-gliders. The head design engineer for the company thought that the company's expertise in designing sails and rigging would apply directly to this popular new product. In addition, many of the retailers who carry the firm's wind-surfing boards are interested in the idea. However, one of them noted that there have been a number of accidents involving hang-gliders--and suggested that the company check into product-liability insurance. When this

was discussed back at the firm, the engineer said that he did not see a big problem. "After all," he said, "our hang-gliders will be as safe as others that are available. And in addition the accidents that occur are invariably the fault of the user. We can't be held responsible for user-errors if the product is properly designed and manufactured."

a. The problem: _____

_____

_____

_____

_____

b. Your recommendation: _____

_____

_____

_____

_____

2. Alka Corporation produces and sells special adhesives used in a variety of industrial manufacturing operations. The firm's initial growth came from a new adhesive that was used by the auto companies to attach rubber guards to metal bumpers. At present, however, most of the products offered by the firm are similar to those available from a variety of other suppliers. Michael Bach, the marketing manager for the company, recently scheduled a meeting with the company president to discuss problems of falling profits. Michael expressed concern that the company did not have a specific person responsible for identifying new products. The president pointed out that few other firms in their industry took such a position--and generally argued that new product thinking was the responsibility of everyone in the firm. After further discussion, the president agreed to let Bach send out a memo to all company employees encouraging them to be alert to new product ideas--and to submit any ideas to the research and development department for analysis of their technical feasibility.

a. The problem: _____

_____

_____

_____

_____

b. Your recommendation: _____

_____

_____

_____

_____

3. Lord Corporation produces a variety of plastic food storage containers and cooking utensils such as spatulas, strainers, and cheese graters. The finance manager at the company recently sent out a memo outlining problems related to the firm's weak financial position. He ended the memo with a plea: "To increase our profits in coming years, we must move ahead aggressively with new product ideas. The president of the company fully backs this thrust. He has established a new-product screening committee with members from different departments of the firm. We want you to submit your ideas. We promise to carry forward with marketing research on every good idea that comes in. Our objective is to really get behind your ideas--and turn them into products."

a. The problem: _____

_____

_____

_____

_____

b. Your recommendation: _____

_____

_____

_____

_____

4. Beta Medical Products Company has developed a promising new non-prescription tablet to relieve the symptoms of allergy sufferers. The idea has successfully passed the screening and idea evaluation stages of the company's new-product development process. The company has also completed concept tests and produced some tablets. Now, the head of the new-product development group has sent the following memo to the marketing department. "Our laboratory tests have satisfied the Food and Drug Administration criteria and we are ready to move ahead with a final test market prior to

commercialization. I want you to start thinking about this now. If the product does well in the test market, we will need to develop the rest of the marketing mix. We will want to come up with an attention-getting package design--one that will really stand out on a drugstore shelf. We will also need to decide on the brand name we would use in a national distribution. For now, we will just price the product in test market at the same price as our cold tablets. So final pricing decisions will also need to be made. And, of course, we will need to decide what type of promotion to use--and what message we want to get across to potential customers. I wanted to alert you to these exciting developments so that you could be getting your ideas together. We want to be ready to move quickly into commercialization if the test market is successful."

a.   The problem: _____

_____

_____

_____

b.   Your recommendation: _____

_____

_____

_____

_____

Question for Discussion

The text emphasizes that many of the new products that are developed and introduced prove to be expensive failures. Who pays the cost of these failures? Is it just the owners of the companies that introduced them?

Exercise 10-3

Growth stage competition

This exercise is based on computer-aided problem number 10--Growth Stage Competition. A complete description of the problem appears on pages 24-25 of *Computer-Aided Problems to Accompany Basic Marketing*.

1. As competition increases over time, AgriChem is likely to get a reduced share of the market. But, at the same time, the overall market will be growing. What market share, unit sales, and profit is AgriChem's marketing manager expecting in the current year and each of the next five years--assuming that the overall market grows at a rate of 200,000 units a year? What will AgriChem's long run profit be (that is, the sum of the profit for the current year and profits for each of the next five years)?

Year	Share (percent)	Unit Sales	Profit
0	_____	_____	_____
1	_____	_____	_____
2	_____	_____	_____
3	_____	_____	_____
4	_____	_____	_____
5	_____	_____	_____

Total Profit _____

2. AgriChem's marketing manager knows that competitors will force prices down over time, and he expects to lose market share as competitors enter the market. But, he also thinks that lower prices will stimulate demand and contribute to growth in the market. In fact, he is thinking about cutting his price to $12.50 now--to try to spur more growth in market demand while he still has a larger share. He thinks that if he cuts his price to $12.50 this year that the annual growth in sales might increase to 280,000 units a year for the current year and each of the next five years. But a price cut now would probably also drive prices down even faster during the next five years. He wants to evaluate the effect of this potential price change on AgriChem's expected long-run profits. Complete the table on the next page to evaluate this situation. (Hint: set the current price on the spreadsheet to $12.50, and set expected unit growth each year to 280,000. Then use the What If analysis to vary years in the future from a minimum of 0 to a maximum of 5 and display the price for each year, unit sales, and profit.)

Year	Price	Unit Sales	Profit
0	$12.50	_____	_____
1	_____	_____	_____
2	_____	_____	_____
3	_____	_____	_____
4	_____	_____	_____
5	_____	_____	_____
		Total Profit	_____

3. How do profits for the current year and the first year in the future compare for the two different pricing/growth situations?

   _____

   _____

   _____

   _____

4. How do long-run profits (say, for the current year and next five years) compare for the two different pricing/growth situations?

   _____

   _____

   _____

   _____

5. Drawing on your analysis, discuss why it is important for a marketing manager to try to anticipate how the market will change over the product life cycle.

   _____

   _____

   _____

   _____

Chapter 11

Place and development of channel systems

What This Chapter Is About

Chapter 11 introduces the strategic decisions in Place--and considers how and why channel systems develop the way they do. These ideas will help you understand the Place-related materials that follow in the next three chapters.

First, the need to adjust discrepancies of quantity and assortment is discussed. This will help you see why channel specialists develop. Later, various types of channel systems are explained--so you will have a better understanding of how channel members work together.

"Ideal" Place objectives are also explained--to emphasize the relevance of potential customers' behavior to Place planning. These ideal Place objectives are related to the product classes introduced in Chapter 9.

At the end of the chapter, the concepts of pushing or pulling within a channel are discussed.

This chapter emphasizes that marketing strategy must consider the whole channel-- and that channel management is an ongoing, dynamic process. As you learn about these strategic Place decisions, think about why a channel captain can play such an important role in leading the channel toward a common product-market commitment.

Important Terms

place, p. 277
channel of distribution, p. 279
discrepancy of quantity, p. 280
discrepancy of assortment, p. 280
regrouping activities, p. 280
accumulating, p. 280
bulk-breaking, p. 280
sorting, p. 281
assorting, p. 281
traditional channel systems, p. 284
vertical marketing systems, p. 285
corporate channel systems, p. 285

vertical integration, p. 285
administered channel systems, p. 286
contractual channel systems, p. 286
ideal market exposure, p. 287
intensive distribution, p. 287
selective distribution, p. 287
exclusive distribution, p. 287
dual distribution, p. 292
pushing, p. 293
pulling, p. 293
channel captain, p. 294

True-False Questions

___ 1. The Place part of the marketing mix is concerned with building channels of distribution and providing the time, place, and possession utilities needed to satisfy target customers.

___ 2. A channel of distribution is any series of firms or individuals who participate in the flow of goods and services from producer to final user or consumer.

___ 3. A marketing manager's decisions on Place have long-range effects and are usually harder to change than Product, Price, and Promotion decisions.

___ 4. Product classes help solve Place problems and in particular how much market exposure will be needed in each geographic area.

___ 5. Discrepancies of quantity exist because producers specialize in making one or a few items--while customers want many items and probably would prefer not to shop at different stores for each item.

___ 6. Because few customers can consume a big part of any producer's output, the large quantities that mass production makes possible generally cause a discrepancy of assortment.

___ 7. Collecting larger quantities of similar products, the accumulating process, creates a discrepancy of quantity but permits economies of scale.

___ 8. Bulk-breaking involves dividing larger quantities into smaller quantities as products get closer to the final market.

___ 9. The sorting process is usually handled by middlemen--when they put together a variety of products to give a target market what it wants.

___ 10. The assorting process means sorting products into the grades and qualities desired by different target markets.

___ 11. Marketing specialists should develop to adjust discrepancies of quantity and assortment only if these discrepancies must be adjusted.

___ 12. Although seldom used, direct-to-user channels are almost always better than channels which use middlemen.

___ 13. In a traditional channel system the various channel members make little or no effort to cooperate with each other.

___ 14. Vertical marketing systems are channel systems in which the whole channel shares a common focus on the same target market at the end of the channel.

___ 15. Corporate channel systems involve corporate ownership all along the channel.

_T_ 16. In regard to the development of the channel system, vertical integration means acquiring firms which operate at different levels of channel activity.

_F_ 17. Any administered channel system--by definition--is also a contractual channel system.

_F_ 18. Because of the importance of Place in a firm's marketing mix, marketing managers should always seek maximum market exposure for their products.

_T_ 19. Ideal market exposure makes a product widely enough available to satisfy the target customers' needs--but not exceed them.

_T_ 20. An intensive distribution policy refers to the marketing manager's desire to sell through all responsible and suitable wholesalers and retailers.

_T_ 21. Since it is not necessary to obtain 100 percent coverage of a market to justify or support national advertising, some firms now using intensive distribution might be wise to switch to selective distribution and use only the better middlemen to distribute and promote their products.

_T_ 22. Exclusive distribution is likely to be used by a producer--to help control prices and the service offered in a channel.

_E_ 23. Following a 1977 Supreme Court ruling, horizontal or vertical arrangements which limit sales by customer or territory may be legal if it can be shown that there are good reasons for such relationships.

_T_ 24. Dual distribution occurs when a manufacturer uses several competing channels to reach the same target market--perhaps using several middlemen in addition to selling directly itself.

_F_ 25. "Pulling a product through the channel" means using normal promotion effort to help sell the whole marketing mix to possible channel members.

_F_ 26. Clearly, a producer should always act as "channel captain"--because he is in the best position to help direct the channel as an integrated system of action.

_F_ 27. A channel system can work well only if its members have accepted a common product-market commitment and are all strongly market-oriented.

1. T, p. 278	10. F, p. 281	19. T, p. 287
2. T, p. 279	11. T, p. 282	20. T, p. 287
3. T, p. 279	12. F, p. 284	21. T, p. 287
4. T, p. 279	13. T, p. 284	22. T, p. 287
5. F, p. 280	14. T, p. 285	23. F, p. 289-90
6. F, p. 280	15. T, p. 285	24. T, p. 292
7. T, p. 280	16. T, p. 285	25. F, p. 293
8. T, p. 280	17. F, p. 286	26. F, p. 294
9. F, p. 281	18. F, p. 287	27. F, p. 296

Multiple-Choice Questions (Circle the correct response)

1. The "Place" variable deals with the creation of:
   a. time and place utilities only.
   b. time, place, possession, and form utilities.
   c. time utility only.
   d. time, place, and possession utilities.
   e. place and possession utilities only.

2. A channel of distribution:
   a. is any series of firms or individuals who participate in the flow of goods and services from producer to final user or consumer.
   b. must include a middleman.
   c. must have at least three members--a manufacturer, a wholesaler, and a retailer.
   d. All of the above are true statements.

3. Marketing specialists develop to adjust "discrepancies" in the marketplace. Which of the following best explains the concept of "discrepancies"?
   a. There are many more consumers than there are producers.
   b. The assortment and quantity of products wanted by a customer may be different than the assortment and quantity of products normally produced by a manufacturer.
   c. Supply and demand is no longer determined by market forces because "big business" is more powerful than the individual consumer.
   d. Price is not always a reliable measure of a product's quality.
   e. Although most manufacturers claim to be marketing-oriented, most firms would rather produce what they want to sell rather than what customers want to buy.

4. If you were a retailer attempting to supply a wide variety of products for the convenience of your customers, which of the following "regrouping activities" would you be *most* involved in?
   a. Sorting
   b. Accumulating
   c. Bulk-breaking
   d. Assorting
   e. Breaking bulk

5. Which of the following statements about channel systems is *true*?
    a. Some administered channel systems have achieved the advantages of vertically integrated systems while retaining more flexibility.
    b. All vertical marketing systems are also contractual channel systems.
    c. The independence of firms in traditional channel systems has led to channel efficiencies because of greater freedom of decision making.
    d. Indirect channel systems seem to be generally more effective than direct channels.
    e. Corporate channel systems are competitively superior to administered channel systems.

6. If K mart were to purchase the Zenith Radio Corporation, this would be an example of:
    a. vertical integration.
    b. internal expansion.
    c. horizontal integration.
    d. an administered channel system.

7. A manufacturer that tries to sell a product through any *responsible* and *suitable* wholesaler or retailer who will stock and/or sell the product is seeking what degree of market exposure?
    a. Exclusive distribution
    b. Intensive distribution
    c. Selective distribution

8. Which of the following statements about "ideal" market exposure is *true*?
    a. A manufacturer should aim for maximum market exposure.
    b. As a firm moves from intensive to exclusive distribution, it loses more and more control over price and service.
    c. It may be necessary to avoid intensive distribution to avoid dealing with middlemen who buy too little compared to the cost of working with them.
    d. Intensive distribution refers to the desire to sell through any and every retail outlet.
    e. All of the above are true statements.

9. Marketing managers should know that:
    a. a Supreme Court ruling prohibits exclusive distribution.
    b. vertical arrangements between manufacturers and middlemen which limit sales by customer or territory may be legal according to a recent Supreme Court ruling.
    c. horizontal arrangements among competing manufacturers or middlemen which limit sales by customer or territory are generally considered legal.
    d. vertical arrangements between manufacturers and middlemen which limit sales by customer or territory are always illegal.
    e. both c and d are true statements.

10. Although some middlemen may resent this approach, a manufacturer may have to use "dual distribution" because:
   a. present channel members are doing a poor job.
   b. the firm desires to reach different target markets.
   c. some customers are widely dispersed geographically.
   d. antitrust regulations prohibit relying on just one channel system.
   e. both a and b above.

11. The Boyd Corporation is introducing a new product next month. To prepare for the introduction, the marketing manager is having his sales force call on distributors to explain the unique features of the new product, how the distributors can best promote it, and what sales volume and profit margins they can reasonably expect. In addition, Boyd is budgeting 2 percent of its estimated sales for magazine advertising. This is an example of:
   a. selective distribution.
   b. a "pulling" policy.
   c. exclusive distribution.
   d. a "pushing" policy.
   e. intensive distribution.

12. Ideally, a "channel captain":
   a. has sufficient market power to force his policies on other channel members.
   b. is a manufacturer.
   c. is a strong retailer or wholesaler.
   d. is assigned this role by majority vote among channel system members.
   e. earns his position by effective leadership.

13. When a channel has a "product-market commitment":
   a. all members focus on the same target market at the end of the channel.
   b. its members attempt to share the various marketing functions in appropriate ways.
   c. there is no need for a channel captain to develop.
   d. all of the above.
   e. a and b above--but not c.

Answers to Multiple-Choice Questions

1. d, p. 278	6. a, p. 285	11. d, p. 293
2. a, p. 279	7. b, p. 287	12. e, p. 294
3. b, p. 280	8. c, p. 287	13. e, p. 295
4. d, p. 281	9. b, p. 289-90	
5. a, p. 283-86	10. a, p. 292	

Exercise 11-1

Evaluating the costs of adjusting discrepancies of quantity and assortment in channel systems

Introduction

If market segmentation were carried to its extreme, every customer would have a set of "tailor-made" goods and services. From an economic standpoint, this normally wouldn't be practical, of course. And fortunately, it isn't necessary--since it's often possible to find reasonably sized groups of consumers having relatively homogeneous needs. This often leads to "economies of scale"--which lower costs to customers.

By their very nature, however, mass production and mass consumption cause discrepancies of quantity and assortment. So, activities for adjusting these discrepancies are needed. The *regrouping activities* are: accumulating, bulk-breaking, sorting, and assorting. These activities can be carried out by the manufacturer or the consumer. Like many activities, however, they are generally performed best by specialists. This is why marketing middlemen develop--and often become important members of channels of distribution.

Assignment

The following case shows the role of marketing middlemen (particularly wholesalers) in creating and adjusting discrepancies of quantity and assortment. Questions appear at various points through the case--to test your understanding of the material. Read the case carefully and answer the questions *as they appear*. It is important that you understand the concepts involved, even though the case has been simplified to aid analysis. So think about the implications for a highly developed economy such as the United States.

NEW TRADE NATION

The New Trade Nation is a small developing country that recently experienced an industrial revolution. The country's 100 basic commodities are produced by 100 specialized firms, each of which makes only one product. All of the products are in turn sold through a network of 2,000 equal-sized retailers who are scattered all around the country.

The Kilroy Company produces widgets (a consumer staple) for the New Trade Nation. Due to large fluctuations in demand, the widgets cannot be manufactured in large quantities--and therefore cost $8 each to produce. Each week Kilroy's salespeople have to call on all of the retailers to solicit their orders for widgets. This results in a relatively high selling cost of $1.00 per each unit sold. Since orders are generally quite small, order processing costs amount to about 40 cents per unit. Finally, the necessity of shipping many small orders to retailers results in transportation costs of 60 cents per unit. The price Kilroy charges for each unit is determined by adding on 50 percent of the *total* unit cost of producing, selling, and delivering the widgets. Each retailer, then, takes a 40 percent markup on the cost they are charged by Kilroy.

1. How much do consumers in the New Trade Nation pay for widgets? Show your work (and label your numbers). The retail price of widgets is _____.

2. What discrepancies of quantity and assortment exist in the New Trade Nation? Be specific.

Consumers in the New Trade Nation complained about the high prices they were being asked to pay for widgets and other commodities. They blamed retailers for the high prices--demanding that the government take some action to reduce the retailers' high markups. However, retailers in turn blamed the high prices on the operating practices of manufacturers. Manufacturers acknowledged inefficiencies in their operations, but contended that such problems were unavoidable given the country's present distribution system.

After thinking over the situation quite carefully, the country's economic advisers concluded that the best solution would be to change the nation's distribution system. They recommended that 10 wholesale establishments be added to facilitate the distribution of manufactured commodities. The welfare minister protested, however, that the addition of more middlemen would only serve to *raise* prices instead of lowering them. Here, the economists countered with the following list to show the advantages of employing wholesalers in the New Trade Nation:

a) The presence of wholesalers would tend to stabilize demand for manufacturers, allowing them to take advantage of mass production techniques. It was estimated that manufacturing costs could be cut in half by producing products in larger quantities.

b) Since manufacturers would only have to deal with 10 wholesalers who buy in large quantities instead of 2,000 retailers, their unit selling costs would decrease by 60 percent. Furthermore, since each wholesaler would only be required to sell to 200 retailers, the wholesale selling costs would amount to only about 20 cents per unit for most commodities.

c) Order processing costs would decrease 50 percent for manufacturers, because wholesalers would order in large quantities. However, it will still cost wholesalers about 20 cents per unit to process each order from the retailers.

d) By shipping bulk quantities to the wholesalers, the manufacturers could take advantage of carload freight rates, thereby cutting their shipping costs to about 20 cents per unit. Also, since their orders would travel shorter distances, the wholesalers could ship products at a rate of 30 cents per unit.

e) Because they deal in large quantities of merchandise, the wholesalers would operate with only a 20 percent markup on total unit cost. Moreover, retailers could cut their markups down to 25 percent, since they would each be dealing with only one wholesaler rather than with 100 manufacturers--and therefore would have lower costs.

3. Assuming that the economist's estimates are accurate, calculate the new retail price for widgets if Kilroy were to distribute them through wholesalers. Show your work (and label your numbers).

The new retail price for widgets would be _____.

4. Should the New Trade Nation adopt the plan to use wholesalers in its distribution system? _____ Yes _____ No
Why?

5.   Explain how the addition of wholesalers would serve to adjust discrepancies of quantity and assortment in the New Trade Nation. Be specific.

Question for Discussion

Which marketing functions were added or eliminated with the addition of wholesalers to the New Trade Nation's macro-marketing system?

Exercise 11-2

Determining market exposure policies

Introduction

Once a producer decides to use middlemen (wholesalers and retailers) to help distribute its products, it must decide what degree of market exposure will be best: *exclusive distribution, selective distribution*, or *intensive distribution.* Contrary to popular opinion, maximum exposure is not always desirable. The ideal market exposure should meet--but not exceed--the needs of target customers. As one moves from exclusive distribution to intensive distribution, the total marketing cost may increase--and the quality of service provided by middlemen may actually decline.

When deciding about the desired market exposure, a marketing manager should consider the functions which middlemen will be asked to perform and the product class for his product. The product classes summarize some of what is known about the product--including what the target customers think of it, their willingness to shop for it, and the amount of personal attention and service they want. The product class often determines the "ideal" market exposure.

Of course, there sometimes is a difference between a firm's *ideal* market exposure and the exposure which it can achieve. Middlemen are not always willing to carry a new product, especially when several similar products are already on the market. The manufacturer must first convince prospective wholesalers and retailers of the product's profit potential. Normally, this is done by using a "pushing" policy. But manufacturers may have to adopt a "pulling" policy to overcome strong channel resistance.

Assignment

This exercise will give you some practice in determining the "ideal" degree of market exposure for a company. Six cases are presented below--with the first serving as an example. Read each case carefully and then indicate (a) the product class which is involved, and (b) the degree of market exposure (intensive, selective, or exclusive) which you think would be "ideal." Then in part (c), explain *why* you think the indicated degree of market exposure would be ideal. State any assumptions which you have made. *Note:* "Ideal" here means the degree of market exposure which will satisfy the target customers' needs (but not exceed them) *and also* will be achievable by the producer. For example, a new producer of "homogeneous" cookies might desire intensive distribution, but agrees to sell to only a few food chains because it knows it will not be able to obtain intensive distribution with its undifferentiated cookies. So its "ideal" is selective distribution, and it will adjust the rest of its marketing mix accordingly.

Note: Exhibits 9-4 and 9-5 on pages 223 and 228 of the text may be helpful in completing this exercise.

1. Boger Mfg., Inc. manufactures a wide line of kitchen dinette sets for sale throughout the United States. The products are distributed through retail outlets. Retailers are supposed to stock a large assortment of dinette sets, along with a large inventory of replacement parts. The tables and chairs are usually shipped to the retailers unassembled. According to a recent cost study, 30 percent of Boger's retailers account for about 80 percent of the company's sales.

    a) Product class: <u>Heterogeneous shopping products</u>

    b) "Ideal" market exposure: <u>Selective distribution</u>

    c) Why? <u>The recent cost study shows that a small percentage of retailers are producing most of the business. These middlemen might do an even better job if given more assistance and less direct competition from retailers carrying the same products. Since customers are willing to shop around, reducing the number of outlets would be possible--and might benefit consumers through larger retail inventories and increased customer service.</u>

2. Storage Equipment, Inc., makes and sells a low-priced line of file cabinets for use in offices. One style of cabinets is designed to store standard size business papers, and another style is designed for computer output. The files are sold directly to universities and other institutions--and indirectly through wholesalers to office equipment dealers. Storage Equipment's files sell to final customers (not the middlemen) at prices ranging from about $90 to $300. Most dealers handle several competing brands of file cabinets, including some "high-quality" brands that sell for as much as $1,000.

    a) Product class: _____

    b) "Ideal" market exposure: _____

    c) Why? _____

        _____

        _____

        _____

        _____

        _____

3. John Deere, Inc. manufactures a full line of farm machinery--including tractors, graders, and materials-handling equipment. John Deere farm products are distributed through over 500 independent dealers scattered throughout the United States. Typically, there is only one Deere dealer near any rural community, although there may be several other dealers who sell competing equipment. Many of John Deere's dealerships are quite small, and the company lacks adequate dealers in several key market areas. To further complicate matters, price wars between dealerships are becoming common as industry sales continue to decline. In fact, some Deere dealers often find themselves competing directly with other Deere dealers--since many farmers travel 100 miles or more to purchase new equipment.

   a) Product class: _____

   b) "Ideal" market exposure: _____

   c) Why? _____

   _____

   _____

   _____

   _____

4. Southern Paper Products Co. (SPPC) recently introduced Absorb, a new double-thick paper towel aimed at families with children. Primarily an industrial products manufacturer, SPPC's had produced paper towels for a few large grocery chains to sell as their own dealer brand. But Absorb was its first attempt at marketing a consumer product under its own brand. So far, results are not encouraging. Only a few wholesalers have taken on the line. Most are very reluctant to handle Absorb, claiming that retail shelves are already overcrowded with paper towels.

   a) Product class: _____

   b) "Ideal" market exposure: _____

   c) Why? _____

   _____

   _____

   _____

   _____

5. Oriental Designs, Ltd., manufactures decorative items for the home. It recently added beaded bamboo curtains to its product line. Designed for use in open doorways or as room dividers, the curtains are available in several colors and can be mounted easily on curtain rods. They are priced at $20 per set and measure six feet long by three feet wide. Like most of the company's products, the curtains are sold in gift shops, hobby shops, and specialty shops such as "Wicker City" franchise outlets. Initial sales for the curtains have been quite promising. The product seems to have good "eye appeal," according to one shop owner. Apparently, the early customers hadn't planned to buy anything like bamboo curtains, but once they saw them displayed in the store, they couldn't resist buying them.

a) Product class: _____

b) "Ideal" market exposure: _____

c) Why? _____

_____

_____

6. Spirit, Inc. designs and manufactures a high-quality line of fashionable clothing that is popular among young women and teenage girls. The line is quite expensive--so most customers are from wealthy families. The clothing is sold through specialty shops which handle only this type of wearing apparel (including competing brands). Spirit will only work with retailers who agree to stock a large variety of sizes and colors of Spirit fashions. They also must agree to promote the Spirit line very aggressively. In return, Spirit agrees not to distribute its line to other retailers within the specialty shop's immediate trading area. Since continuing promotion seems to be necessary in this highly competitive market, advertisements for Spirit clothes appear regularly in fashion magazines targeted at young women.

a) Product class: _____

b) "Ideal" market exposure: _____

c) Why? _____

_____

_____

Question for Discussion

How do you think each firm should try to achieve the "ideal" degree of market exposure you discussed above? Are there any legal constraints they should consider?

Exercise 11-3

Intensive vs. selective distribution

This exercise is based on computer-aided problem number 11--Intensive vs. Selective Distribution. A complete description of the problem appears on pages 25-26 of *Computer-Aided Problems to Accompany Basic Marketing*.

1. Hydropump's marketing manager thinks that the type of channel relationship possible with selective distribution would make it possible to get a large share (40 percent) of the pumps sold by its hot-tub dealers. But he realizes that the actual percent might vary. He thinks that the percent could be as low as 35 percent, or go as high as 45 percent. He wants to evaluate the effect that this might have on expected profits. Do a What If analysis, based on the selective distribution alternative, varying Hydropump's percent of dealer unit sales between 35 percent and 45 percent and displaying Hydropump's profit, and then complete the missing numbers in the table below.

Hydropump's percent of Dealer Unit Sales	Hydropump's Expected Unit Sales	Hydropump's Expected Profit
35	_____	_____
37	_____	_____
_____	9,880	193,200
43	_____	_____
44	_____	_____
45	_____	_____

2. How important is it that Hydropump win at least a 40 percent share of the dealers' unit sales? Explain your reasons.

_____

_____

_____

_____

_____

3. Hydropump's marketing manager thinks that the hot-tub dealers will pay more attention to the company's product if they get a higher than normal level of attention and help from Hydropump sales reps. However, a sales rep would only be able to spend the extra time with each dealer if he is responsible for fewer accounts. If each rep is assigned only 47 dealers, instead of 70, how many more sales reps would be needed, and how much would personal selling costs increase?

    _____ number of sales reps needed at 47 dealers per rep

    _____ personal selling cost for this number of sales reps

    -___$72,000___ personal selling cost for 4 sales reps

    _____ increase in personal selling cost

4. With this change in the sales force, Hydropump's manager is confident that the firm will get at least 40 percent--and perhaps as high as 50 percent--of the pumps sold by the dealers. Evaluate Hydropump's likely profit in this situation--and then compare it with your previous analysis (above). Would you recommend that Hydropump add the extra sales reps? Discuss your reasons.

    _____

    _____

    _____

    _____

    _____

    _____

    _____

    _____

Chapter 12

Retailing

What This Chapter Is About

Chapter 12 looks at the many changes, sometimes called "scrambled merchandising," which have been taking place in retailing.

Try to understand why and how retailers behave--because retailing probably will continue to change in the future. In particular, try to see why there are so many different types of retailers--and why some seem to be doing well while others have serious problems.

Don't just memorize the definitions of the various types of retailers. Instead, study what each is doing for some group of target customers. A diagram is presented later in the chapter to help organize your thinking.

It is useful to think of retailers from their point of view--rather than only as outlets for manufacturers' products. Most retailers see themselves as buyers for their customers, rather than selling arms of manufacturers. Try to look at retailing the way they do. This should increase your understanding of this vital part of our marketing system.

Important Terms

retailing, p. 299
convenience store, p. 301
shopping stores, p. 301
specialty stores, p. 301
general stores, p. 303
single-line (limited-line) stores, p. 303
specialty shop, p. 303
department stores, p. 305
mass merchandising concept, p. 305
supermarket, p. 306
catalog showroom retailers, p. 306
discount houses, p. 307
mass merchandisers, p. 308
super-stores, p. 308
convenience (food) stores, p. 309

automatic vending, p. 309
telephone and direct-mail
    retailing, p. 310
door-to-door selling, p. 311
scrambled merchandising, p. 312
wheel of retailing theory, p. 313
corporate chain store, p. 317
cooperative chains, p. 317
voluntary chains, p. 317
franchise operation, p. 318
planned shopping center, p. 319
neighborhood shopping centers, p. 319
community shopping centers, p. 319
regional shopping centers, p. 320

True-False Questions

T 1. Retailing covers all of the activities involved in the sale of products to final consumers.

F 2. More than three-fourths of all new retailing ventures fail during the first year.

F 3. A consumer's choice of a retail store appears to be based almost entirely on emotional needs--economic needs have almost no influence.

T 4. By definition, a convenience store would not stock shopping products or specialty products.

F 5. The major attraction of a shopping store would be the width and depth of its merchandise assortment.

F 6. A specialty store is one that handles an assortment of unusual or exotic merchandise.

T 7. A hundred and fifty years ago, general stores--that carried anything they could sell in reasonable volume--were the main retailers in the United States.

F 8. A limited-line store will typically carry a broader assortment than a single-line store.

F 9. Limited-line stores may carry several lines of merchandise--but with a very limited assortment of products within each line.

T 10. A specialty shop is a type of limited-line store that usually is small, has a distinct personality, and aims at a carefully defined market segment by offering knowledgeable salespeople, better service, and a unique product assortment.

F 11. A specialty shop would probably be viewed by most customers as a specialty store that stocks primarily specialty goods.

F 12. Department stores are becoming less important and they now account for only about 1 percent of retail sales.

T 13. Conventional retailers believe in a fixed demand for a territory and have a "buy-low and sell-high" philosophy.

T 14. The mass merchandising concept says that retailers should offer low prices to get faster turnover and greater sales volumes--by appealing to larger markets.

T 15. A well-managed supermarket can generally count on a net profit level of only about 1 percent of sales.

___F___ 16. Catalog showroom retailers have become quite successful in the United States using their strategy of stocking little inventory and delivering by mail.

___T___ 17. While discount selling generally involves price cutting on a limited assortment of products, many modern discount houses are fast-turnover, price-cutting operations that offer full assortments, better locations, and more services and guarantees.

___F___ 18. The average mass merchandiser has a store that is about the same size as an average supermarket.

___F___ 19. Super-stores are simply large mass merchandisers that carry more shopping products.

___F___ 20. Convenience food stores limit their assortment to those "pickup" or "fill-in" items that are needed between major shopping trips to a supermarket, and thus earn smaller profits as a percent of sales.

___F___ 21. Automatic vending has low operating costs because labor costs are very low.

___F___ 22. Telephone and mail-order retailing grew for a while but now seems to have leveled off at less than 2 percent of retail sales.

___T___ 23. Although it's an expensive method of selling--door-to-door retailers may be especially useful for the sale of unsought products.

___T___ 24. "Scrambled merchandising" is a way of describing the activities of modern retailers who are willing to carry "unconventional" assortments of products--anything they can sell profitably.

___F___ 25. All major retailing developments can be explained by the "Wheel of Retailing" theory--which describes a recurring retail cycle from low cost and low prices to higher cost and higher prices.

___T___ 26. Less than 5 percent of all retail stores have annual sales of 2.5 million dollars or more--but these stores account for more than 50 percent of all retail sales.

___T___ 27. On average, retail net profits as a percentage of sales are less than 5 percent.

___T___ 28. One of the incentives to chain store development is the availability of economies of scale.

___F___ 29. Voluntary chains are formed by independent retailers in their efforts to compete with corporate chains--while cooperative chains operate similarly except that they are sponsored by wholesalers.

___F___ 30. The very high failure rate among franchise operations explains why franchises are becoming less popular.

___ 31. By the year 2000 franchise holders will account for one-half of all retail sales.

___ 32. A good example of a planned shopping center is the central business district found in most large cities.

___ 33. Neighborhood shopping centers consist primarily of convenience stores.

___ 34. Although community shopping centers may provide a variety of convenience products--their major emphasis is on shopping products.

___ 35. Regional shopping centers typically serve 40,000 to 150,000 people within a radius of 3-4 miles.

___ 36. In the future, in-home shipping and electronic retailing are both expected to become more popular.

Answers to True-False Questions

1. T, p. 299	13. T, p. 305	25. F, p. 314
2. T, p. 300	14. T, p. 305	26. T, p. 315
3. F, p. 300	15. T, p. 306	27. T, p. 316
4. F, p. 301	16. F, p. 306	28. T, p. 317
5. T, p. 301	17. T, p. 307	29. F, p. 317
6. F, p. 301	18. F, p. 308	30. F, p. 318
7. T, p. 303	19. F, p. 308	31. T, p. 318
8. F, p. 303	20. F, p. 309	32. F, p. 319
9. F, p. 303	21. F, p. 309	33. T, p. 319
10. T, p. 303	22. F, p. 310	34. F, p. 319
11. F, p. 304	23. T, p. 311	35. F, p. 320
12. F, p. 305	24. T, p. 312	36. T, p. 321

Multiple-Choice Questions (Circle the correct response)

1. Which of the following best describes what "retailing" involves?
   a. The sale of consumer products to wholesalers, retailers, or final consumers.
   b. The performance of all merchandising activities except promotion and pricing.
   c. The sale of both industrial and consumer products.
   d. The sale of products to final consumers.
   e. All of the above describe what retailing involves.

2. Retail stores can be classified as convenience stores, shopping stores, and specialty stores. This classification is based on:
   a. the size of the store.
   b. the customers' image of the store.
   c. the location of the store.
   d. the type of products the store carries.
   e. All of the above.

3. A small privately owned men's clothing store in a university town has stressed personal services (e.g., free 90-day credit) and first-name relationships with student customers. The store carries only expensive, well-known brands of clothing and offers the largest selection of such merchandise in the area. Which of the following classifications is this retailer attempting to achieve?
   a. Specialty store--shopping products
   b. Shopping store--specialty products
   c. Specialty store--convenience products
   d. Shopping store--shopping products
   e. Convenience store--convenience products

4. Which of the following are *not* "conventional retailers" according to the text?
   a. General stores
   b. Single-line stores
   c. Supermarkets
   d. Limited-line retailers
   e. All of the above

5. Which of the following would be considered a *limited-line* retailer?
   a. Supermarket
   b. Gas station
   c. Mass merchandiser
   d. Drugstore
   e. Bakery shop

6. Specialty shops:
   a. generally try to become well known for the distinctiveness of their line and the special services offered.
   b. generally carry complete lines--like department stores.
   c. carry specialty products almost exclusively.
   d. generally achieve specialty store status.
   e. All of the above are true.

7. Department stores:
   a. are often frowned upon by the retailing community because they provide too many customer services.
   b. normally are large stores which emphasize depth and distinctiveness rather than variety in the lines they carry.
   c. achieve specialty store status with some consumers--and thus may be the only way to reach these market segments.
   d. account for less than 1 percent of the total number of retail stores--but over half of total retail sales.
   e. All of the above are true statements.

8. Large departmentalized retail stores that are larger than supermarkets and follow the discount house's philosophy of emphasizing lower margins to achieve faster turnover are called:
   a. department stores.
   b. mass merchandisers.
   c. planned shopping centers.
   d. specialty shops.
   e. box stores.

9. Which of the following statements about supermarkets is *true*?
   a. Supermarkets should be classified as "conventional retailers."
   b. Net profits after taxes in supermarkets usually run about 1 percent of sales--or less.
   c. The minimum annual sales volume for a store to be classified as a supermarket is $500,000.
   d. They typically carry 25,000 products items.
   e. All of the above are true statements.

10. Catalog showroom retailers:
    a. are essentially mail-order sellers.
    b. must charge above-average prices to cover the costs of printing and distributing catalogs to consumers.
    c. stress convenience as their most distinguishing feature.
    d. minimize handling costs by keeping their inventories in backroom warehouses until customer orders are placed.
    e. All of the above are true statements.

11. The "super-store concept":
    a. is just another name for the mass merchandising concept.
    b. essentially refers to large department stores which have adopted supermarket-style operating procedures and methods.
    c. is concerned with providing all of the customer's routine needs at a low price.
    d. probably will not be accepted by mass merchandisers.
    e. All of the above are true.

12. The modern convenience (food) stores are successful because they offer:
    a. wide assortments.
    b. low prices.
    c. expanded customer service.
    d. the right assortment of "fill-in" items.
    e. All of the above.

13. Which of the following statements about telephone and mail-order retailing is *true*?
    a. Most large mail-order houses aim at special-interest target markets.
    b. Mail-order houses tend to have lower operating costs than conventional retailers.
    c. All mail-order houses offer both convenience products and shopping products.
    d. Although mail-order houses have declined in number in the United States, they have achieved more than 15 percent of total U.S. retail sales.
    e. Mail-order retailers place their primary emphasis on low-price merchandise.

14. Electronic (cable TV) shopping:
    a. yielded sales of about $200 million in 1986.
    b. has come on strong on cable TV where whole channels are devoted to it.
    c. allows shoppers to order almost any kind of product from their home by phone.
    d. All of the above are true statements.
    e. None of the above are true statements.

15. Which of the following concepts is best illustrated by a retail bakery that sells wristwatches?
    a. The "super-store"
    b. Scrambled merchandising
    c. Time-sharing
    d. The "Wheel of Retailing" theory
    e. Mass merchandising

16. The "Wheel of Retailing" theory suggests that:
    a. retail stores do not have life cycles.
    b. retailing profits tend to be cyclical.
    c. only the largest retailers have a chance to survive in a fast-moving economy.
    d. new types of retailers enter as low-price operators and eventually begin to offer more services and charge higher prices.
    e. only discounters can survive in the long run.

17. Census data indicate that:
    a. less than 5 percent of all retail establishments have annual sales of $2.5 million or more.
    b. there are more manufacturers and wholesalers than there are retailers in the United States.
    c. retailing is no longer a field made up mostly of small businesses.
    d. the really large retailers account for a rather small percentage of total retail sales.
    e. all of the above are true.

18. A group of retailers banding together to establish their own wholesaling organization would be known as a:
    a. cooperative chain.
    b. voluntary chain.
    c. consumer cooperative.
    d. corporate chain.
    e. franchise.

19. Franchisers:
    a. are similar to voluntary chain operators.
    b. often provide franchise holders with training.
    c. usually receive fees and commissions from the franchise holder.
    d. reduce their risk of starting a new retailing business.
    e. All of the above are true statements.

20. A new shopping center has been built in an area which allows it to serve about 80,000 people with a five- to six-mile radius. It is composed of a supermarket, drugstore, hardware store, beauty shop, laundry and dry-cleaning store, a gas station, and a small department store. This center would be considered:
    a. a community shopping center.
    b. a neighborhood shopping center.
    c. a central business district.
    d. a regional shopping center.

21. Which of the following is *least likely* to occur in retailing in the future?
    a. Conventional retailers will continue to feel a profit squeeze.
    b. Scrambled merchandising will decline.
    c. There will be more vertical arrangements between producers and retailers.
    d. There may be an increase in in-home shopping.
    e. Stores will continue to make shopping more convenient.

Answers to Multiple-Choice Questions

1. d, p. 299	8. b, p. 305	15. b, p. 312
2. b, p. 301	9. b, p. 306	16. d, p. 313
3. a, p. 302	10. d, p. 306	17. a, p. 315
4. c, p. 303	11. c, p. 308	18. a, p. 317
5. e, p. 303	12. d, p. 309	19. e, p. 318
6. a, p. 303	13. b, p. 310	20. a, p. 319
7. c, p. 305	14. d, p. 311	21. b, p. 320

Exercise 12-1

Analyzing store-product combinations

Introduction

In Chapter 9, consumer products were classified--as convenience products, shopping products, specialty products, and unsought products--based on how different consumers think about and buy products. But just as the same *product* can mean different things to different people, the same *retail store* may also be seen differently by different target customers. Thus, in Chapter 12--building on the earlier discussion of consumer behavior and product classes--retail stores are classified as convenience stores, shopping stores, and specialty stores.

Because marketing planners should consider both product- and store-related needs, it is helpful to put the products and store classes together to form store-product combinations. (See Exhibit 12-2 on page 302 of the text.)

This exercise illustrates how different customer needs and shopping behavior for basically the same product--in this case, men's shirts--can result in different target customers seeking different store-product combinations. As you do the exercise, try to think about the strategic implications of store-product combinations--both for retailers as well as for manufacturers and wholesalers.

Assignment

The needs and shopping behavior of potential customers for men's shirts are described in the following cases. Assume in each case that the customer being described is representative of a group of customers having similar needs and shopping behavior. Read each case carefully and then: (a) indicate which of the following store-product combinations is most relevant and (b) briefly explain your answer in the space provided. The first case is answered for you as an example.

1. Convenience store selling convenience products
2. Convenience store selling shopping products
3. Convenience store selling specialty products
4. Shopping store selling convenience products
5. Shopping store selling shopping products
6. Shopping store selling specialty products
7. Specialty store selling convenience products
8. Specialty store selling shopping products
9. Specialty store selling specialty products

1. Bob Moore was about to start a new sales job and needed about a dozen new dress shirts--in varying styles and colors--to fill out his wardrobe. He decided to buy all of the shirts at Dayton's Department Store because Dayton's was the only store in town where Bob had a charge account.

    a) Store-product combination: <u>Specialty store selling shopping products</u>

    b) Explanation: <u>He prefers a particular store (Dayton's) because he has a charge account there, but also because he needs an adequate assortment of shirts from which to choose.</u>

2. Mike Beard's girlfriend is an accountant at Dayton's Department Store. When he met her at the store to go to lunch, she pointed out that his felt-tip pen had leaked all over the pocket of his shirt. Since he had an important business appointment right after lunch, he quickly stopped in the Dayton's shirt department and bought a standard white shirt.

    a) Store-product combination: _____

    b) Explanation: _____

    _____

    _____

    _____

3. When Cathy Strong asked her husband what he would like for his birthday, he said that he wanted a white Arrow brand dress shirt to wear with his new gold cuff links. The next day, Cathy stopped in Dayton's Department Store to buy some sheets that were on sale. On the way out of the store, the men's shirt department caught her eye and she found the exact shirt her husband wanted. She was pleased that she didn't have to search at a number of other stores.

    a) Store-product combination: _____

    b) Explanation: _____

    _____

    _____

    _____

4. George Denver had been looking for a shirt that would go well with his new suit. As he was looking through Esquire magazine, he saw an ad for an Alexander Julian designer shirt that was just right. Knowing exactly what he wanted, he went from store to store until he found the shirt at Dayton's Department Store.

a)   Store-product combination: _____

b)   Explanation: _____

_____

_____

_____

5.   Nick Deydow decided to buy a colorful sport shirt to wear to his fraternity's cookout. He didn't have any particular style or color in mind, but from past experience he was sure he could find something that he would like at Dayton's Department Store or one of the many men's clothing stores right around Dayton's.

        a)   Store-product combination: _____

        b)   Explanation: _____

                _____

                _____

                _____

6.   Doug Bermen is a weightlifter and has trouble buying dress shirts that fit well across his chest and shoulders. Most stores carry sizes only for "normal" size men. Thus, Doug buys all his dress shirts at Dayton's Department Store--which stocks a special line of shirts for men with athletic builds.

        a)   Store-product combination: _____

        b)   Explanation: _____

                _____

                _____

                _____

7.   Pete Right dislikes white shirts, but has to wear them five days a week in his job as a buyer at Dayton's Department Store. When his white shirts wear out, Pete buys a whole box of Dayton's own brand of shirts at one time--taking advantage of his 20 percent employee discount plus a quantity discount.

        a)   Store-product combination: _____

        b)   Explanation: _____

                _____

_____

_____

8. After spilling his morning cup of coffee all over his white shirt, advertising agency executive Frank Longino telephoned all the nearby clothing stores to find one that was willing to deliver a new shirt in time for Frank to attend an important luncheon meeting. Dayton's Department Store told him they would send a clerk right over with a shirt.

    a) Store-product combination: _____

    b) Explanation: _____

    _____

    _____

    _____

9. On Saturday morning, while shopping at Dayton's Department Store, Steve Hammermesh suddenly remembered that he didn't have a tennis shirt to wear for his match later in the day. He quickly walked over to the sportswear department to see if he could find a casual shirt that he would like.

    a) Store-product combination: _____

    b) Explanation: _____

    _____

    _____

    _____

Question for Discussion

How might a retailer such as Dayton's Department Store use the above store-product combinations in planning its marketing strategies? Are these combinations also relevant for wholesalers and manufacturers?

Name: _____ Course & Section: _____

Exercise 12-2

Identifying and analyzing retail stores

Introduction

Retailing involves the sale of products to final consumers. There are almost two million retail stores in the United States. However, as discussed in the text, there are many different types of retailers which vary both in size and method of operation. Marketing managers of consumer products at all channel levels must understand retailing--for if the retailing effort is not effective, the products may not be sold and *all* members of the channel will suffer. Likewise, consumers must be concerned with retailing--because their standard of living is partly dependent on how well retailing is done.

The purpose of this exercise is to focus your attention on the retailers who serve *your* community. What types of stores are there? How do they operate? Who are their target customers? Why might there be different types of retailers selling *basically* the same kind of products?

Assignment

Listed below are several types of retail stores which were discussed in the text. For each type:

a) Give the name and address of a store in your community that illustrates this type.

b) Briefly describe the store in terms of its *width* and *depth* of assortment. Is it a single-line or limited-line store or a "scrambled merchandiser"? Does the store stress high turnover or low turnover products?

c) Briefly describe the store in terms of its price/service blend (is the store price-oriented or service-oriented) and estimate whether the store's gross margin is in the *low range* (below 20 percent), *medium range* (20-35 percent), or *high range* (over 35 percent).

Note: If your community does not have a particular store type, write "none" under part (a) and then answer parts (b) and (c) in terms of how you *think* that type of store would operate.

1. *Limited-Line "Conventional" Retailer*

    a) Store name and address: _____

    b) Assortment: _____

    c) Price/Service blend: _____

        Gross margin range: _____

2. *Department Store*

    a) Store name and address: _____

    b) Assortment: _____

    c) Price/Service blend: _____

        Gross margin range: _____

3. *Supermarket*

    a) Store name and address: _____

    b) Assortment: _____

    c) Price/Service blend: _____

        Gross margin range: _____

4. *Convenience (Food) Store*

    a) Store name and address: _____

    b) Assortment: _____

    c) Price/Service blend: _____

        Gross margin range: _____

5. *Catalog Showroom*

    a) Store name and address: _____

    b) Assortment: _____

    c) Price/Service blend: _____

        Gross margin range: _____

6. *Mass Merchandiser*

   a) Store name and address: _____

   b) Assortment: _____

   c) Price/Service blend: _____

   Gross margin range: _____

Question for Discussion

Why are there so many different types of retailers in the United States? What implications does this have for marketing strategy planning?

Exercise 12-3

Mass merchandising

This exercise is based on computer-aided problem number 12--Mass Merchandising. A complete description of the problem appears on pages 26-27 of *Computer-Aided Problems to Accompany Basic Marketing*.

1.   The wholesaler's estimates of what quantity of the toy PlayTime could expect to sell at different markups were based on the average sales of other toy stores that the wholesaler sells to. But PlayTime's manager knows that the exact amount he sells at a particular markup might vary. For example, the wholesaler indicated that the smallest quantity of Brand A that any store sold at the $1.50 markup was 23, and that the largest quantity of Brand B sold at that markup was 33.

PlayTime's manager is interested in how profit contribution per inch of shelf space for Brand A might vary for different quantities in the 23 to 33 range. Prepare an analysis that provides this information--and complete the table below. (Hint: change the markup for Brand A to $1.50 on the spreadsheet and then use the What If analysis to vary the quantity sold at that markup between a minimum of 23 and a maximum of 33. Select contribution per inch of shelf as the value to display.)

Brand A Quantity	Contribution Per Inch
24	_____
25	_____
26	_____
27	_____
28	_____
29	_____
30	_____
31	_____
32	_____
33	_____

2. The wholesaler also had more detailed information about different stores that had sold Brand B at a $1.00 markup. The smallest quantity sold at that markup was 36, and the largest quantity sold was 54. Evaluate Brand B's contribution per inch for different quantities in this range, and complete the table below.

Brand B Quantity	Contribution Per Inch
36	_____
38	_____
40	_____
42	_____
44	_____
46	_____
48	_____
50	_____
52	_____
54	_____

3. It is hard to predict the exact quantity PlayTime might sell of either brand. It might be that its sales would be toward the low end for one, but toward the high end for the other. Even so, the manager must make a decision and he is thinking about stocking Brand A and selling it with a $1.50 markup. Based on the analyses you have just completed, does this seem like a good decision? Why?

_____

_____

_____

_____

_____

_____

_____

Chapter 13

Wholesaling

What This Chapter Is About

Chapter 13 discusses various kinds of specialized wholesalers who have developed to provide "wholesaling functions"--really just variations of the basic marketing functions. You should become familiar with the various types: what they do, and roughly what they cost.

Wholesalers are not guaranteed a place in channel systems. Some have been eliminated. Others probably will be. And other wholesalers have been making a "comeback" in some lines. Try to understand why.

Like other firms, wholesalers must develop market-oriented strategies. But wholesalers are channel specialists--so think of them as members of channel systems--rather than as isolated firms. This will help you see why wholesalers are very important members of *some* channel systems--while they are not used at all in other channels.

Important Terms

wholesaling, p. 326
wholesalers, p. 326
merchant wholesalers, p. 330
service wholesalers, p. 330
general merchandise wholesalers, p. 330
single-line (or general-line)
  wholesalers, p. 330
specialty wholesalers, p. 330
limited-function wholesalers, p. 331
cash-and-carry wholesalers, p. 331
drop-shippers, p. 331
truck wholesalers, p. 332
mail-order wholesalers, p. 333
producers' cooperatives, p. 333
rack jobbers, p. 334
agent middlemen, p. 334
manufacturers' agent, p. 334

brokers, p. 335
commission merchants, p. 336
selling agents, p. 336
auction companies, p. 337
export agents, p. 337
import agents, p. 337
export commission houses, p. 337
import commission houses, p. 337
export brokers, p. 337
import brokers, p. 337
combination export manager, p. 337
manufacturers' sales branches, p. 338
factors, p. 338
field warehouser, p. 338
sales finance companies, p. 339
floor planning, p. 339

True-False Questions

F   1.   A producer who uses a direct channel system normally is also considered a wholesaler--because he must take over the wholesaling functions that an independent wholesaler might provide.

F   2.   All wholesalers perform the following functions for their customers: anticipate needs, regroup products, carry stocks, deliver products, grant credit, provide information and advisory service, provide part of buying function, and own and transfer title to products.

T   3.   A wholesaler might help a producer by reducing the producer's need for working capital.

F   4.   The typical merchant wholesaler's operating expenses amount to about 20 percent of sales.

T   5.   Merchant wholesalers don't necessarily provide all of the wholesaling functions, but they do take title to the products they sell.

T   6.   A general merchandise service wholesaler may represent many different kinds of manufacturers and supply many different kinds of retailers.

T   7.   Drop shippers own the products they sell--but do not actually handle, stock, or deliver them.

T   8.   Service wholesalers provide all of the wholesaling functions--while limited-function wholesalers provide only certain functions.

T   9.   Cash-and-carry wholesalers operate like service wholesalers, except that the customer must pay cash.

T   10.   Truck wholesalers' operating costs are relatively high because they provide a lot of service relative to how much they sell.

T   11.   Mail-order wholesalers should probably be classified as retailers--since they sell out of catalogs.

F   12.   Producers' cooperatives are limited-function wholesalers that specialize in supplying consumer cooperatives at the retail level.

T   13.   Rack jobbers are limited-function wholesalers, with relatively high operating costs, who help retailers offer a more attractive assortment of products--especially nonfood items.

T   14.   A manufacturer who has the capability of operating its own distribution facilities but lacks customer contacts should consider the use of agent middlemen to facilitate the buying and selling functions.

F   15.   The key role of manufacturers' agents is to provide well-established customer contacts for new products--while assuming all the risks of taking title to the products they handle.

                                                      McCarthy and Perreault

___ 16. A broker's "product" is information about what buyers need--and what supplies are available.

___ 17. Probably the most important function of a commission merchant is anticipating the needs of its customers.

___ 18. A small manufacturer with limited financial resources whose only skills are in production should probably consider contracting with a selling agent to act, in effect, as the firm's marketing manager.

___ 19. The primary advantage of auction companies is that they facilitate buying by description.

___ 20. Agent middlemen are less common in international trade than in U.S. markets because merchant wholesalers can both sell products and handle the financing.

___ 21. The fact that many manufacturers have set up their own sales branches suggests that the use of wholesalers usually makes distribution costs unnecessarily high.

___ 22. A small manufacturer of textiles with limited financial resources should probably consider selling its accounts receivable to a factor.

___ 23. A manufacturer who wants to maintain an inventory of goods in a sparsely populated rural area should seek the services of a field warehousing organization.

___ 24. Many appliance dealers do not own outright any of the appliances on their display floor--instead the inventories are financed by sales finance companies as part of an arrangement called "floor planning."

___ 25. Many manufacturers and retailers have realized that wholesaling functions are not always necessary, so wholesalers have been eliminated at an increasing rate in recent years.

___ 26. Most modern wholesalers have become more streamlined in their operations, more computerized in controlling their inventories, and more selective in their distribution policies.

___ 27. Recent trends in wholesaling indicate that wholesaling will survive, even though some wholesalers may disappear.

1. F, p. 326	10. T, p. 332	19. F, p. 337
2. F, p. 326	11. F, p. 333	20. F, p. 337
3. T, p. 327	12. F, p. 333	21. F, p. 338
4. F, p. 328	13. T, p. 334	22. T, p. 338
5. T, p. 330	14. T, p. 334	23. F, p. 338
6. T, p. 330	15. F, p. 334	24. T, p. 339
7. T, p. 331	16. T, p. 335	25. F, p. 340
8. T, p. 331	17. F, p. 336	26. T, p. 341
9. T, p. 331	18. T, p. 336	27. T, p. 342

Multiple-Choice Questions (Circle the correct response)

1. Which of the following is *not* a typical wholesaling function?
   a. provide market information to a producer.
   b. grant credit to customers.
   c. supply capital to pay the cost of carrying inventory.
   d. all of the above are typical wholesaling functions.
   e. none of the above is a typical wholesaling function.

2. Which of the following types of wholesalers has the *highest* operating expenses as a percent of sales?
   a. Manufacturers' agents
   b. Manufacturers' sales branches
   c. Brokers
   d. Commission merchants
   e. Merchant wholesalers

3. The two basic types of merchant wholesalers are:
   a. single-line and specialty.
   b. service and limited-function.
   c. service and general merchandise.
   d. single-line and limited-function.
   e. agents and brokers.

4. Which of the following statements about merchant wholesalers is *true*?
   a. The major distinguishing characteristic of merchant wholesalers is that they take title to the products they handle.
   b. Merchant wholesalers are the most numerous type of wholesaling establishment--but handle only about 25 percent of wholesale sales.
   c. General merchandise wholesalers operating in the consumer products area handle a broad variety of nonperishable items--usually including only convenience products.
   d. A specialty wholesaler generally would limit himself to the industrial products area--as distinguished from the consumer products area.
   e. All of the above statements are true.

5. Which of the following types of wholesalers do *not* carry stocks for their customers?
   a. Cash-and-carry wholesalers.
   b. Rack jobbers.
   c. Truck wholesalers.
   d. Drop-shippers.
   e. Mail-order wholesalers.

6. Which of the following statements about rack jobbers is *true*?
   a. Rack jobbing is a relatively high-cost operation--costing more than the average for merchant wholesaling.
   b. Rack jobbers provide retailers with specialized information about consumer preferences.
   c. Rack jobbers are practically full-service wholesalers--except they usually do not grant credit.
   d. Rack jobbers developed because many grocers did not wish to bother with reordering and maintaining displays of nonfood items.
   e. All of the above are true statements.

7. A type of middleman that does *not* take title to the products is known as:
   a. an agent middleman.
   b. a limited-function wholesaler.
   c. a rack jobber.
   d. a merchant wholesaler.
   e. a drop-shipper.

8. Which of the following statements is *false*?
   a. Agent middlemen generally do not take title to products they sell.
   b. Manufacturers' agents usually do not represent competing manufacturers.
   c. Brokers are often used because of the seasonal nature of production or demand.
   d. Manufacturers' agents generally have more authority over prices and terms of sale than do selling agents.
   e. Agent middlemen are very common is international trade.

9. The Jory Co. handles the entire output of several small clothing manufacturers on a national basis. The firm has almost complete control of pricing, selling, and advertising. In addition, Jory often provides working capital to the producers, who have very limited financial resources. In return, Jory is paid a substantial commission on all sales. The Jory Co. is a:
   a. selling agent.
   b. commission merchant.
   c. full-service wholesaler.
   d. manufacturers' agent.
   e. broker.

10. The principal function of a broker is to:
    a. transport acquired products.
    b. facilitate inspection of products.
    c. establish a central market.
    d. bring buyers and sellers together.
    e. distribute grocery products.

11. Manufacturers' sales branches:
    a. have very low sales per branch.
    b. are mainly used in weak market areas, where there is not enough business for other types of wholesalers.
    c. operating costs would be even lower than they are now if manufacturers didn't "charge" them with extra expenses.
    d. handle about a third of all wholesale sales.
    e. serve the same basic needs as do brokers.

12. The Perlman Corp. manufactures and distributes a specialized line of textile products. An opportunity has arisen for Perlman to expand its product line. However, most of Perlman's working capital is tied up due to slow payment of accounts receivable--and management does not wish to take on any additional debt at this time. Perlman should consider employing the services of a:
    a. sales finance company.
    b. field warehouseman.
    c. factor.
    d. floor planner.
    e. any of the above.

13. Which of the following statements is *least relevant* in explaining the "Comeback of the Wholesaler"?
    a. It is due to a natural rise in the need for wholesaling services.
    b. It is caused in part by the fact that wholesalers are now more "retailer-minded."
    c. It has been aided by more selective choice of customers--as many small retailers were clearly unprofitable.
    d. Many wholesalers no longer require each customer to pay for all of the services they provide *some* customers.
    e. Greater emphasis has been placed on training and advising retailer-customers.

Answers to Multiple-Choice Questions

1. d, p. 326-27	6. e, p. 334	11. d, p. 338
2. e, p. 328	7. a, p. 334	12. c, p. 338
3. b, p. 330	8. d, p. 334	13. a, p. 340-42
4. a, p. 330	9. a, p. 336	
5. d, p. 331	10. d, p. 335	

Exercise 13-1

Choosing the right kind of wholesaler

Introduction

Wholesalers are less dominant than they once were, but they are still a very important part in our economy. Wholesalers have become more specialized, so a marketing manager who must select a wholesaler must be concerned not only with finding a "good one," but also finding the right *type* of wholesaler.

There are two important types of wholesalers--*merchant wholesalers* and *agent middlemen*. The most important difference between the two types is that merchant wholesalers take title to (own) the products they handle, while agent middlemen do not. There are several types of merchant wholesalers and agent middlemen--and each performs different tasks. A marketing manager should select the type best suited to his marketing strategy. The various types of wholesalers are:

A. *Merchant Wholesalers*
  1. *Service Wholesalers*--including general merchandise, single-line and specialty wholesalers.
  2. *Limited-function Wholesalers*--including cash and carry, drop shippers, truck wholesalers, mail-order wholesalers, producers' cooperatives, and rack jobbers.

B. *Agent Middlemen*--including auction companies, brokers, commission merchants, manufacturers' agents, and selling agents.

Assignment

This exercise will give you some practice in choosing the right type of wholesaler. Each of the following cases describes a situation in which a buyer or seller *might* want to use one or more types of merchant wholesalers or agent middlemen. Read each case carefully and then indicate which type(s) of wholesaler(s) would be most appropriate for each situation. Then explain your answer.

The first case is answered for you as an example.

1. Jack Miller, a farmer in Indiana, has six truckloads of pumpkins that he wants to sell before Halloween. Local auction prices have been low, however, and Miller hopes that selling the pumpkins in Chicago may bring higher prices. Unfortunately, he is too busy with the rest of his fall harvest to bring the pumpkins to Chicago's central market and search for the best price.

a) Type of Wholesaler: <u>Agent middleman--commission merchant</u>

b) Explanation: <u>The farmer needs a low-cost wholesaler on a temporary basis to represent him in a distant market--providing market contacts, aggressive selling including price negotiation, and transporting. [Note: in the long run, the farmer might be better off joining a producers' cooperative--if one is operating.]</u>

2. Sol Feferman recently developed a patented recycling process for diseased trees. Officials from nearby cities--lacking any ecologically acceptable alternatives for disposing of trees that have been cut down--have agreed to deliver their trees free of charge to Feferman's plant. There, the trees are processed and converted into products such as wood chips for landscaping, bark mulch, railroad ties, and patio blocks. However, Feferman has little marketing experience and know-how. Usually buyers come to him by word of mouth--and then he is not sure how to price his products. The firm is in trouble financially and may have to declare bankruptcy unless Feferman can locate a steady and sizable market for his products. But, he has no funds to hire a sales rep or to promote his products.

a) Type of Wholesaler: _____

b) Explanation: _____

_____

_____

3. Bob Miles and his wife Jane had been managing an oyster bar at the beach. That seemed like an interesting thing to do when they graduated from college, but now they wanted to start their own business. They thought that the growing interest in health food opened up some interesting opportunities. And using money from the sale of their house, they made a down payment on a bakery which formerly belonged to a local cookie manufacturer. As their first product, they decided to produce a unique sesame seed and honey snack bar. They "discovered" the recipe for this unusual product while traveling in Greece, and they were certain that it could be a profitable item if they could distribute it through health food stores and nutrition centers. A number of the health food stores in their area had already expressed interest in carrying the bars. But the Miles know that they would need to obtain wider distribution--i.e., outside their present area--to be successful. One of the problems with expanding distribution, however, is that the bars use no preservatives--so they are perishable.

a) Type of Wholesaler: _____

b) Explanation: _____

_____

_____

4. Chemco Corporation--a large manufacturer of chemical products for paper manufacturing--has decided to produce and sell a new line of automobile tires. The company deliberately avoided the highly competitive tire market in the past--but now feels that it has a product that is much safer than any tires currently on the market. Chemco plans to distribute its new tires through gasoline service stations, automotive stores, hardware stores, department stores, mass merchandisers, and perhaps even through supermarkets. At the present time, the company has very limited financial resources--due to the cost of expanding its manufacturing facilities to produce the new line of tires.

    a) Type of Wholesaler: _____

    b) Explanation: _____

    _____

    _____

5. Nortex, Inc. is an established company that sells a full line of grinding equipment, sandpapers, and polishing compounds to a variety of industrial accounts. Recently Nortex developed a special compound for an auto producer to use to polish out small scratches on the paint of new cars. The new polish proved to be very effective and easy to use. Nortex decided that the polish might do well in the consumer market. The polish was test marketed in Atlanta, Ga. recently--and met with considerable success. Now Nortex has decided to sell the polish in other large cities--including New York, Cleveland, Detroit, Chicago, and Los Angeles. Nortex has adequate resources to finance the manufacturing and physical distribution of the product to these areas. However, the company does not have any established contacts with auto supply retailers in the new markets. Further, Nortex is reluctant to hire and train new sales reps to promote its only consumer product.

    a) Type of Wholesaler: _____

    b) Explanation: _____

    _____

    _____

6. Collins Packing Company of Salem, Oregon recently bought several small fruit packers. This greatly expanded its processing capacity beyond the quantity of fruit it has been selling under its own brand. It was able to buy the packers at a very low price because they had not been able to find enough business at profitable prices and were near bankruptcy. Collins Packing hopes to expand sales of its own brand over the next few years, but does not expect sales to increase much this year. Therefore, it is looking for some way to quickly "get rid of" fairly large quantities of canned sweet cherries, pears, plums, and several kinds of berries.

a)   Type of Wholesaler: _____

b)   Explanation: _____

_____

_____

7.   Goodco, Inc. makes "Made-Rite" potato chips--the best selling brand of potato
chips in the metropolitan New York area. The company has grown
considerably since it was started during the 1930s. In fact, Made-Rite potato
chips have become so popular among customers that the company is now
planning to expand its market coverage into the Midwest. New plants will be
opened in Cleveland and Chicago. However, company officials doubt that
Goodco can afford to operate its own plant-to-retailer delivery service in the
new market areas--as it now does in the New York area.

a)   Type of Wholesaler: _____

b)   Explanation: _____

_____

_____

8.   Koppers Fiberglass Works produces a line of fiberglass shingles that are used
for residential and commercial roofing. It supplies home builders, large roofing
contractors, and lumber yards throughout a three-state area. Koppers uses its
own trucks for deliveries within a hundred miles--and ships carload quantities
by railroad. Currently, four sales reps call directly on its present customers.
The company is faced with large swings in demand, however, and has had
difficulty finding new customers.

a)   Type of Wholesaler: _____

b)   Explanation: _____

_____

_____

Question for Discussion

Why are there so many different types of wholesalers?

Exercise 13-2

Analyzing channels of distribution

Introduction

A channel of distribution consists of different people performing different functions. They are linked together by a common interest in marketing products that someone needs and wants. At one end of the channel are manufacturers and at the other end are customers, and often there are "middlemen" in between.

Most products are *not* distributed directly from the manufacturer to the consumer or final user. In fact, the variety of middlemen has actually increased over the years. Middlemen exist because they perform some necessary functions--often more efficiently and economically than could either manufacturers or consumers.

This exercise focuses on several important types of middlemen. The objective is to determine what specific functions and activities each middleman performs--and to understand the role each plays in the distribution channel. Further, the exercise illustrates that while one type of middleman can sometimes be substituted for another--in other situations different types of middlemen perform complementary functions. Thus, while one channel may be longer than some others, it may also be faster, more economical, or more effective.

Assignment

The activities of several types of middlemen are described below in five cases. For each middleman described:

A. Identify the *general type* of middleman (a full-service merchant wholesaler, a limited-function merchant wholesaler, or an agent middleman) *and* the *specific type* of middleman (rack jobber, broker, etc.).

B. Diagram the channel or *channels* of distribution that are described in the case, using the following symbols.

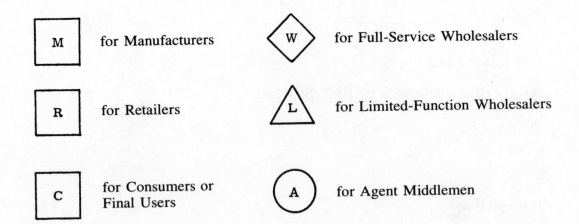

M	for Manufacturers	W	for Full-Service Wholesalers
R	for Retailers	L	for Limited-Function Wholesalers
C	for Consumers or Final Users	A	for Agent Middlemen

The first case has been completed as an example.

1.   Ralph Brown sells carload quantities of chemicals to industrial users--for several chemical manufacturers. Brown takes title to the products he sells. But he does not take physical possession of them, although he often arranges for transporting the products. One part of his business that is costly is the frequent need to provide credit to the small customers.

   a)   General Type: Brown is a limited-function merchant wholesaler.

         Specific Type: drop-shipper

   b)   Diagram of the Channel:

2.   Sellco, Inc.--in Athens, Georgia--operates as the "marketing manager" for several manufacturers. For example, it handles the entire output of a small fabric manufacturer whose products are distributed through selected retail outlets in the Southeast. While the fabric manufacturer provides transportation for its products, Sellco handles pricing, selling, advertising, billing and collecting, and even product design. This arrangement was made to relieve a strain on the financial and administrative resources of the manufacturer. Sellco earns a large commission on all sales.

a) General Type: _____

   Specific Type: _____

b) Diagram of the Channel:

3. Pesto Produce Company sells fresh fruits and vegetables that are grown (by others) in the Midwest and shipped to Pesto in Chicago. It sells to food processors, food chains, and full-service and limited-function wholesalers. In general, Pesto doesn't work with any producer on a continuous basis, but rather earns commissions on seasonal products of variable quality that are available in large quantities and that need immediate buyers. Pesto handles the products, negotiates prices, and completes the sale for the producers.

   a) General Type: _____

      Specific Type: _____

   b) Diagram of the Channel:

4. Top Valu is a wholesale grocer who sponsors a voluntary chain of independent retailers. In addition to the usual wholesaling functions, Top Valu provides special services for its stores: its own "dealer brand" products at very competitive prices, merchandising assistance, employee training programs, store location and design assistance, and accounting aid. Merchandise economies are achieved through group buying, and a modern distribution center is used to lower operating costs.

   Some retailers are too small to benefit from membership in the chain. For these customers, Top Valu operates a subsidiary to provide a smaller assortment of canned products and other household needs. Perishables are not stocked, and retailers must provide their own transportation. The products are priced attractively--considering the small order quantities--but no credit is offered.

a)   General Type: _____

Specific Type: _____

b)   Diagram of the Channel:

5.   Mead, Johnson & Company--a manufacturer of drug products--also produces Pablum, a baby food. Some years ago, Pablum was sold only to wholesale druggists because it was "logical" to send a new product through the company's present distribution channels--even though consumers bought such products mainly in grocery stores. Retail grocers bought the product from wholesale grocers, who in turn bought it from wholesale druggists. Mead wanted to eliminate the problem of Pablum carrying two wholesale margins, but did not want to risk irritating the wholesale druggists by "withdrawing" the product from them. Instead, the company chose to also use the services of people like Donald Tell to help it sell directly to grocery middlemen. Tell works with wholesale and retail grocers in the Boston area, handling noncompeting lines of several manufacturers. He promotes products very aggressively to earn about a 5 percent commission on sales. In general, Tell does not handle the physical distribution of Pablum.

(Note: Diagram both channels in this case.)

a)   General Type: _____

Specific Type: _____

b)   Diagram of the Channel   Diagram of the Channel
     with Wholesale Druggists: with Wholesale Grocers:

Question for Discussion

Are salespeople middlemen? Where are salespeople shown in channel diagrams?

Exercise 13-3

Merchant vs. agent wholesaler

This exercise is based on computer-aided problem number 13--Merchant vs. Agent Wholesaler. A complete description of the problem appears on page 27 of *Computer-Aided Problems to Accompany Basic Marketing*.

After further discussion, the owner of Giftware Distributing--the merchant wholesaler--says that he might take on some, or even all, of the responsibility for advertising the Art Glass items to gift stores--if Art Glass will sell to him at a lower price--to help cover the advertising expense. Art Glass is considering this idea--and trying to decide what type of arrangement makes the most sense.

1. Art Glass' marketing manager has decided that it will help him analyze the decision if he first figures out how much Giftware will earn under the current arrangement--assuming that Giftware sells 4,500 units. Although he did not include this calculation in the spreadsheet, he can calculate the total dollar markup because he knows how much Giftware would pay for each item and Giftware's selling price. What is the total dollar markup (contribution to profit) for Giftware?

    Giftware's selling price: $_____

    Art Glass' selling price to Giftware: -$_____

    Giftware's dollar markup per unit: $_____

    multiplied times the total units sold: _____4,500_____

    Total $ markup (contribution to profit)
    earned by Giftware: $_____

2. Since Art Glass is considering spending $8,000 on advertising to support Giftware's marketing effort, and since Giftware is expected to sell about 4,500 units, what is the expected advertising cost per unit?

    Advertising cost per unit: $_____

3. Use the spreadsheet to calculate the profit contribution to Art Glass if it sells to Giftware at $10.25 a unit, and Giftware does the advertising needed to sell 4,500 units (that is, so that Art Glass has no advertising expense). Would this be a better arrangement for Art Glass than what it was originally considering? Briefly explain why or why not?

    Art Glass' Total Contribution to Profit with this plan: $_____

Explanation: _____

_____

_____

_____

4. Art Glass' marketing manager thinks that Giftware would be more likely to agree to an arrangement in which Art Glass pays for some of the "up front" advertising expense. He is thinking about offering to pay half of the proposed $8,000 advertising expense. If this plan is used (and Giftware sells 4,500 units), what price should Art Glass charge to enable it to make the same profit contribution as it would if it paid for all of the advertising and sold to the wholesaler at the $12.00 price? (Hint: change the advertising expense on the spreadsheet, and use the What If analysis to vary Art Glass' selling price).

Art Glass' selling price to make about the same contribution if it pays for only half of the advertising expense:

$_____ price to Giftware

$_____ total profit contribution to Art Glass

5. At Art Glass' price in question 4, how much would Giftware have left as a "contribution to profit" if it sold 4,500 units and paid $4,000 for advertising expense? (Please show your calculations below. Please label the numbers you use.)

Giftware's "contribution to profit": $_____

6. Art Glass' marketing manager wants to know how this advertising cost-sharing arrangement would compare to the original proposal (that is, with Art Glass paying all of the advertising expense but getting a higher price from Giftware) if Giftware were able to sell 5,000 units, rather than the expected 4,500.

Art Glass' contribution to profit:

from 5,000 units sold at $12.00 with $8,000 ad expense: $_____

from 5,000 units sold at $_____
with $4,000 in advertising expense: $_____

7. Would Giftware be motivated to work harder at selling Art Glass' products under the proposed ad cost-sharing arrangement than it would if it bought at the higher price but with Art Glass paying all the advertising expense)? Briefly explain why or why not?

_____

_____

_____

_____

_____

_____

_____

Chapter 14

Physical distribution

What This Chapter Is About

Chapter 14 is concerned with the "invisible" part of marketing--the physical movement and storing of products. These activities account for about half the cost of marketing.

This chapter covers some important details on transporting and storing. But the major focus is on integrating transporting and storing into one coordinated effort-- to provide the appropriate physical distribution customer service level at the lowest total cost.

The total cost approach to physical distribution, the physical distribution concept, and customer service level are important ideas which have significantly improved some companies' marketing strategy planning. But they are not yet well accepted. Try to see why. Helping to apply these ideas may offer a breakthrough opportunity for you.

Important Terms

physical distribution (PD), p. 346
customer service level, p. 346
transporting, p. 349
ton-mile, p. 351
pool car service, p. 352
diversion in transit, p. 353
containerization, p. 355
piggy-back service, p. 355

freight forwarders, p. 355
storing, p. 356
inventory, p. 356
private warehouses, p. 357
public warehouses, p. 358
distribution center, p. 359
physical distribution (PD) concept, p. 360
total cost approach, p. 361

True-False Questions

____ 1. Physical distribution--which is the transporting and storing of goods within individual firms and along channel systems--accounts for nearly half the cost of marketing.

____ 2. Customer service level is a measure of how rapidly and dependably a firm can deliver what customers want.

____ 3. Marketing managers should be careful to avoid offering customers a level of physical distribution service that might increase storing or transporting costs.

    4.   Transporting--which is the marketing function of moving goods--provides time, place, and possession utilities.

    5.   The value added to products by moving them should be greater than the cost of the transporting, or there is little reason to ship in the first place.

    6.   Since 1980, there has been much more government regulation over transporting.

    7.   Based on ton-mile measurements, it is obvious that railroads are the backbone of the U.S. freight transportation system--followed in order of importance by trucks, airways, barges, and oil pipelines.

    8.   Railroad pool car service appeals mainly to very large shippers who are transporting to only a few locations.

    9.   Railroads offering "diversion-in-transit" enable shippers to ship commodities away from the source, stop them along the way for processing, and then start them moving again, as long as the final destination stays the same.

    10.   In contrast to railroads which are best suited for moving heavy and bulky freight over long distances, the flexibility of trucks make them especially suitable for moving small quantities of goods short distances.

    11.   Water transportation is very important to international trade, but it plays a small role within the U.S. market.

    12.   Trucking rates are roughly one-half of airfreight rates.

    13.   An important advantage of using airfreight is that the cost of packing and unpacking goods for sale may be reduced or eliminated.

    14.   Even though freight forwarders usually do not own their own transporting facilities, they can obtain low transporting rates by combining small shipments into more economical quantities.

    15.   The fact that rates on less-than-full carloads or truckloads are often much higher than those on full carloads or truckloads is one reason for the development of wholesalers.

    16.   When a firm's small shipments have to be moved by varied transporters, it probably should consider employing the services of freight forwarders.

    17.   While transporting provides time utility, the storing function provides place utility.

    18.   Inventory means the amount of goods being stored.

____ 19. The storing function offers several ways to vary a firm's marketing mix-- and its channel system--by: (1) adjusting the time goods are held, (2) sharing the storing costs, and (3) delegating the job to a specialized storing facility.

____ 20. Unless a large volume of goods must be stored regularly, a firm should probably choose public warehouses over private warehouses--even though public warehouses do not provide all the services that could be obtained in the company's own branch warehouses.

____ 21. The distribution center concept is based on the assumption that--unless storage creates time utility--reducing storage and increasing turnover will lead to bigger profits.

____ 22. According to the physical distribution concept, a firm might lower its total cost of physical distribution by selecting a higher cost transportation alternative.

____ 23. The total cost approach to PD involves evaluating each possible PD system--and identifying all of the costs of each alternative.

____ 24. When a firm decides to minimize total costs of physical distribution, it may also be settling for a lower customer service level and lower sales and profits.

____ 25. A higher physical distribution service level may mean both higher costs and higher profits.

____ 26. Improved order processing can sometimes have the same effect on customer service levels as faster, more expensive transportation.

Answers to True-False Questions

1. T, p. 346	10. T, p. 353	19. T, p. 357
2. T, p. 346	11. F, p. 354	20. F, p. 358
3. F, p. 347	12. T, p. 354	21. T, p. 359
4. F, p. 349	13. T, p. 354	22. T, p. 360
5. T, p. 349	14. T, p. 355	23. T, p. 361
6. F, p. 350	15. T, p. 355	24. T, p. 361
7. F, p. 351	16. T, p. 355	25. T, p. 361
8. F, p. 353	17. F, p. 356	26. T, p. 362
9. F, p. 353	18. T, p. 356	

Multiple-Choice Questions (Circle the correct response)

1. The physical distribution service level is important because:
   a. it is a measure of how rapidly and dependably a firm delivers what its customers want.
   b. it may result in lost sales if it is too low.
   c. it may result in lower profits if it is too high.
   d. All of the above.
   e. None of the above.

2. Performance of the physical distribution functions provides:
   a. time utility.
   b. place utility.
   c. possession utility.
   d. All of the above.
   e. Only a and b above.

3. Based on ton-miles carried, which of the following sets of rankings (from high to low) correctly indicates the relative importance of each mode of intercity freight transportation?
   a. Railways, pipelines, motor vehicles, inland waterways, airways
   b. Motor vehicles, railways, inland waterways, pipelines, airways
   c. Inland waterways, railways, motor vehicles, airways, pipelines
   d. Railways, motor vehicles, inland waterways, pipelines, airways
   e. Motor vehicles, railways, airways, pipelines, inland waterways

4. Which of the following transportation modes is "best" regarding "number of locations served"?
   a. Rail
   b. Water
   c. Truck
   d. Pipeline
   e. Air

5. A railroad shipping process which allows redirection of carloads already in transit is called:
   a. diversion in transit
   b. freight forwarding
   c. transloading privileges
   d. pool car shipping
   e. piggy-back service

6. Berry Bros. wants to ship a somewhat bulky, high-valued commodity a short distance--and it is seeking low-cost and extremely fast service. Berry should use:
   a. airfreight.
   b. railroads.
   c. inland waterways.
   d. trucks.
   e. None of the above.

7. Compared to other forms of transportation, airfreight may result in:
   a. a lower total cost of distribution.
   b. less damage in transit.
   c. higher transportation rates.
   d. lower packing costs.
   e. All of the above.

8. Grouping individual items into an economical shipping quantity and sealing them in protective containers for transit to the final destination is called:
   a. containerization
   b. pool car service
   c. freight forwarding
   d. piggy-back service
   e. all of the above

9. Freight forwarders:
   a. are not very active in international shipping because they are unwilling to handle all the paperwork necessary in overseas shipments.
   b. generally own their own transportation facilities--including pickup and delivery trucks.
   c. can be especially helpful to the marketing manager who ships in large quantities.
   d. accumulate small shipments from shippers and then reship them in larger quantities to obtain lower transportation rates.
   e. All of the above are true statements.

10. Storing:
    a. is related to Place--but has no effect on Price.
    b. is necessary because production does not always match consumption.
    c. must be performed by all members of a channel system.
    d. facilitates mass production.
    e. All of the above are true statements.

11. A manufacturer having irregular need for regional storage of bicycles should use which one of the following?
    a. A private warehouse to be sure of adequate space
    b. Public warehouses to provide flexibility and low unit cost
    c. Merchant wholesalers
    d. Agent middlemen
    e. Commission houses

12. A distribution center is designed to:
    a. stockpile goods for long periods and avoid rising prices.
    b. buy low and sell high.
    c. reduce inventory turnover.
    d. speed the flow of goods and avoid unnecessary storing.
    e. all of the above.

13. According to the "physical distribution concept":
    a. transporting and storing are independent activities.
    b. all transporting and storing activities of a business and a channel system should be thought of as part of one system.
    c. inventories should be based on production requirements.
    d. the production department should be responsible for warehousing and shipping.
    e. the lowest-cost distribution system is the best alternative.

14. The "total cost approach" to physical distribution management:
    a. emphasizes faster delivery service and thus favors the use of airfreight over railroads.
    b. often ignores inventory carrying costs.
    c. might favor a high-cost transportation mode if storage costs are reduced enough to lower total distribution costs.
    d. seeks to reduce the cost of transportation to its minimum.
    e. All of the above are true.

15. A marketing-oriented physical distribution manager would *insist* that:
    a. the storage function be eliminated to reduce inventory costs.
    b. efficiency in physical distribution can be best achieved by minimizing costs.
    c. emphasis must be on maximizing the customer service level.
    d. both customer service level and total distribution costs be considered.
    e. none of the above.

Answers to Multiple-Choice Questions

1. d, p. 346-47	6. d, p. 353	11. b, p. 358
2. e, p. 346	7. e, p. 354	12. d, p. 359
3. a, p. 351	8. a, p. 355	13. b, p. 360
4. c, p. 353	9. d, p. 355	14. c, p. 361
5. a, p. 353	10. b, p. 356	15. d, p. 361

Exercise 14-1

Evaluating physical distribution alternatives

Introduction

Physical distribution costs sometimes make up a large percentage of a product's final selling price. In fact, high distribution costs may block a company from competing effectively in distant markets. On the other hand, a firm may obtain a big competitive advantage if it can keep distribution costs to a minimum. However, it is not easy to pick the lowest cost distribution alternative. One must consider the nature of the products to be shipped, the distances the products will travel, the quantities to be shipped, and the rate structures.

This exercise gets you into the mechanics of selecting the "best" method of distribution when several alternatives are available. Here, the emphasis is on choosing the alternative which minimizes the *total* cost of distribution.

Assignment

Assume that you are physical distribution manager for the ABC Company and that you are considering the following alternative methods of distributing your company's products into a new market. You would like to develop a simple graph to show management that different alternatives may become more economical as the annual quantities shipped change. The estimated costs of the various methods of physical distribution are shown in Table 14-1, on the next page.

Alternative methods of physical distribution:

A. *Rail and local warehouse*--Ship products by railroad to leased warehouse in new territory and use leased trucks to deliver products to customers.
B. *Direct rail*--Store products in plant until ordered and then ship directly to customers by combination of rail and local trucking companies.
C. *Trucks*--Store products in plant until ordered and then ship directly to customers by truck (common carriers).
D. *Airfreight*--Store products in plant until ordered and then ship directly to customers by combination of airfreight and local trucking companies. (Inventories would be smaller due to the speed of airfreight.)

1. To help you plot a graph, calculate the total cost of each alternative for the following annual quantities shipped: (a) zero tons and (b) 50,000 tons.

Show your answers in Table 14-2. Answers for alternative A have already been calculated as an example.

Hint:
   total cost = fixed cost + (variable cost/ton) x (number of tons shipped)

TABLE 14-1
Costs of Distribution Alternatives

Distribution Alternative	Fixed Cost of Alternative	Variable Cost/Ton of Alternative
A. Rail and Local Warehouse	$3,500,000	$ 50
B. Direct Rail	$1,900,000	$ 80
C. Trucks	$1,600,000	$110
D. Airfreight	$1,000,000	$160

TABLE 14-2
Total Costs of Physical Distribution Alternatives
for Selected Shipping Quantities

Distribution Alternative	Total Cost of Quantity Shipped	
	Zero Tons	50,000 Tons
A. Rail and Local Warehouse	$3,500,000	$6,000,000
B. Direct Rail	$_____	$_____
C. Trucks	$_____	$_____
D. Airfreight	$_____	$_____

2. Using Figure 14-1, construct a graph that will show which transportation alternative has the lowest total cost for any annual quantity shipped up to 70,000 tons.

   Hint: For each transportation alternative, plot the two total cost estimates which you calculated in Table 14-2 for quantities of (a) zero tons and (b) 50,000 tons. Then connect the two points you have plotted with a straight line and extend the line out to a shipping quantity of 70,000 tons. Each straight line will then represent the total cost--for a particular alternative--of shipping quantities up to 70,000 tons. The total cost of using a particular alternative is represented by a straight line--because the variable shipping cost per ton is constant.

The total cost line for alternative A has already been drawn as an example.

FIGURE 14-1

Total Costs of Physical Distribution Alternatives for Shipping Quantities up to 70,000 Tons

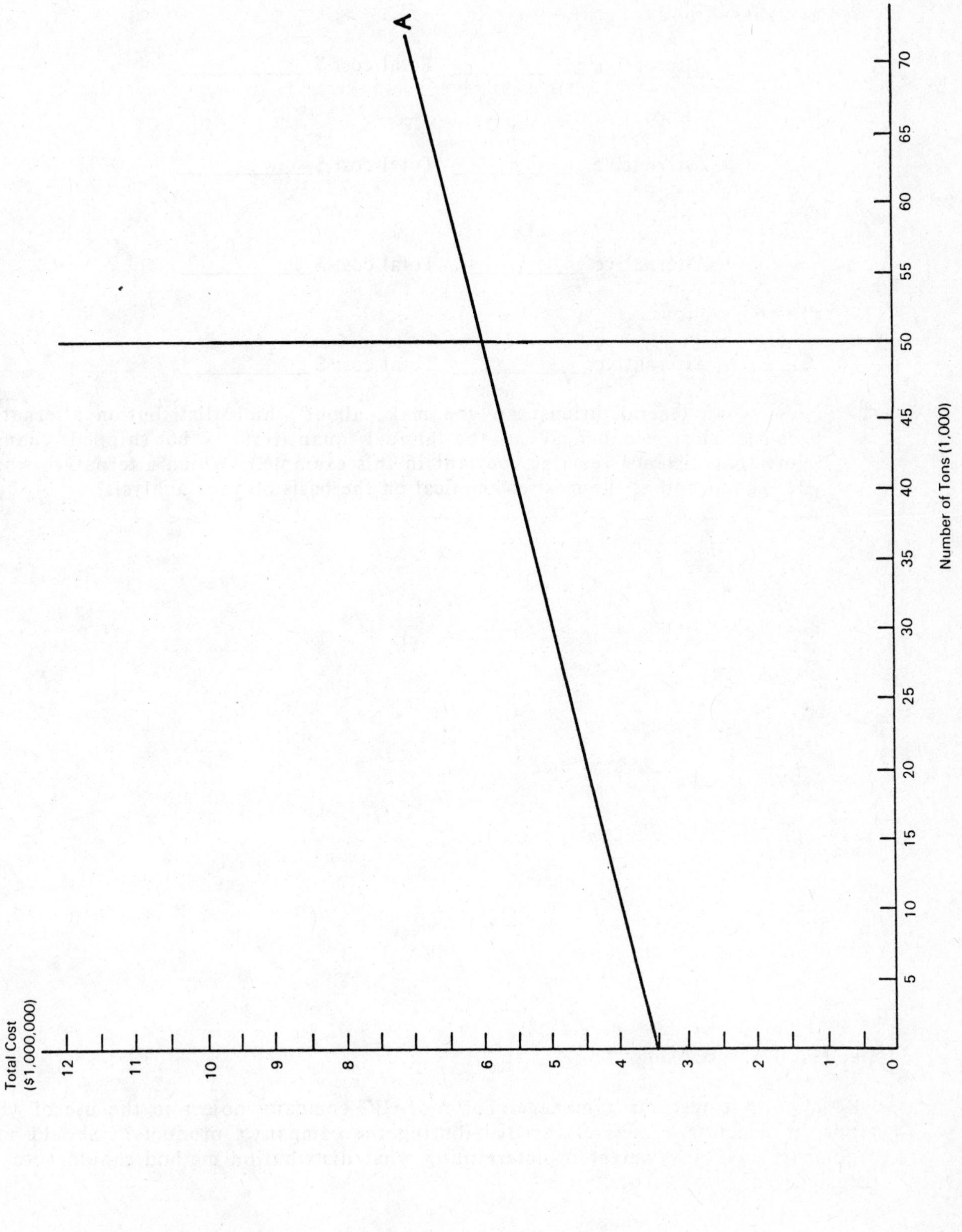

3. Reading off of your graph, indicate which distribution alternative offers the *lowest total cost* for each of the following annual quantities shipped and show (estimate) the total cost:

    a) 5,000 tons:

        Alternative _____ Total cost $_____

    b) 15,000 tons:

        Alternative _____ Total cost $_____

    c) 40,000 tons:

        Alternative _____ Total cost $_____

    d) 60,000 tons:

        Alternative _____ Total cost $_____

4. Now, what generalizations can you make about which distribution alternative becomes most economical as the annual quantities to be shipped change? (Note that distance remains constant in this example.) Which alternative would you recommend as the most economical on the basis of your analysis?

Question for Discussion

Why might the marketing manager for the ABC company object to the use of your graph in selecting a method for distributing the company's products? Should such arguments have any weight in determining what distribution method should actually be employed?

Exercise 14-2
Strategic planning for customer service level

Introduction

Within the framework of marketing strategy planning, physical distribution managers seek to provide the level of customer service that satisfies the needs of the firm's target market. Given some specified level of customer service, it is also the physical distribution manager's job to provide that service at the lowest cost possible. This total cost approach is based on the idea of "tradeoffs" among parts of the distribution system.

For example, a physical distribution manager may be making a tradeoff when he decides to lower his transportation costs, because such a move usually results in larger inventory costs. Following the total cost approach, he would not try to minimize with transportation *or* inventory costs. Instead, he would operate his physical distribution system in a way that would *minimize the total cost of offering the desired customer service level*. The following exercise will illustrate this idea in greater detail.

Assignment

Read the following case and answer the questions that follow.

ACME COMPANY

The Acme Company is studying its physical distribution system to see if the system needs to be remodeled. Currently, whatzits (an industrial product) are manufactured at Acme's plant in Chicago and then shipped by train to several branch warehouses across the United States. When an order is received at the Chicago plant, the order is relayed to the branch warehouse closest to the customer. The products are then shipped directly to the customer by truck. Acme tries to maintain a 60 percent customer service level--that is, it tries to deliver 60 percent of its orders to the customer within three days after the orders are received.

Recently, several company managers have expressed dissatisfaction with the present distribution system. Acme's sales manager feels that the 60 percent service level is inadequate--and should be increased to at least 80 percent by adding more warehouses. The production manager wants to cut the service level to 20 percent, to even out his production schedule--although the traffic manager claims this will increase transportation costs too much. Finally, the finance manager has suggested that the firm try to minimize its total distribution costs by providing whatever level of customer service it can while operating at the lowest possible total cost.

To help resolve this conflicting advice from his top managers, Acme's president ordered his assistant to analyze the relationship between alternative customer service levels and physical distribution costs. The results of this analysis are shown in Figure 14-2.

FIGURE 14-2

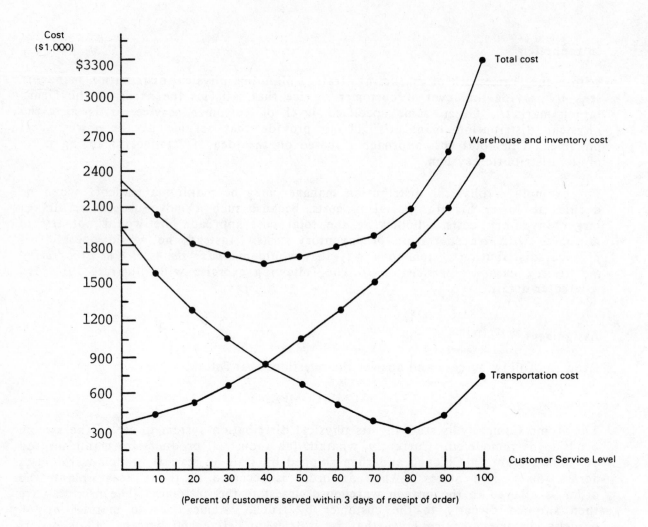

(Percent of customers served within 3 days of receipt of order)

1. According to Figure 14-2, what is Acme's total cost of physical distribution at its present 60 percent customer service level? $_____

2. What would the total cost be if a 80 percent service level were adopted? $_____

3. What would the total cost be if a 20 percent service level were adopted? $_____

McCarthy and Perreault

4. At what customer service level would the total cost of distribution be *minimized*? What would the minimum total cost be?

    Customer service level _____% Total cost $_____

5. What would the *total cost* be if Acme attempted to *minimize* its:

    a) transportation costs $_____

    b) warehouse and inventory costs $_____

6. What would the total cost be if Acme were to *maximize* its customer service level? $_____

7. Obviously, the optimal customer service level for Acme would be _____ percent because:

8. As marketing manager for the Acme Company, what advice would you give the president concerning the customer service level decision?

Question for Discussion

Suppose you were the warehouse manager for the Acme Company and would have to account for an increase in warehouse and inventory costs of 65 percent if the sales department's plans to increase the service level were implemented. If you were responsible for minimizing warehouse and inventory costs--and this were your only area of responsibility--you would look bad. How would you explain this to your boss? What are the implications of your answer for company organization?

Exercise 14-3

Total distribution cost

This exercise is based on computer-aided problem number 14--Total Distribution Cost. A complete description of the problem appears on page 28 of *Computer-Aided Problems to Accompany Basic Marketing*.

Bay Shore's marketing manager is trying to decide what distribution system to use to reach new target customers on the other side of the country. Although he is concerned about the total cost of distribution, he is also concerned about the physical distribution customer service level. Better customer service may cost more--but it may also help to win customers in this distant market. And these customers may be willing to pay a higher price for a marketing mix with better service.

1. Using a distribution system involving railroad transportation at $2.00 a unit, 2 warehouses at $5,000 per year each, and a 10 per cent inventory carrying cost would make it possible to deliver 95 percent of all orders within 7 days. What is the total cost of distribution in this situation--if Bay Shore expects to sell 15,000 units per year at a price of $21.00 a unit? What is the total revenue? How much money is left after the total cost of distribution is subtracted from revenue?

   $_____ total revenue

   minus $_____ total cost of physical distribution

   equals $_____ total revenue after cost of distribution

2. If Bay Shore uses airfreight that costs $4.68 a unit, maintains an inventory level with a carrying cost of 5 percent, and pays $4,000 per year for space in one warehouse, it would be possible to deliver 95 percent of all orders within 3 days. What is the total cost of distribution in this situation--if Bay Shore expects to sell 15,000 units per year and keep the price at $21.00 a unit? What is the total revenue? How much is left after the distribution cost is subtracted from revenue?

   $_____ total revenue

   minus $_____ total cost of physical distribution

   equals $_____ total revenue after cost of distribution

3. How do these two distribution systems (1 and 2 above) compare in terms of total cost? In terms of customer service level?

   _____

   _____

4. The comparison in question 3 assumes that all customers will be charged the same price regardless of which system is used. But marketing research suggests that customers might pay more for a marketing mix with better customer service. The results of the research are not precise, but it appears that customers would be willing to pay somewhere between $22.00 and $23.00. Approximately how high a price would customers have to be willing to pay for the airfreight system to enable Bay Shore to make more money than it would by using the railroad system? To get started, show the difference between total revenue and total distribution cost for the railroad-based distribution system (from previous page)?

$_____ difference between revenue and total PD cost for railroad system

5. Next, do a What If analysis in which you vary the selling price for the airfreight system. Record the total revenue and total physical distribution (PD) cost at each price in the columns below. Then, for each price, fill in the final column by subtracting the total cost from total revenue.

Airfreight Selling Price ($)	Airfreight Total Revenue	Airfreight Total PD Cost	Your calculation: Revenue minus PD Costs
$22.00	_____	_____	_____
_____	_____	_____	_____
_____	_____	_____	_____
_____	_____	_____	_____
_____	_____	_____	_____
_____	_____	_____	_____
_____	_____	_____	_____
_____	_____	_____	_____
_____	_____	_____	_____
$23.00	_____	_____	_____

Compare your calculations with the number you recorded for the railroad system (in question 4), and decide at what price airfreight would be better than railroad.

$_____ = price at which higher-cost airfreight would be better than railroad.

Chapter 15

Promotion--Introduction

What This Chapter Is About

Chapter 15 introduces Promotion--the topic of Chapters 15-17. Be sure to see that Promotion is only one of the four Ps--*not* the whole of marketing. Promotion tries to carry out promotion objectives--just as the other Ps have their own specific objectives.

This chapter looks at promotion objectives and methods from a strategic viewpoint--with emphasis on developing a good promotion blend. Early in the chapter, much attention is given to the communication process and the adoption of new ideas. These theoretical concepts should be studied carefully. They provide a solid base for strategy planning of personal selling (Chapter 16) and mass selling (Chapter 17).

Although some of the material appears theoretical, it is important because not all promotion decisions are "just common sense." Poor decisions here could lead to "mass marketing" and the use of a "shotgun" rather than a "rifle" approach to Promotion. This chapter should help you bring a rifle to promotion planning--to practice "target marketing."

Important Terms

promotion, p. 367
personal selling, p. 368
mass selling, p. 368
advertising, p. 368
publicity, p. 369
sales promotion, p. 370
communication process, p. 373
source, p. 373
receiver, p. 373
noise, p. 373
encoding, p. 374
decoding, p. 374
message channel, p. 374
AIDA model, p. 374

adoption curve, p. 376
innovators, p. 376
early adopters, p. 377
early majority, p. 377
late majority, p. 378
laggards, p. 378
non-adopters, p. 378
primary demand, p. 381
selective demand, p. 382
sales managers, p. 388
advertising managers, p. 388
public relations, p. 388
sales promotion managers, p. 388

True-False Questions

T 1. Promotion is communicating information between seller and potential buyer--to influence attitudes and behavior.

F 2. Advertising is any form of nonpersonal presentation of ideas, goods, or services.

F 3. Sales promotion refers to activities such as personal selling, advertising and publicity.

F 4. All sales promotion is aimed at final consumers or users.

T 5. Sales promotion aimed at middlemen--sometimes called trade promotion--stresses price-related matters.

T 6. The overall objective of promotion is to affect behavior.

T 7. The three basic objectives of promotion are to inform, persuade, and/or remind.

T 8. Much of what we call promotion is really wasted effort because it does not really communicate.

T 9. A major advantage of personal selling is that the source can get immediate feedback to help direct subsequent communication efforts.

F 10. The term "noise" refers only to distorting influences within the message channel which reduce the effectiveness of the communication process.

F 11. If the right message channel is selected, problems related to encoding and decoding in the communication process will be avoided.

T 12. The communication process is complicated by the fact that receivers are usually influenced not only by the message but also by the source and the message channel.

F 13. The AIDA model consists of four promotion jobs: attention, information, desire, and action.

T 14. The adoption curve focuses on the process by which an individual accepts new ideas.

T 15. Publicity in technical journals is likely to be a more effective method of promotion than personal selling for reaching extremely innovative business firms.

T 16. The late majority are influenced more by other late adopters--rather than by advertising.

T 17. Opinion leaders are often very difficult to identify, especially since different people may be opinion leaders for different products.

McCarthy and Perreault

_F_ 18. Salespeople should usually be expected to do the whole promotion job for industrial products.

_T_ 19. Special considerations which may affect the promotion blend are the size of the promotion budget, the stage of the product life cycle, the nature of competition, the target of the promotion, and the nature of the product.

_T_ 20. During the market introduction stage of product life cycles, promotion must pioneer acceptance of the product idea--not just the company's own brand--to stimulate primary demand.

_F_ 21. In the market growth stage of the product life cycle, promotion emphasis must begin to shift from stimulating selective demand to stimulating primary demand for the company's own brand.

_T_ 22. Firms in monopolistic competition may favor mass selling because they have differentiated their marketing mixes somewhat--and have something to talk about.

_T_ 23. The large number of potential customers practically forces producers of consumer products and retailers to emphasize mass selling and sales promotion.

_F_ 24. Industrial customers are much less numerous than final consumers--and therefore it becomes more practical to emphasize mass selling in the promotion blends aimed at these markets.

_T_ 25. One reason personal selling is important in promotion to retailers is that marketing mixes often have to be adjusted from one geographic territory to another.

_T_ 26. Promotion to employees is especially important in service-oriented industries where the quality of the employees' efforts is a big part of the product.

_T_ 27. In total, personal selling is several times more expensive than advertising.

_F_ 28. Typically, manufacturers selling well-branded consumer products through established channels have promotion blends which rely almost exclusively on advertising to consumers.

_F_ 29. Planning of promotion blends can be best accomplished by placing specialists in charge of each promotion method; for example, the firm might appoint a sales manager, an advertising manager, and a sales promotion manager to weigh the pros and cons of the various approaches and come up with an effective blend.

_F_ 30. To avoid conflicts, it is usually best for sales promotion to be handled by a firm's advertising manager and sales manager--not by a sales promotion specialist.

31. Spending on sales promotion is growing, but in total it is still only about one-third as much as is spent on advertising.

32. Sales promotion aimed at final consumers usually is trying to increase demand and speed up the time of purchase.

Answers to True-False Questions

1. T, p. 367	12. T, p. 374	23. T, p. 383
2. F, p. 368	13. F, p. 374	24. F, p. 384
3. F, p. 370	14. F, p. 376	25. T, p. 385
4. F, p. 370	15. T, p. 376	26. T, p. 386
5. T, p. 370	16. T, p. 378	27. T, p. 387
6. T, p. 370	17. T, p. 378	28. F, p. 387
7. T, p. 371	18. F, p. 380	29. F, p. 388
8. T, p. 372	19. T, p. 380	30. F, p. 389
9. T, p. 373	20. T, p. 381	31. F, p. 390
10. F, p. 373	21. F, p. 382	32. T, p. 390
11. F, p. 374	22. T, p. 383	

Multiple-Choice Questions (Circle the correct response)

1. Promotion does *not* include:
   a. personal selling.
   b. advertising.
   c. publicity.
   d. sales promotion.
   e. Promotion includes all of the above.

2. Personal selling is more appropriate than mass selling when:
   a. the target market is large and scattered.
   b. there are many potential customers and a desire to keep promotion costs low.
   c. flexibility is not important.
   d. immediate feedback is desirable.
   e. All of the above are true.

3. Sales promotion can be aimed at:
   a. final consumers or users.
   b. middlemen.
   c. the company's own sales force.
   d. all of the above.
   e. only a and b above.

4. Promotion is intended to make a firm's demand curve:
   a. become more elastic--while shifting it to the right.
   b. become more inelastic--while shifting it to the left.
   c. become more elastic--while shifting it to the left.
   d. become more inelastic--while shifting it to the right.

5. Which basic promotion objective should be emphasized by a firm whose product is very similar to those offered by many competitors?
   a. Communicating
   b. Persuading
   c. Reminding
   d. Informing

6. Which of the following is *not* one of the basic elements in the communication process?
   a. Feedback
   b. Receiver
   c. Encoding
   d. Dissonance
   e. Message channel

7. Communication is *most difficult* to achieve when:
   a. the source and the receiver are not in face-to-face contact with each other.
   b. immediate feedback is not provided.
   c. any trace of "noise" remains in the message channel.
   d. the source and the receiver do not have a common frame of reference.
   e. the encoder does not do the decoding.

8. The AIDA model's four promotion jobs are getting:
   a. awareness, interest, demand, action.
   b. attention, interest, desire, action.
   c. action, interest, desire, acceptance.
   d. awareness, interest, decision, acceptance.

9. Mary Jones is strongly influenced by her peer group--and she often adopts a new product only after they have pressured her to try it. She makes little use of mass media and salespeople as sources of information. In terms of the adoption curve, she would be in what category?
   a. Laggard
   b. Late majority
   c. Early adopter
   d. Innovator
   e. Early majority

10. During the market introduction stage of the product life cycle, the basic objective of promotion is to:
    a. spend more money on promotion than competitors.
    b. remind customers about the firm and its products.
    c. inform the potential customers of the product.
    d. stimulate selective demand.
    e. persuade the early majority to buy the product.

11. Which of the following statements about the *target of promotion* and promotion blends is *true*?
   a. Promotion to wholesalers is very similar to promotion to retailers--except that wholesalers are more numerous and perhaps less aware of demand and cost.
   b. Mass selling is seldom necessary or useful in the industrial products field.
   c. Personal selling is generally quite important for closing the sale in retail stores--regardless of how much mass selling is attempted.
   d. Promotion to retailers is primarily informative--although some persuasion is also needed.
   e. The vast number of potential customers forces consumer products manufacturers and retailers to rely exclusively on mass selling in their promotion blends.

12. Deciding on the appropriate promotion blend is a job for the firm's:
   a. advertising agency.
   b. marketing manager.
   c. advertising manager.
   d. sales manager.
   e. sales promotion manager.

13. Sales promotion:
   a. is currently a weak spot in many firms' marketing strategies.
   b. spending is growing rapidly.
   c. involves a wide variety of activities which often require the use of specialists.
   d. can make the personal selling job easier.
   e. All of the above are true statements.

14. Sales promotion:
   a. to consumers usually is trying to increase demand or speed up the time of purchase.
   b. aimed at middlemen is sometimes called trade promotion.
   c. might include free samples of a product.
   d. aimed at employees is common in service firms.
   e. all of the above.

Answers to Multiple-Choice Questions

1. e, p. 368-69
2. d, p. 368
3. d, p. 370
4. d, p. 371
5. b, p. 372

6. d, p. 373
7. d, p. 374
8. b, p. 374-75
9. b, p. 378
10. c, p. 381

11. d, p. 385
12. b, p. 388
13. e, p. 389
14. e, p. 390-91

Name: _____ Course & Section: _____

Exercise 15-1

The communication process in promotion

Introduction

Promotion must communicate effectively--or it's wasted effort. Yet it is often difficult to achieve effective communication. The communication process can break down in many different ways.

Understanding the whole communication process can improve promotion. As discussed in more detail in the text (see pages 372-374 and Exhibit 15-4), the major elements of the communication process include:

> a source,
> encoding,
> a message channel,
> decoding,
> a receiver,
> feedback, and
> noise.

Each of these different elements can influence the effectiveness of a firm's promotion effort--so marketing managers need to consider each element when planning or modifying their promotion. The whole promotion effort may fail because of a failure in just one element.

This exercise is designed to enhance your understanding of the communication process in promotion planning. The focus here is on specific elements of the process.

Assignment

Listed below are several descriptions of different promotion situations. In each case, there is a problem with the promotion effort. For some reason, communication has not been effective. You may see different elements of the promotion process that may be related to the problem. But, the focus of each situation is on a specific element of the process. So, for each situation, write down *one* element (from the list above) that you think is the major problem. Then, briefly explain why you think that element is a problem, and how the communication process might need to be changed to correct the problem. (Note: your recommendation may include changing one or more elements of the communication process other than the one that you noted as the major problem.)

1. A magazine publisher has a list of customers whose subscriptions are about to expire. The company has hired sales reps to telephone these customers and ask them if they would like to renew their subscriptions. Research shows that most customers appreciate this service--since it means that there will not be a lapse in their subscription. The company has screened and hired sales reps carefully. Each salesperson has been trained concerning the prices for different subscriptions. The company leaves it to each sales rep to decide what to say--so that the presentation will be as natural as possible. But, the inexperienced salespeople have trouble getting the conversation started--and often the customer hangs up before the point of the call is clear.

   Problem element of the communication process: _____

   Explanation: _____

   _____

   _____

   _____

   _____

   _____

2. A company has been doing advertising for its line of weight-loss diet supplements. The supplements are targeted to overweight, middle-aged men and women. The company's ads appear on TV exercise programs that are viewed by the same target market. In the ad, a trim professional model explains the product and how safely and effectively it works. But the ads do not seem to be effective. Apparently the overweight viewers don't believe that a trim model really knows about the difficulties of losing weight.

   Problem element of the communication process: _____

   Explanation: _____

   _____

   _____

   _____

   _____

   _____

McCarthy and Perreault

3.   A local YMCA wants to promote membership growth. Research shows that many nonmembers are hesitant to join because they think the YMCA dues are higher than is actually the case. The Y has put up a large poster at the front door of its building that shows clearly how little it actually costs to use the YMCA facilities. But so far response has been very poor.

Problem element of the communication process: _____

Explanation: _____

_____

_____

_____

_____

_____

_____

_____

4.   A company that produces baby food wants to sell its product in a developing nation where packaged baby food has not previously been available. Because most of the target customers could not read or write, the package showed a picture of a smiling baby to promote the product. But the effort was a failure because target customers were accustomed to seeing pictures of a package's contents on the label. Most target customers didn't understand what the product was--and some horrified customers even thought that the small bottles contained ground-up babies.

Problem element of the communication process: _____

Explanation: _____

_____

_____

_____

_____

_____

_____

_____

Question for Discussion

Does market segmentation make it easier--or more difficult--to develop effective promotion communications? Why?

Exercise 15-2

Using the adoption curve to develop promotion blends

Introduction

We have continually stressed that each of the "four Ps" should be matched with the needs and characteristics of target markets. But marketing mix planning can get more complicated in the promotion area. Even though a target market may have fairly homogeneous needs--*groups of people within this market may differ considerably in their sources of information and how quickly they adopt new products.* Therefore, marketing managers may need to use several promotion blends--over time--to communicate effectively with this target market.

Promotion blend planning should use the adoption curve--which shows when different groups accept ideas. Five adopter groups are commonly used: innovators, early adopters, the early majority, the late majority, and laggards.

As outlined in the text (see pages 376-79), a unique pattern of communication exists within and between each of these adopter groups. Therefore, each may require its own promotion blend.

Assignment

This exercise is designed to show how an understanding of the adoption curve can be helpful when planning promotion blends. Read the following case and then *develop a promotion blend for each adopter group* within the firm's target market. Outline in detail what kind of mass selling, personal selling, and sales promotion you would use, if any, to reach each adopter group. Be specific. For example, if you decide to advertise in magazines, give examples of the magazines you would use. Above all, be creative--it's expected of you!

After you outline your promotion blend for each adopter group, explain *why* you chose that particular blend in the space marked "Comments." Here, you should consider some of the important characteristics of each adopter group--as discussed in the text.

Note that you are only being asked to focus on *promotion to final consumers.* The firm would also have to do some promotion work in the channels--just to obtain distribution--and adoption curve thinking should be applied to middleman adoption, too. But all of this promotion activity should be ignored here--because we want to focus on the way that final consumers would accept the product and its impact on promotion planning.

VISUALS, LTD.

Visuals, Ltd.--one of the world's largest manufacturers of cameras--has just announced the introduction of a revolutionary new 35-mm camera called the VisiMax. Aimed primarily at the "serious amateur" market, the VisiMax features *automatic focusing*--which means that the user does not have to manually adjust the focus before every shot. The camera does this automatically. Further, the camera has *automatic exposure*--so the camera electronically selects the lens opening and the shutter speed to provide for perfect exposures. While such features can be found on larger 35-mm cameras, the VisiMax is the first pocket-sized 35-mm camera to offer these features--making it the world's most sophisticated "point and shoot" camera.

The VisiMax also includes two other "firsts" among pocket 35-mm cameras. There is a built-in motorized winder capable of advancing the film three frames per second. In addition, there is a built-in "pop up" electronic flash unit which automatically adjusts itself to different film speeds and lens openings, and which tilts to allow the user to "bounce" the flash off of ceilings and walls for softer, more natural lighting effects.

The VisiMax also has a unique zoom lens which permits wide-angle to moderate-telephoto shots as well as close-ups of objects as near as 5 inches from the lens. And since the VisiMax is a "single lens reflex" camera, the user sees exactly what the lens sees when he or she looks through the viewfinder.

The VisiMax has a manufacturer's suggested list price of $359--but it is expected to retail for about $220. This price is not out of line when one considers the unique capabilities of the VisiMax--but the price is much higher than consumers are used to paying for a pocket camera. Therefore, promotion may be critical for the new camera--which will be distributed through camera stores, department stores, and mass merchandisers.

Visuals, Ltd. managers are not sure what promotion blend to use to introduce this new camera. One manager has noted that some customers will adopt the VisiMax faster than others--and therefore the promotion blend may have to vary over time. So, they are asking you to advise them.

Suggested Promotion Blends for Communicating with Potential Consumers in Each Adopter Group

1.   Innovators

   a)   Market characteristics: _____

   _____

   _____

   _____

b) Promotion blend: _____

_____

_____

_____

c) Comments: _____

_____

_____

_____

2. Early adopters

    a) Market characteristics: _____

_____

_____

_____

    b) Promotion blend: _____

_____

_____

_____

    c) Comments: _____

_____

_____

_____

3. Early majority

    a) Market characteristics: _____

_____

_____

_____

b)   Promotion blend: _____

_____

_____

c)   Comments: _____

_____

_____

_____

4.   Late majority

a)   Market characteristics: _____

_____

_____

_____

b)   Promotion blend: _____

_____

_____

_____

c)   Comments: _____

_____

_____

_____

5.   Laggards

a)   Market characteristics: _____

_____

_____

_____

b)   Promotion blend: _____

_____

_____

_____

c)   Comments: _____

_____

_____

_____

Question for Discussion

Which of the adopter categories is probably the most important from the viewpoint of the marketing strategy planner? That is, which is most crucial in launching a successful new product? Why?

Exercise 15-3

Sales promotion

This exercise is based on computer-aided problem number 15--Sales Promotion. A complete description of the problem appears on pages 28-29 of *Computer-Aided Problems to Accompany Basic Marketing*.

1. The PTA likes the idea of the T-shirt promotion, but is concerned about the "front-end" costs. Thus, it has decided to order only 400 T-shirts at $2.40 each, the minimum order from the supplier. In addition, the PTA has decided to evaluate a variation of the president's idea--offering a choice of a regular ticket at $5.00 or a ticket with a T-shirt at $6.50. If the PTA used this approach and sold 400 tickets with T-shirts and 200 tickets without T-shirts, how much money--net--would the PTA earn? How would this compare with what the PTA would earn if it sold the same total number of tickets at $5.00 each--with the first 400 purchasers getting a free T-shirt.

    $_____ money earned by PTA using 2 prices (with and without T-shirt)

    $_____ money earned by PTA selling all tickets at $5.00 and giving away 400 T-shirts

2. Another possibility is that the game would attract the "normal" number of ticket buyers at $5.00 a ticket, but that not all of the higher priced tickets with a T-shirt would be sold. If 300 tickets were sold at $5.00 and only 300 people bought the higher priced tickets with the T-shirt, how much money would the PTA earn?

    $_____ money earned by the PTA.

3. Spreadsheet analysis helped the PTA evaluate various possibilities, but it is still uncertain how to proceed. The group thinks there will be a lot of interest in the T-shirts--but they worry that they will cause dissatisfaction and lose potential ticket sales if they order the minimum and then run out of T-shirts. One member of the group has proposed an idea that might solve the problem.

    He recommends a "sweepstakes" approach. Specifically, he suggests that they sell all the tickets at a regular price of $5.50--but that every person who has a ticket with a winning number will be given a T-shirt at the game. 400 winning numbers will be drawn from a bowl during the game. He thinks this will stimulate the most interest--and allow the PTA to place the minimum T-shirt order.

    If the PTA uses this approach, how many tickets will it have to sell to pay for the T-shirt promotion?

_____ tickets to pay for the T-shirt promotion

If 700 tickets are sold, how much money will be earned for the PTA?

$_____ money earned if 700 tickets are sold.

4. If the PTA earns $3,000 from the game, they will be able to buy new uniforms for the school band. If they use the sweepstakes approach, about how many tickets would they have to sell to be able to buy the new uniforms? (Hint: use the What If analysis to vary the number of tickets sold, and display the amount of money earned.)

_____ number of tickets to sell to be able to buy new uniforms

5. Based on your analysis of this problem, briefly comment on the following quote: "Companies spend too much money on sales promotion. It just adds to the cost of marketing."

_____

_____

_____

_____

_____

_____

Chapter 16

Personal selling

What This Chapter Is About

Chapter 16 is concerned with the strategic decisions in the personal selling area.

It is important to see that not all sales jobs are alike. This is why a good understanding of the three basic sales tasks--order getting, order taking, and supporting--is important. The blend of these tasks in a particular sales job has a direct bearing on the selection, training, and compensation of salespeople.

Making an effective sales presentation is an important part of personal selling. Three approaches are explained. Each can be useful--depending on the target market and the products being sold.

Try to see that the strategic personal selling decisions are a part of the whole marketing strategy planning effort. Our earlier discussion of buyer behavior and communication theory is applied here. Be sure to see how materials are being tied together. This chapter continues the strategy planning emphasis which has been running through the text.

Important Terms

basic sales tasks, p. 399
order getters, p. 399
order getting, p. 399
order takers, p. 402
order taking, p. 402
supporting salespeople, p. 404
missionary salespeople, p. 405
technical specialists, p. 406
team selling, p. 406

national accounts sales force, p. 406
sales territory, p. 407
job description, p. 408
prospecting, p. 413
telephone selling, p. 414
sales presentation, p. 415
prepared sales presentation, p. 415
need-satisfaction approach, p. 416
selling formula approach, p. 416

True-False Questions

F 1. It should be the responsibility of the sales manager--not the marketing manager--to make final decisions about how many and what kind of salespeople are needed.

F 2. Personal selling has declined in importance to the point that there are now more Americans employed in advertising than in personal selling.

_T_ 3. Professional salespeople don't just try to sell the customer--they try to help him buy.

_T_ 4. Some salespeople are expected to act as marketing managers for their own geographic territories and develop their own marketing mixes and strategies.

_T_ 5. Three basic sales tasks are found in most sales organizations--although in some situations one salesperson might have to do all three tasks.

_T_ 6. High-calibre order getters are essential in sales of industrial installations and accessory equipment.

_T_ 7. Sales representatives for progressive merchant wholesalers often serve as advisors to their customers--not just as order takers.

_T_ 8. Unsought consumer products often require order getters--to convince customers of the product's value.

_T_ 9. A wholesaler's order takers handle so many items that they usually will not--and probably should not--give special attention to any particular items.

_F_ 10. A consumer products manufacturer using an indirect channel system has little need to use missionary salespeople.

_T_ 11. An industrial products manufacturer may benefit considerably by using technical specialists, even though a direct channel of distribution and order getters are used.

_T_ 12. A national accounts sales force sells directly to very large accounts.

_T_ 13. A sales territory is a geographic area that is the responsibility of one salesperson or several working together.

_T_ 14. The first step in deciding how may salespeople are needed is to estimate how much work can be done by one person in some time period.

_F_ 15. A good job description should not be too specific--since the nature of the sales job is always changing.

_F_ 16. All new salespeople should receive the same kind of sales training.

_T_ 17. A written job description can be helpful in setting the level of compensation for salespeople, because it shows whether any special skills or responsibilities are required that will command higher pay levels.

_F_ 18. A sales manager's control over a salesperson tends to vary directly with what proportion of his compensation is in the form of salary.

_F_ 19. A combination compensation plan will usually provide the greatest incentive for a salesperson to increase sales.

F 20. The most popular compensation method is the straight commission plan.

T 21. Many firms set different sales objectives--or quotas--to adjust the compensation plan to differences in potential in each territory.

T 22. Basically, prospecting involves following down all the "leads" in the target market--and deciding how much time to spend on which prospects.

T 23. Telephone selling is becoming more common because it is an efficient way to find out about a prospect's interest in the company's marketing mix-- and even to make a sales presentation or take an order.

T 24. Some kind of priority system is needed to guide sales prospecting-- because most salespeople will have too many prospects.

T 25. The prepared (canned) sales presentation probably would be appropriate for the majority of retail clerks employed by convenience stores.

T 26. An effective office equipment salesperson might use a selling formula sales presentation.

F 27. The need-satisfaction approach requires less skill on the part of the salesperson than the prepared approach.

F 28. The AIDA sequence is helpful for planning a need-satisfaction sales presentation--but not for a selling formula sales presentation.

Answers to True-False Questions

1. F, p. 395
2. F, p. 396
3. T, p. 397
4. T, p. 398
5. T, p. 399
6. T, p. 400
7. T, p. 400
8. T, p. 401
9. T, p. 403
10. F, p. 405

11. T, p. 406
12. T, p. 406
13. T, p. 407
14. T, p. 407
15. F, p. 408
16. F, p. 409
17. T, p. 410
18. T, p. 411
19. F, p. 411
20. F, p. 411

21. T, p. 412
22. T, p. 413
23. T, p. 414
24. T, p. 414
25. T, p. 415
26. T, p. 416
27. F, p. 416
28. F, p. 417

Multiple-Choice Questions (Circle the correct response)

1. Which of the following statements about personal selling is *true*?
   a. As a representative of his company, a salesperson's job is to sell the customer rather than to help him buy.
   b. Today's salesperson is really only responsible for "moving products."
   c. The modern salesperson's sole job is to communicate his company's story to customers.
   d. Some sales representatives are expected to be marketing managers in their own geographic territories.
   e. A beginning salesperson could not expect to be responsible for a sales volume as large as that achieved by many retail stores.

2. A salesperson might have to perform three basic sales tasks. Choose the *correct* description of these tasks from the following:
   a. *Supporting:* the routine completion of sales made regularly to the target customers.
   b. *Order getting:* aggressively seeking out potential buyers with a well-organized sales presentation designed to sell a product.
   c. *Order taking:* purpose is to develop goodwill, stimulate demand, explain technical aspects of product, train the middleman's salespeople, and perform other specialized services aimed at obtaining sales in the long run.
   d. All of the above are correct.
   e. None of the above are correct.

3. Order-getting salespeople would be required for which one of the following jobs?
   a. Helping a buyer plan and install a computer system.
   b. Helping drug retailers find new ways to display and promote their products.
   c. Seeking orders from food retailers for a new brand of cake mix which has been added to the company's line.
   d. "Helping" an indecisive supermarket customer select the kind of meat she should buy for dinner.
   e. All of the jobs call for order takers.

4. A large appliance manufacturer has adequate wholesale and retail distribution--but is concerned that the middlemen do not push its products aggressively enough--because they also carry competitive lines. The manufacturer should hire some:
   a. missionary salespeople.
   b. order getters.
   c. order takers.
   d. technical specialists.

5. Which of the following statements is *false*?
   a. Team selling involves different specialists--to handle different parts of the selling job.
   b. A national accounts sales force is used to sell to small retailers who are not covered by wholesalers in the channel.
   c. Carefully selected sales territories can reduce the cost of sales calls.
   d. The first step in deciding how many salespeople are needed is to estimate how much work can be done by one person in some time period.

6. With regard to the level of compensation for salespeople, a marketing manager should recognize that:
   a. order takers generally are paid more than order getters.
   b. the appropriate level of compensation should be suggested by the job descriptions.
   c. a good order getter will generally be worth less to a firm than a good technical specialist.
   d. the firm should attempt to pay all its salespeople at least the going market wage for order getters.
   e. salespeople should be the highest-paid employees in the firm.

7. The sales manager of the Bubba Beanbag Corp. wishes to compensate his sales force in a way which will provide some security, incentive, flexibility, and control. The company should offer its sales force:
   a. straight salaries.
   b. straight commissions.
   c. a combination plan.

8. Regardless of the sales volume, the least expensive type of sales force compensation system is always:
   a. straight salary.
   b. straight commission.
   c. a combination plan.
   d. None of the above.

9. Wilma Rogers works as a telephone salesperson for the Catalog Division of Sears, Roebuck. Her primary job is to call customers with Sears charge accounts to inform them about sales items and ask if they would like to order the sales items. Which of the following kinds of sales presentations would be best for Wilma to use?
   a. Prepared sales presentation.
   b. Selling formula approach.
   c. Need-satisfaction approach.

10. Bill White sells life insurance for a large Texas firm. He locates customers by selecting names out of a telephone directory and calling to arrange an appointment. He begins each presentation by explaining the basic features and merits of his product--eventually bringing the customer into the conversation to clarify the customer's insurance needs. Then he tells how his insurance policy would satisfy the customer's needs and attempts to close the sale. Bill's sales presentation is based on the:
    a. need-satisfaction approach.
    b. selling formula approach.
    c. canned presentation approach.

Answers to Multiple-Choice Questions

1. d, p. 398
2. b, p. 399
3. c, p. 399
4. a, p. 405

5. b, p. 407
6. b, p. 410
7. c, p. 411
8. d, p. 413

9. a, p. 415
10. b, p. 416

Exercise 16-1

Analyzing the nature of the personal selling task

Introduction

Personal selling may involve three basic tasks: (1) *order getting*, (2) *order taking*, and (3) *supporting*. Each task may be done by different individuals--or the same person may do all three. While we use these terms to describe salespeople by referring to their *primary* task, it is important to keep in mind that many salespeople do all of the three tasks to some extent.

Consider, for example, a sales rep for a manufacturer of an established consumer good which is distributed through wholesalers. Since the product is established in the marketplace, the sales rep's primary task would probably be order taking-- obtaining routine orders from regular wholesale customers. The same rep may also be expected to do other secondary tasks, however. For example, he may be expected to get orders from new wholesale customers--and so he would also do order getting at times. Further, he might also spend part of his time helping the wholesaler's sales force--by informing retailers about his company's product, building special store displays, and so forth. In this case, the sales rep would be doing a supporting task.

This exercise focuses on the basic differences among the three selling tasks. In some cases, these differences may be rather clear. In other cases, the differences may be quite difficult to see. To determine what kind of sales rep is needed to handle a particular personal selling job, we will try to distinguish between the *primary* and *secondary* selling tasks. *Note: the words "primary" and "secondary" are used in this way in this exercise only--they do not appear in the text.*

Assignment

Six cases are presented below to show how the selling tasks may vary. In some of the cases, the sales rep will perform both primary and secondary selling tasks, while in others only the primary selling task will be discussed. Read each case and then indicate (a) the *primary* selling task *usually required to effectively carry out the specified job* and (b) any secondary selling task(s) which *may also be described in the case.* Then explain your answer in the space marked "Comments." The first case is answered for you as an example.

1. Jane Smith, a sophomore at Midwestern University, works part time at the Campus Drug Store. During the week, Jane works afternoons waiting on

customers at the lunch counter. On weekends, she usually operates the cash register at the candy and cigarette counter--in addition to handling bills for public utilities. According to her boss, Jane is a very good worker.

a)   Primary selling task: <u>Order taking</u>

b)   Secondary selling task(s): <u>Possibly order getting</u>

c)   Comments: <u>No order getting is specifically mentioned, but she may do some occasionally. For example: "Would you like to try some of our fresh strawberry pie today? It's delicious!"</u>

2.   Robert Kelman is a sales rep for Smith Brothers, a large merchant wholesaler that distributes chain saws, lawn mowers, and other outdoor power equipment. Smith Brothers sells to retailers and also sells direct to large end-users--such as golf courses, and cemeteries. Recently Smith Brothers decided to target local government (city and country) buyers--who purchase equipment to maintain parks, roadside areas, and public schools and hospitals. In the past, these buyers often just purchased equipment from local retailers. Kelman was assigned responsibility for identifying who influenced these purchase decisions, and for persuading them either to buy from Smith Brothers or at least allow Smith Brothers to bid on their next order. In addition, Kelman has been successful in getting Smith Brothers on the state government list of approved vendors. That means that various state agencies can select equipment from the Smith Brothers catalogue and submit a purchase order without a lot of additional red tape. Kelman follows up with the warehouse manager to make certain that these orders are shipped promptly.

a)   Primary selling task: _____

b)   Secondary selling task(s): _____

c)   Comments: _____

_____

_____

_____

3.   Francis Stewart, a marketing major in college, went to work for Procter & Gamble as soon as she graduated. While she hopes to become a brand manager some day, Pat is a district sales representative--calling on supermarkets, grocery stores, and drugstores. Her job is to build special displays, inform store managers of new products, provide merchandising assistance, review customer complaints, and occasionally to suggest special orders for the stores she visits. Pat is paid a straight salary--plus a bonus when sales in her district are good. (Note: P&G uses merchant wholesalers to distribute its products.)

a)   Primary selling task: _____

b) Secondary selling task(s): _____

c) Comments: _____

_____

_____

_____

4. Dick Sparrow is a manufacturers' agent for several noncompeting producers of specialized plumbing parts and components. His customers include producers of mobile homes, recreational vehicles, and hot-tubs, as well as specialty plumbing contractors (for example, who install special plumbing fixtures in hospitals). He also calls on a number of very large plumbing supply wholesalers. Dick has been a manufacturer's agent for 20 years--and he knows most of his customers really well. Over this time, he has drifted into selling a large variety and assortment of products. Because of the complexity and variety of his lines, he has found it desirable to spend much of his time checking his customers' parts inventories. This gives him continual customer contact--and provides a useful service. He also finds some time to seek new customers--and is always looking for new producers to represent.

Recently, however, one of Dick's large producers decided that Dick's services were no longer required. Apparently the producer felt that Dick had not been aggressively promoting its products over the last few years--and had failed to open up enough new accounts. Dick was quite bitter over losing the account. "I built their West Coast business from scratch--and now they're dropping me without a second thought," he complained. "I handle too many products to worry about just one manufacturer's offerings."

a) Primary selling task: _____

b) Secondary selling task(s): _____

c) Comments: _____

_____

_____

_____

5. Mac Wozniak is a "sales engineer" with Sealed Air Corporation--which specializes in foam and air "bubble" packaging materials. Producers use these packaging materials to protect their products inside shipping cartons during shipping. Sealed Air has a line of standard products but also will produce custom packaging materials if that is what a customer needs. Sealed Air does advertising in trade magazines, and each ad includes a response card. When a prospect calls to inquire about Sealed Air products, Wozniak is sent out to analyze the customer's packaging needs. He determines how much protection is needed and which Sealed Air product would be best. After finishing his

work, Wozniak reports back to his sales manager--who assigns another sales rep to handle the rest of the contacts with the customer.

a) Primary selling task: _____

b) Secondary selling task(s): _____

c) Comments: _____

_____

_____

_____

6. Steve Britt has just started a landscaping company. Business is going well, but he needs extra money to buy some additional equipment. So he also is working as a house-to-house sales rep for AmWay (household cleaning products). At first, he did not like selling products door-to-door, but lately Steve has been doing very well. "Once you learn the knack of getting your foot in the door," says Steve, "sales come easily and the commissions add up fast. After all, people do like our products."

a) Primary selling task: _____

b) Secondary selling task(s): _____

c) Comments: _____

_____

_____

_____

Question for Discussion

Three different kinds of sales presentations are discussed in the text: the *prepared*, *need-satisfaction*, and *selling formula* presentations. Which of these three kinds of sales presentations would be most appropriate for each of the sales reps described in Exercise 16-1? Why?

Exercise 16-2

Selecting the appropriate kind of salesperson

Introduction

Many people believe that a good salesperson must always be an aggressive, extroverted type of individual with highly developed persuasive skills. Such is not the case, however. Studies have shown, for example, that middle-class shoppers often prefer salespeople who tend to be passive and impersonal. Thus--like all other ingredients of a firm's marketing mix--the kind of salesperson needed depends on the needs and attitudes of the firm's target market.

In addition, the firm must keep its basic promotion objectives in mind. The selling task is not always one of persuasion--but may involve informing or reminding target customers about the company's products and/or the company itself. Therefore, it is often desirable to use order takers--or supporting salespeople--rather than order getters.

Selecting the right kind of salesperson is an important strategic decision. Using the wrong kind of salesperson to handle a specific selling situation may do a firm more harm than good.

Assignment

This exercise will give you practice in selecting the appropriate kinds of salespersons. Several situations involving a need for personal selling are described below. For each situation, indicate which of the following kinds of salespeople would be *most* appropriate--and then explain *why* in the space provided.

> A. Order getter
> B. Order taker
> C. Missionary salespeople
> D. Technical specialist

The first situation is answered for you as an example.

1. Someone is needed to operate an established home-delivered milk route in a suburban area.

    a) Kind of salesperson: <u>Order taker</u>

b) Explanation: <u>Since the route has already been established, the job will mainly involve the routine completion of sales made regularly to the same or similar customers.</u>

2. The Mitushi Alarm Company has developed a new line of electronic smoke and fire detectors that hook into a central computerized alarm system. The new alarm system is much safer than the older units it is designed to replace, and it is intended for use in remodeling old hotels, office buildings, and hospitals.

   a) Kind of salesperson: _____

   b) Explanation: _____

   _____

3. A small manufacturer of industrial component materials is hoping to sell a unique, small hand tool it is importing from Japan--with exclusive distribution rights--to hardware retailers in the United States.

   a) Kind of salesperson: _____

   b) Explanation: _____

   _____

4. A producer of a line of dental products--including dental floss, fluoride tablets, and denture cleaners--needs some people to provide free samples and information about new products to dentists.

   a) Kind of salesperson: _____

   b) Explanation: _____

   _____

5. A large snack food producer that sells to retail food stores through manufacturers' agents (called "food brokers") and truck wholesalers wants to introduce a new line of snack products.

   a) Kind of salesperson: _____

   b) Explanation: _____

   _____

6. An insurance company wishes to sell life insurance to college students.

   a) Kind of salesperson: _____

   b) Explanation: _____

   _____

7. A new movie theatre needs a person to operate its snack counter.

    a) Kind of salesperson: _____

    b) Explanation: _____

    _____

8. A specialty wholesaler distributes a full line of cleaning supplies to local businesses and maintenance service firms.

    a) Kind of salesperson: _____

    b) Explanation: _____

    _____

Question for Discussion

What kind of sales compensation plan--straight salary, straight commission, or a combination plan--would be appropriate in the above situations? Why? What factors must be considered in choosing a sales compensation plan?

Exercise 16-3

Sales compensation

This exercise is based on computer-aided problem number 16--Sales Compensation. A complete description of the problem appears on page 30 of *Computer-Aided Problems to Accompany Basic Marketing*.

Yale's sales manager is going to use a combination plan--but he is considering changes from the salary and commission percents shown in the initial spreadsheet. These changes would increase the amount of the rep's total compensation that comes from salary.

1. If he increases the salary component to $15,200--and other values remain as on the initial spreadsheet--what would the rep's total compensation be? The total "profit contribution" to the company?

    _____ rep's total compensation

    _____ total "profit contribution"

2. The sales manager thinks that the possibility in question 1 is too much compensation for the "profit contribution" generated. So he wants to see how lowering the commission percents will affect the sales rep's compensation. Specifically, he is considering a 4 percent commission on Product B. He originally planned that the commission percent for Product A would be 60 percent of the commission percent for Product B. (Note that 3 percent is .6 times 5 percent.) If he wanted the new commission percents to maintain the same ratio, what percent would he set for Product A? With commissions set this way, what would the rep's total compensation be? Total profit contribution to the firm?

    _____% sales commission for Product A

    $_____ total sales compensation

    $_____ total profit contribution

3. The sales manager has concluded that the possibility in question 2 is a reasonable compensation plan. But he is also wondering if he should give the new sales rep the authority to cut prices on Product A. That would give the rep more flexibility to change the price to make a sale, e.g., a lower price might be needed to be competitive. But cutting price might mean more units sold at lower profits. After analyzing his records for other territories, the sales manager estimates that the sales rep will on average sell Product A at $95 a unit if he is allowed to cut prices--and that he might increase the units of A sold by 10 percent--to 3,960 units. If that were to happen, what would

the rep's total compensation be? The total profit contribution to the firm?
Briefly discuss the implications of these results.

$_____$ rep's total sales compensation

$_____$ total profit contribution

_____

_____

_____

_____

_____

4. After much consideration, the sales manager has decided not to allow price
cutting to get sales in the new territory. In addition, he has offered the new
territory to a Yale sales rep who has been working in an established territory.
The manager has told him that an "average" rep should be able to earn about
$30,000 to $32,000 in the territory. The rep is very interested in the job, but
he wants to get some idea what the compensation will be if he does an
outstanding job--not just an average one. The sales manager is confident that
an excellent job would result in sales of 1,400 units of Product B, and between
3,960 and 4,200 units of Product A. Given these estimates (and a salary of
$15,200, a commission on Product A of 2.4 percent and on Product B of 4.0
percent), what would you tell the rep he could make if he is excellent?
Briefly explain why.

$_____$ rep's compensation with "excellent" performance

Explanation: _____

_____

_____

_____

_____

_____

_____

Chapter 17

Mass selling

What This Chapter Is About

Chapter 17 focuses on advertising--the main kind of mass selling--and the strategic decisions which must be made.

The importance of specifying advertising objectives is emphasized. Advertisements and advertising campaigns cannot be effective unless we know what we want done.

Next, the kinds of advertising which can be used to reach the objectives are explained. Then, how to deliver the message--via the "best" medium, and what is to be communicated--the copy thrust--is discussed.

Advertising agencies are treated also. They often handle the mass-selling details for advertisers--under the direction of the firm's advertising manager. Avoiding deceptive advertising is also treated. Increasingly, this has strategic importance-- because the FTC can proceed against both the advertiser and its agency.

Try to see how advertising would fit into a promotion blend--and be a part of a whole marketing strategy. Advertising is not an isolated topic. It can be a vital ingredient in a marketing strategy.

Important Terms

product advertising, p. 425
institutional advertising, p. 425
pioneering advertising, p. 425
primary demand, p. 425
competitive advertising, p. 426
selective demand, p. 426
direct type advertising, p. 426
indirect type advertising, p. 426

comparative advertising, p. 427
reminder advertising, p. 428
advertising allowances, p. 428
cooperative advertising, p. 429
direct-mail advertising, p. 433
copy thrust, p. 434
advertising agencies, p. 436
corrective advertising, p. 440

True-False Questions

_F_ ___ 1. Advertising expenditures grew continuously from World War II until 1975, but since then the trend has been down.

_F_ ___ 2. U.S. corporations spend an average of 20 percent of their sales on advertising--with the largest share of this going to television.

T   3. Advertising objectives should be very specific--even more specific than personal selling objectives.

F   4. A firm whose objective is to help buyers make their purchasing decision should use institutional advertising.

F   5. Pioneering advertising should be used in the market introduction stage of the product life cycle to develop selective demand for a specific brand.

T   6. The objective of competitive advertising is to develop selective demand--demand for a specific brand.

F   7. Direct competitive advertising involves making product comparisons with competitive brands, while indirect competitive advertising focuses solely on the advertiser's products.

F   8. The Federal Trade Commission has banned comparative advertising that involves specific brand comparisons using actual product names.

T   9. Reminder advertising is likely to be most useful when the firm has achieved brand preference or brand insistence for its products.

T 10. Advertising allowances are price reductions to firms further along in the channel to encourage them to advertise or otherwise promote the firm's products locally.

F 11. The main reason cooperative advertising is used is that large manufacturers usually can get lower media rates than local retailers.

F 12. Regardless of a firm's objectives, television advertising is generally more effective than newspaper or magazine advertising.

F 13. A major advantage of using "cost per thousand" data to aid in media selection is that this approach is very helpful for target marketing.

T 14. A firm that wants to send a specific message to a clearly identified target market probably should seriously consider using direct-mail advertising.

F 15. Some advertising media are "must buys"--meaning that the FTC requires firms to use such media.

T 16. Copy thrust means what is to be communicated by an ad's words and illustrations.

T 17. The first job in message planning is to determine how to get attention.

T 18. Advertising agencies are specialists in planning and handling mass selling details for advertisers.

F 19. With the growth of mega-agencies, it will only be a matter of time before small agencies disappear.

___ 20. Normally, media have two prices: one for national advertisers and a lower rate for local advertisers.

___ 21. The 15 percent commission system of ad agency compensation is most favored by large national advertisers of consumer products.

___ 22. Advertising effectiveness can be measured quite simply and accurately just by analyzing increases or decreases in sales.

___ 23. The Federal Trade Commission has the power to control deceptive or false advertising.

___ 24. Corrective advertising and affirmative disclosures are methods used by the FTC to control false or deceptive advertising.

___ 25. Unfortunately, no effort at self-regulation by advertisers has ever been successful in either shaping advertising guidelines or in stopping problem ads.

Answers to True-False Questions

1. F, p. 422	10. T, p. 428	19. F, p. 437
2. F, p. 423	11. F, p. 429	20. T, p. 438
3. T, p. 424	12. F, p. 431	21. F, p. 439
4. F, p. 425	13. F, p. 432	22. F, p. 439
5. F, p. 425	14. T, p. 433	23. T, p. 440
6. T, p. 426	15. F, p. 433	24. T, p. 440
7. F, p. 426	16. T, p. 434	25. F, p. 441
8. F, p. 427	17. T, p. 435	
9. T, p. 428	18. T, p. 436	

Multiple-Choice Questions (Circle the correct response)

1. The largest share of total advertising expenditures in the United States goes for:
   a. newspaper advertising.
   b. television advertising.
   c. magazine advertising.
   d. direct-mail advertising.
   e. radio advertising.

2. Which of the following statements about advertising objectives is *false*?
   a. They should be as specific as possible.
   b. They should be more specific than personal selling objectives.
   c. They usually are quite clear from the nature and appearance of an advertisement.
   d. They should flow from the overall marketing strategy.
   e. They should set the framework for an advertising campaign.

3. Bill Smith developed an innovative machine to make a more effective and less expensive bottle cap. He found a backer, produced a model, photographed it, and placed an advertisement in a food canners' magazine explaining how caps could be made as needed--right in the canner's plant. Much of the ad copy tried to sell the convenience and inventory cost-saving features of in-plant production as needed, rather than purchasing large quantities. Smith's advertising was trying to develop:
   a. selective demand.
   b. primary demand.
   c. derived demand.
   d. elastic demand.

4. The message "Drink milk every day" is an example of which type of advertising?
   a. Pioneering
   b. Competitive
   c. Indirect action
   d. Reminder
   e. Direct action

5. "Better things for better living through chemistry" is an example of:
   a. pioneering advertising.
   b. reminder advertising.
   c. competitive advertising.
   d. institutional advertising.
   e. cooperative advertising.

6. Comparative ads:
   a. have been encouraged by the Federal Trade Commission.
   b. attempt to develop primary demand.
   c. have been banned on television because of their tendency to deceive consumers.
   d. have consistently pleased consumers.
   e. that actually name the competitor's brand are illegal.

7. "Cooperative" advertising refers to the practice of:
   a. producers and middlemen sharing in the cost of advertising which is done by the producer.
   b. producers doing some advertising and expecting their middlemen to cooperate by providing the rest of the promotion blend.
   c. the producer paying for all of the advertising which is done by its middlemen.
   d. middlemen doing advertising which is partially paid for by the producer.
   e. middlemen picking up the promotion theme of the producer and carrying it through.

8. The choice of the "best" advertising medium depends upon:
   a. the promotion objectives.
   b. the budget available.
   c. the target markets.
   d. the characteristics of each medium.
   e. All of the above.

9. To communicate a very specific message to a very select, well-identified group of consumers, one probably should use:
   a. magazines aimed at special-interest groups.
   b. newspapers.
   c. television.
   d. direct mail.
   e. radio.

10. Which of the following statements about advertising agencies and compensation methods is *true*?
    a. The 15 percent commission system is no longer required--and some advertisers have obtained discounts or fee increases.
    b. The traditional compensation arrangements between advertisers and agencies might make it difficult for an agency to be completely objective about low cost media.
    c. Some advertisers--especially industrial products manufacturers--were quite satisfied with the traditional compensation arrangements whereby the agency did the advertiser's advertising work in return for the normal discount allowed by the media.
    d. The agencies earn commissions from media only when time or space is purchased at the national rate (as opposed to local rates).
    e. All of the above are true statements.

11. Which of the following statements about measuring advertising effectiveness is *false*?
    a. The most reliable approach is to check the size and composition of media audiences.
    b. Some progressive advertisers are now demanding laboratory or market tests to evaluate the effectiveness of advertisements.
    c. No single technique or approach has proven most effective.
    d. When specific advertising objectives are set, then marketing research may be able to provide feedback on the effectiveness of the advertising.
    e. Ideally, management should pretest advertising before it is run rather than relying solely on the judgment of creative people or advertising "experts."

12. Advertisers should keep in mind that:
    a. Congress has prohibited the FTC from using charges of "unfairness" against an individual company.
    b. only false or deceptive ads can be controlled by the FTC.
    c. the FTC does not have the power to require corrective advertising or affirmative disclosures.
    d. there are very clear-cut guidelines concerning how to substantiate ad claims.
    e. ads which are not false or deceptive may still be ruled illegal if they are shown to be "unfair."

13. Efforts at self-regulation by advertisers
    a. have often failed because of their inability to enforce guidelines.
    b. have been ineffective, so the government formed the NAD--a government agency to regulate ads.
    c. is hindered because there is no way to get inputs from consumers or government agencies.
    d. All of the above are true.
    e. None of the above are true.

Answers to Multiple-Choice Questions

1. a, p. 422	6. a, p. 427	11. a, p. 439-40
2. c, p. 424	7. d, p. 429	12. e, p. 440-44
3. b, p. 425	8. e, p. 430-34	13. a, p. 441
4. a, p. 425	9. d, p. 433	
5. d, p. 425	10. e, p. 438-39	

Exercise 17-1

Identifying different kinds of advertising

Introduction

Perhaps because of the high cost of advertising, some companies try to use multi-purpose ads to reach several promotion objectives at the same time. Studies have shown, however, that such ads often fail to produce *any* of the desired effects. On the contrary, several special-purpose ads are much more likely to stimulate positive responses than a single multi-purpose ad. Thus, a marketing manager usually should use different kinds of advertising to accomplish different promotion objectives.

This exercise is designed to show the different kinds of advertising which can be used--and to show the various objectives an advertisement might have. While doing the assignment, you should see that promotion objectives may be only indirectly concerned with increasing sales--and that a firm may have other reasons for advertising. Try to guess what these "other reasons" are--and how they might relate to a company's overall marketing mix.

Assignment

Using recent magazines and newspapers, find advertisements to *final consumers* which illustrate the following kinds of advertising (as defined in the text):

        A.   Institutional
        B.   Pioneering
        C.   Direct competitive
        D.   Indirect competitive
        E.   Comparative
        F.   Reminder

Clip out the ads--and for each ad attach a separate sheet of paper indicating:

a)   what kind of advertising the ad illustrates.
b)   what target market, if any, the ad appears to be aimed at.
c)   the general and specific objectives of each ad--e.g., to inform consumers (general) about three new product improvements (specific).
d)   the name of the magazine or newspaper in which the ad appeared.

Question for Discussion

When one overall objective of a company's marketing activities must be to sell its products, why would advertisements have objectives such as those you indicated for your examples?

Exercise 17-2

Determining advertising objectives and the appropriate kind of advertising

Introduction

About 1910 George Washington Hill--president of the American Tobacco Company--is said to have made this now-famous quote: "I am convinced that 50 percent of our advertising is sheer waste, but I can never find out which half." Today, there are many business executives who would probably share Mr. Hill's feelings. Billions of dollars are spent each year creating clever--and sometimes annoying--ads which often appear to be poorly designed and largely ineffective.

Actually, it is extremely difficult to measure the effectiveness of advertising--because companies often lack clearly defined advertising objectives. In hopes of remaining competitive, advertisers often budget some fixed percent of their sales dollars to advertising without any specific objectives in mind--other than to just "promote the product."

Like all business expenditures, however, there is no reason for making advertising expenditures unless the company has some specific purpose in mind. Since the advertising objectives selected will largely determine the kind of advertising that is needed, companies should set specific advertising objectives which are tied to their overall marketing strategies.

Assignment

This exercise will give you some practice determining the kind of advertising that may be needed to obtain some specific advertising objectives. Described below are several situations in which some kind of advertising may be necessary or desirable. For each situation: (a) indicate what *general* (i.e., inform, persuade, and/or remind) and *specific* objectives the advertising probably would be meant to achieve; and (b) indicate which of the following kinds of advertising would be *most* appropriate to accomplish that objective.

> A. Pioneering advertising
> B. Direct competitive advertising
> C. Indirect competitive advertising
> D. Reminder advertising
> E. Institutional advertising

The first situation is answered for you as an example.

1. The Harper Life Insurance company is planning to place ads in college newspapers to tell students about the importance of owning a well-planned life insurance program--and to explain how its agents are trained to help plan an insurance program that fits their needs.

    a) Advertising objectives: <u>To INFORM prospects about the company's name and the merits of its products, and to "open the door" for the company's sales reps.</u>
    b) Kind of advertising: <u>Indirect competitive</u>

2. Bucklin's Clothing Store has lost its lease after 20 successful years in the same location. Jack Bucklin has found a new store in a shopping center that is just being built. He is going to have a sale to reduce his inventory before the move--and he worries about whether his customers will "follow him" to his new location.

    a) Advertising objectives: _____

    _____

    _____

    b) Kind of advertising: _____

3. The California Grape Growers Association recently held a meeting to discuss ways of increasing per-capita raisin consumption. They decided to target young children and their baby boom parents--most of whom wouldn't think of raisins as "snack food." The ad agency for the Association proposed a series of TV ads featuring animated raisins dancing and singing "I Heard It through the Grapevine," a song that was very popular in the 1960s.

    a) Advertising objectives: _____

    _____

    _____

    b) Kind of advertising: _____

4. Volvo, the Swedish auto manufacturer, has an outstanding reputation among European buyers for building the safest cars available. But marketing research reveals that most American buyers think of Oldsmobiles, Lincolns, and Mercedes as the safest cars available in the country. Volvo dealers in the U.S. complain that many safety-conscious consumers never even consider Volvo.

    a) Advertising objectives: _____

    _____

    _____

    b) Kind of advertising: _____

5. Merrill Lynch, the financial services firm, received much bad publicity when some of its executives were involved in illegal activities. Few customers were directly affected--but many individual investors responded to the news reports by closing their accounts. The firm's president held a press conference at which he promised to rebuild faith in the firm and its many fine products.

   a) Advertising objectives: _____

   _____

   _____

   b) Kind of advertising: _____

6. National Supermarket is dropping its "full-service" approach and switching to a discount selling operation.

   a) Advertising objectives: _____

   _____

   _____

   b) Kind of advertising: _____

7. International Wood--which cuts down large stands of trees all over the Northwest--wishes to tell concerned citizens about the steps it is taking to replant trees and protect the environment.

   a) Advertising objectives: _____

   _____

   _____

   b) Kind of advertising: _____

8. Front Row, Inc. is one of the leading producers of stereo speakers in the United States. Unlike the technological advances in other types of stereo components, there has been little change in speakers in the last 30 years. Front Row, however, has just patented a revolutionary new way to reproduce sound through a speaker. The new Front Row speaker produces music that is significantly better. Some industry sources predict that by 1995 the new technology will capture 40 to 50 percent of the stereo speaker market.

   a) Advertising objectives: _____

   _____

   _____

   b) Kind of advertising: _____

9. "Students are tired of hard-sell radio commercials," argues one sales executive. "They know our name and products anyway. Why don't we give them a few seconds of good music--and then mention our name?"

a) Advertising objectives: _____

_____

_____

b) Kind of advertising: _____

Question for Discussion

Would there be difficulties in evaluating the effectiveness of ads for the situations mentioned in Exercise 17-2? Why?

Exercise 17-3

Advertising media

This exercise is based on computer-aided problem number 17--Advertising Media. A complete description of the problem appears on pages 30-31 of *Computer-Aided Problems to Accompany Basic Marketing.*

Peter Troy had almost decided to go with advertising on FM radio--given the numbers on the original spreadsheet. This would result in a "cost per buyer" of about $8.65. At that point, the sales rep for the magazine space called and suggested that Troy consider some new information.

1. First, the rep said it was hard to verify the actual number of readers--but that some of his 200,000 magazines are actually read by two or three people. He stressed that, when this "pass-along circulation" is included, the actual number of readers is greater than 200,000--probably between 230,000 and 250,000. Troy decided to evaluate this new information with his spreadsheet. Do you think it should influence his decision? Briefly explain why.

    _____

    _____

    _____

    _____

2. The magazine's sales rep also told Troy about a new "quantity discount." The magazine has reduced the rate for a one page ad to $1,500 when an advertiser agrees to place five or more ads in one year. How does the lower ad rate affect the two kinds of costs? (Note: do this analysis and subsequent analyses assuming 240,000 readers--for the reasons described in the question above.)

    $_____ cost per aware prospect $_____ cost per buyer

3. As in question 2, companies that do more advertising often get lower advertising rates. Briefly discuss how this might affect their ability to compete with other firms.

    _____

    _____

    _____

    _____

4. The magazine's sales rep has also told Troy that the magazine has just started to include a "reader service" card in each issue--so readers can follow up on advertising of interest by simply returning the postage-paid card. Troy will receive all of the names--and his salespeople can follow up with personal phone calls. Troy is optimistic that this could help identify good prospects and increase the percentage of "awares" converted to buyers from a low of the expected 1.5 percent to as high as 2.5 percent. Given the increased number of readers due to pass-along circulation, the rate discount for placing five or more ads, and the reader interest card, evaluate the "new" situation--regarding use of the magazine. How does it compare with the original spreadsheet proposal for the radio campaign? Briefly summarize your conclusions based on your analysis. (Hint: one approach is to do a What If analysis--varying the percent of awares who will buy and comparing these results with the results for the radio ad.)

_____

_____

_____

_____

_____

_____

_____

_____

_____

_____

Chapter 18

Pricing objectives and policies

What This Chapter Is About

Chapter 18 talks about the strategic decisions in the Price area. You should see that there is much more to Price than accepting the "equilibrium price" set by the interaction of supply and demand forces (as discussed in Appendix A). The actual price paid by customers depends on many factors. Some of these are discussed in this chapter. They include: the trade, quantity, and cash discounts offered; trade-ins; who pays the transportation costs; and what actually is included in the marketing mix.

The chapter begins with a discussion of possible pricing objectives--which should guide price setting. Then, the marketing manager's decisions about price flexibility and price level over the product life cycle are discussed.

The marketing manager must also set prices which are legal. This chapter discusses what can and cannot be done legally.

Clearly, there is much more to pricing than the simple economic analysis which we used earlier to understand the nature of competition. Chapter 18 is an important chapter--and deserves very careful study.

Important Terms

price, p. 446
target return objective, p. 448
profit maximization objective, p. 449
sales-oriented objective, p. 449
status quo objectives, p. 451
non-price competition, p. 451
administered prices, p. 451
one-price policy, p. 452
flexible-price policy, p. 452
skimming price policy, p. 453
penetration pricing policy, p. 454
introductory price dealing, p. 454
basic list prices, p. 455
discounts, p. 456
quantity discounts, p. 456
cumulative quantity discounts, p. 456
noncumulative quantity discounts, p. 456
seasonal discounts, p. 456
net, p. 457

cash discounts, p. 457
trade (functional) discount, p. 459
allowances, p. 459
trade-in allowance, p. 459
advertising allowances, p. 459
push money (or prize money)
   allowances, p. 460
trading stamps, p. 460
rebates, p. 461
F.O.B., p. 462
zone pricing, p. 462
uniform delivered pricing, p. 463
freight absorption pricing, p. 463
unfair trade practice acts, p. 463
phony list prices, p. 464
Wheeler-Lea Amendment, p. 464
price fixing, p. 464
Robinson-Patman Act, p. 465
price discrimination, p. 465

True-False Questions

F   1. Any business transaction in our modern economy can be thought of as an exchange of money--the money being the Price--for something of greater value.

T   2. The "something" that Price buys is different for consumers or users than it is for channel members.

T   3. A target return objective is often used in a large company to evaluate several different divisions or products.

F   4. Profit maximization objectives are undesirable from a social viewpoint, because profit maximization necessarily leads to high prices.

F   5. Instead of setting profit-oriented objectives, a marketing manager should follow sales-oriented objectives because--in the long run--sales growth leads to big profits.

T   6. Market share objectives provide a measurable objective--but an increase in market share does not always lead to higher profits.

F   7. Status quo pricing objectives don't ever make sense if the firm intends to develop an overall marketing strategy that is aggressive.

T   8. Instead of letting daily market forces determine their prices, most firms set their own administered prices.

T   9. A one-price policy means offering the same price to all customers who purchase products under essentially the same conditions and in the same quantities.

F   10. Flexible pricing is seldom used anymore in the United States because it does not aid selling.

F   11. A skimming pricing policy is especially desirable when economies of scale reduce costs greatly as volume expands--or when the firm expects strong competition very soon after introducing its new product.

T   12. A penetration pricing policy might be indicated where there is no "elite" market--that is, where the whole demand curve is fairly elastic--even in the early stages of the product's life cycle.

F   13. Introductory price dealing is the same thing as using a penetration pricing policy.

F   14. A firm involved in an oligopoly situation can usually increase profits by pricing higher than the market.

T   15. Sellers who may appear to emphasize below-the-market prices in their marketing mixes may really be using different marketing strategies--not different price levels.

___ 16. Basic list prices are the prices final consumers (or industrial customers) are normally asked to pay for products.

___ 17. Discounts from the list price may be granted by the seller to a buyer who either gives up some marketing function or provides the function for himself.

___ 18. Noncumulative quantity discounts apply only to individual orders.

___ 19. Cumulative quantity discounts tend to encourage larger single orders than do noncumulative quantity discounts.

___ 20. The following is an example of a seasonal discount: A local supermarket gives a free half gallon of milk with every order of $10.00 or more, provided the purchases are made on either Monday, Tuesday, or Wednesday--which normally are slow days in the food business.

___ 21. Cash discounts are used to encourage buyers to pay their bills quickly-- meaning they are granted to buyers who pay their bills by the due date.

___ 22. The following terms of sale appear on an invoice: 2/10, net 30. A buyer who fails to take advantage of this cash discount offer is--in effect-- borrowing at an annual rate of 36 percent a year.

___ 23. A mass merchandiser that allows government employees to purchase products at 10 percent below the store's normal selling prices is using a trade or functional discount.

___ 24. Allowances are typically given only to consumers, not to middlemen customers.

___ 25. Trade-in allowances are price reductions given for used products when similar new products are bought.

___ 26. PMs are given to retailers by manufacturers or wholesalers to pass on to their salespeople in return for aggressively selling particular items.

___ 27. Because trading stamps cost money, retailers who give them to customers must charge higher prices.

___ 28. A retailer is usually willing to redeem a producer's coupons since they increase his sales to consumers and also because he's paid by the producer for handling the coupons.

___ 29. Rebates give the producer a way to be sure that final consumers, instead of middlemen, get an intended price reduction.

___ 30. F.O.B. pricing simplifies a seller's pricing--but may narrow his target market because customer located farther from the seller must pay more for transporting costs and may buy from nearby suppliers.

_T_ 31. With zone pricing, an average freight charge is made to all buyers within certain geographic areas.

_F_ 32. Uniform delivered pricing--which is used when the seller wishes to sell his products in all geographic areas at one price--is most often used when transportation costs are relatively high.

_T_ 33. Freight absorption pricing means absorbing freight cost so that a firm's delivered price will meet the nearest competitor's.

_T_ 34. The practical effect of the unfair trade practices acts is to protect certain limited-line retailers from the kind of "ruinous" competition that full-line stores might offer if they sold certain products below cost for long time periods.

_T_ 35. Phony list prices are prices that customers are shown to suggest that the price they are to pay has been discounted from "list."

_F_ 36. The Wheeler-Lea Amendment bans price fixing in interstate commerce.

_F_ 37. Price fixing is illegal if it raises or stabilizes prices--but not if it results in lower prices.

_F_ 38. Although price fixing is illegal under the Sherman Act and the Federal Trade Commission Act, there are no penalties for managers who ignore these laws.

_F_ 39. The Robinson-Patman Act makes it illegal--under any conditions--to offer price differences to different buyers of products of "like grade and quality."

_T_ 40. In the *Borden* case, the U.S. Supreme Court upheld the FTC's position that products are of "like grade and quality" if their physical characteristics are similar--even if sold under different labels.

_T_ 41. A producer could legally refuse to give a wholesale discount to a large retail grocery chain that buys direct--although the chain might handle a larger volume than small wholesalers.

_F_ 42. Under the Robinson-Patman Act, it is legal for a firm to provide push money, advertising allowances, or other promotion aids to its customers, as long as such allowances are made available to all customers in equal dollar amounts.

1. F, p. 446	15. T, p. 455	29. T, p. 461
2. T, p. 447	16. T, p. 455	30. T, p. 462
3. T, p. 448	17. T, p. 456	31. T, p. 462
4. F, p. 449	18. T, p. 456	32. F, p. 463
5. F, p. 450	19. F, p. 456	33. T, p. 463
6. T, p. 450	20. T, p. 456	34. T, p. 463
7. F, p. 451	21. F, p. 457	35. T, p. 464
8. T, p. 451	22. T, p. 457	36. F, p. 464
9. T, p. 452	23. F, p. 459	37. F, p. 464
10. F, p. 452	24. F, p. 459	38. F, p. 464
11. F, p. 453	25. T, p. 459	39. F, p. 464
12. T, p. 454	26. T, p. 460	40. T, p. 464
13. F, p. 454	27. F, p. 460	41. T, p. 465
14. F, p. 454	28. T, p. 460	42. F, p. 466

Multiple-Choice Questions (Circle the correct response)

1. Which of the following would be *least likely* to be included in the "something" part of the "price equation" as seen by channel members?
   a. Quantity discounts
   b. Rebates
   c. Price-level guarantees
   d. Sufficient margin to allow chance for profit
   e. Convenient packaging for handling

2. If a marketing manager for a large company wants to compare the performance of different divisions of his firm, which of the following pricing objectives would he be most likely to pursue?
   a. Status quo
   b. Market share
   c. Target return
   d. Profit maximization
   e. Sales growth

3. With respect to pricing objectives, a marketing manager should be aware that:
   a. profit maximization objectives generally result in high prices.
   b. status quo pricing objectives can be part of an extremely aggressive marketing strategy.
   c. target return objectives usually guarantee a substantial profit.
   d. sales-oriented objectives generally result in high profits.
   e. All of the above are true statements.

4. Prices are called "administered" when:
    a. they are determined through negotiations between buyers and sellers.
    b. they fall below the "suggested list price."
    c. a marketing manager has to change his strategy every time a customer asks about the price.
    d. government intervenes to ensure that prices fluctuate freely in response to market forces.
    e. firms set their own prices for some period of time--rather than letting daily market forces determine their prices.

5. In contrast to flexible pricing, a one-price policy:
    a. means that the same price is offered to all customers who purchase products under the same conditions.
    b. involves setting the price at the "right" level from the start--and holding it there.
    c. generally results in rigid prices which change very infrequently.
    d. means that delivered prices will be the same to all customers.
    e. All of the above.

6. Which of the following factors would be *least favorable* to a skimming price policy?
    a. The firm has no competitors.
    b. The quantity demanded is very sensitive to price.
    c. The product is in the market introduction stage of its life cycle.
    d. The firm follows a multiple target market approach.
    e. The firm has a unique, patented product.

7. The Gill Corp. is introducing a new "me-too" brand of shampoo in market maturity. To speed its entry into the market--without encouraging price competition with other shampoo producers--Gill should consider using:
    a. a penetration pricing policy.
    b. a flexible-price policy.
    c. a skimming price policy.
    d. introductory price dealing.
    e. an above-the-market price-level policy.

8. The Stark Corporation purchases large quantities of iron castings from a well-known producer. Stark receives a discount which increases as the total amount ordered during the year increases. What type of discount is involved here?
    a. Seasonal discount
    b. Cumulative quantity discount
    c. Brokerage allowance
    d. Noncumulative quantity discount
    e. Cash discount

9. The terms "3/20, net 60" mean that:
    a. in effect, the buyer will pay a 27 percent interest rate if he takes 60 days to pay the invoice.
    b. the buyer must make a 3 percent down payment--with the balance due in 20 to 60 days.
    c. a 3 percent discount off the face value of the invoice is permitted if the bill is paid within 60 days--otherwise, the full face value is due within 20 days.
    d. the invoice is dated March 20 and must be paid within 60 days.
    e. None of the above is a true statement.

10. The Bowman Co., a manufacturer of sports equipment, gives its retailers a 2 percent price reduction on all products with the expectation that the dealers will advertise the products locally. Apparently, Bowman believes that local promotion will be more effective and economical than national promotion. This is an example of:
    a. "push money."
    b. a brokerage allowance.
    c. a cash discount.
    d. a trade discount.
    e. an advertising allowance.

11. Some manufacturers give _____ to retailers to pass on to the retailers' salesclerks in return for aggressively selling particular items or lines.
    a. brokerage commissions
    b. advertising allowances
    c. trade discounts
    d. "push money" allowances
    e. cash discounts

12. Regarding trading stamps, a retailer should be aware that:
    a. the use of trading stamps usually gives a retailer a long-lasting competitive advantage.
    b. trading stamps generally cost retailers about 5-10 percent of sales.
    c. there has been a steady increase in the use of stamps since the 1950s.
    d. the use of trading stamps does not necessarily result in higher retail prices.
    e. All of the above are true statements.

13. A manufacturer in North Carolina sold some furniture to a firm in Baltimore. If the *seller* wanted title to the products to pass immediately--but still wanted to pay the freight bill--the invoice would read:
    a. F.O.B. delivered.
    b. F.O.B. seller's factory--freight prepaid.
    c. F.O.B. Baltimore.
    d. F.O.B. seller's factory.
    e. F.O.B. buyer's warehouse.

14. Which of the following statements about geographic pricing policies is *true*?
   a. Zone pricing penalizes buyers closest to the factory.
   b. Uniform delivered pricing is more practical when transportation costs are relatively low.
   c. Freight absorption pricing may increase the size of market territories.
   d. F.O.B. pricing tends to reduce the size of market territories.
   e. All of the above are true statements.

15. A main purpose of "unfair trade practice acts" is to:
   a. prevent manufacturers from taking high markups.
   b. eliminate price competition on manufacturers' brands.
   c. require some minimum percentage markup on cost.
   d. permit different types of retail outlets to charge different retail prices.
   e. guarantee retailers some profit.

16. Price fixing:
   a. is always illegal.
   b. is prohibited by the Robinson-Patman Act.
   c. is illegal if it raises or stabilizes prices--but not if it lowers prices.
   d. is technically illegal--but there is very little that the federal government can do about it.
   e. All of the above are true statements.

17. According to the _____ Act, it is unlawful in interstate commerce to practice price discrimination between different purchasers of "commodities of like grade and quality" which may tend to injure competition.
   a. Magnuson-Moss
   b. Fair-Trade
   c. Sherman Antitrust
   d. Robinson-Patman
   e. Celler-Kefauver

18. A manufacturer might try to defend himself against charges of illegal price discrimination by claiming that:
   a. the price discrimination occurred as a defensive measure to "meet competition in good faith."
   b. the price differentials did not actually injure competition.
   c. the price differentials were justified on the basis of cost differences in production and/or distribution.
   d. his products were not of "like grade and quality."
   e. Any of the above could make price discrimination legal.

McCarthy and Perreault

19. Which of the following price-related actions by a manufacturer *most likely* would be a violation of the Robinson-Patman Act?
   a. Offering a lower price to only one buyer to match a competitor's price.
   b. Selling to all its customers at uniform prices.
   c. Granting a lower price to a buyer because of a large-quantity purchase.
   d. Giving a special advertising allowance to a retailer that was having difficulty competing in its local market.

Answers to Multiple-Choice Questions

1. b, p. 447	8. b, p. 456	15. c, p. 463
2. c, p. 448	9. a, p. 457	16. a, p. 464
3. b, p. 451	10. e, p. 459	17. d, p. 464
4. e, p. 451	11. d, p. 460	18. e, p. 464-66
5. a, p. 452	12. d, p. 460	19. d, p. 466
6. b, p. 453	13. b, p. 462	
7. d, p. 454	14. e, p. 462-63	

Exercise 18-1

Using discounts and allowances to improve
the marketing mix

Introduction

Most price structures have a basic list price from which various discounts and allowances are subtracted. *Discounts* (not to be confused with discount selling) are reductions from list price that are given by a seller to a buyer who either gives up some marketing function or provides the function himself. Several types of discounts are commonly used, including:

> a) Cumulative quantity discounts
> b) Noncumulative quantity discounts
> c) Seasonal discounts
> d) Cash discounts
> e) Trade (functional) discounts

Allowances are similar to discounts. They are given to final consumers, customers or channel members for doing "something" or accepting less of "something." Different types of allowances include:

> a) Trade-in allowances
> b) Advertising allowances
> c) Push money or prize money allowances

While many firms give discounts and allowances as a matter of custom, they should be viewed as highly useful tools for marketing strategy planning. As outlined in the text, each type is designed for a specific purpose. Thus, some firms offer buyers a choice of several discounts and allowances.

The purpose of this exercise is to illustrate how discounts and allowances can be used in marketing strategy planning. The emphasis will be on recognizing opportunities to improve a firm's marketing mix. In Exercise 18-2, we will discuss various legal restrictions which may affect a firm's policies regarding discounts and allowances.

Assignment

Presented below are five cases describing situations in which a firm *might* want to add or change some discount or allowance--as part of its marketing mix. Read each case carefully and then answer the questions which follow.

1. Athletic Footwear Company produces a high-quality line of Lightfoot brand men's and women's running shoes. Lightfoot shoes are distributed nationally through a network of carefully selected sporting stores and runners' stores. When jogging first became popular, Lightfoot sales grew rapidly--in part because of its ongoing advertising in national magazines. Now, however, sales are flat--and in some areas falling. Most retailers now carry several competing brands of shoes--and the company is concerned about what it considers "a lack of adequate promotion support at the retail level."

    Could Athletic Footwear Company use discounts or allowances to obtain additional promotion support at the retail level? Why? If so, what type would you recommend? Why?

2. Richmond Auto Supply sells a wide assortment of products to gas stations and auto service centers in the Richmond, Virginia, area. Richmond's line includes almost everything its customers might need--ranging from tune-up parts, mufflers, batteries, tires, brake repair items, automobile paint, hand cleaner, and a wide variety of mechanic's tools and equipment. In addition, like most other auto parts wholesalers in the area, Richmond offers free delivery. Despite Richmond's efforts to promote itself as "the most economical source for all your needs," most of its customers split their business among a number of different auto supply wholesalers. When Richmond's owner complained about this, one of his counter clerks offered an explanation: "The garage owners don't care what parts house gets the business--so the different mechanics just call whoever comes to mind first."

    Could discounts or allowances be useful to Richmond Auto Supply? Why? If so, what type would be best? Explain.

3.   Hunt Electric Co. manufactures a large assortment of electrical parts and supplies. Hunt's products are sold through merchant wholesalers (distributors) who supply builders, electrical contractors, hardware stores, and lumber yards. Hunt's production manager recently complained to the firm's marketing manager that "the sales force needs to do a better job of smoothing out sales. In the fall and winter--when there is little building activity--we have extra capacity. Then, late in the spring all of the orders come in at once--and we have to pay overtime to get everything produced. It's not just a matter of putting items in our warehouse. We need to get the orders. We have bills to pay."

Could Hunt's problem be due in part to a lack of appropriate discounts or allowances? Why? Is so, what type might be best for the company to adopt? Explain.

4.   Bosa Co. manufactures expensive stereo speakers which are sold through manufacturers' agents to selected retailers who specialize in high-quality stereo component systems. Most of Bosa's speakers are sold on credit. In fact, Bosa usually does not get paid until its retailers manage to sell the speakers themselves. While this service is convenient and necessary for most of its customers, it places a heavy financial burden on Bosa. Recently, for example, the company was forced to postpone production of a promising new product due to a lack of cash.

Should Bosa Co. consider using discounts or allowances to solve its financial problem? Why? If so, what type would be best? Why?

5. The Smart-Set Dress Shop has just purchased $5,000 worth of women's dresses from the Vogue Manufacturing Company. The invoice for the dresses included the terms "2/10, net 30."

a) What do the terms 2/10, net 30 mean?

b) Suppose Smart-Set pays the invoice 10 days after receipt. What amount should it pay Vogue Manufacturing?

c) If Smart-Set does not pay the invoice until 30 days after receipt, it will in effect be borrowing money at a fairly high interest rate. Calculate what the effective interest rate would be in this case. (Assume a 360 day year.)

d) What conditions would make it sensible for Vogue Manufacturing to offer these terms?

Question for Discussion

Do discounts and allowances really offer marketing managers a great deal of flexibility in varying their marketing mixes? Explain.

Exercise 18-2

How legislation affects pricing policies

Introduction

Pricing legislation is a very complex area. Even legal experts cannot always provide their clients with clear-cut advice in pricing matters. This is due in part to the vague way in which many laws have been written by legislators--and in part to the fact that no two situations are ever exactly alike. It is up to the courts and administrative bodies, such as the Federal Trade Commission, to interpret pricing legislation. And their interpretation of laws has tended to vary a lot, depending on the political environment.

Nevertheless, a marketing manager should try to understand the legal environment-- and know how to work within it. Legislation and legal cases often tend to focus on pricing matters, because prices are highly visible elements of the marketing mix. Business managers have much freedom to charge whatever prices they choose-- subject to the forces of competition. But they must be aware of and work with the restrictions which do exist. Ignorance of the law is no excuse. The penalties for violating pricing laws are tough--even jail!

This exercise is designed to increase your understanding of the basic federal laws (Sherman Act, Robinson-Patman Act, Federal Trade Commission Act, Wheeler-Lea Amendment) related to pricing matters. The intent is not to make you a legal expert--but rather to be sure you understand the kinds of pricing activities which *might* be illegal.

Assignment

The following four cases describe pricing activities which *might* be judged illegal in certain circumstances. Study each case carefully and then answer the questions which follow. Be sure to identify the law (or laws) which are *most relevant* to each situation *as it is described*.

1. Medico, Inc.--a large manufacturer of pharmaceuticals--sells its consumer products exclusively through drug wholesalers--who sell to retail druggists. Wholesalers are allowed a "chain discount" of 35 percent and 10 percent off of the manufacturer's suggested retail list prices. The wholesalers are then expected to pass the 35 percent discount on to retailers. Recently a large retail drug chain approached Medico about buying direct. Medico agreed to sell direct to the chain--and offered a discount of 35 percent. However, the chain wanted the additional 10 percent usually given to wholesalers. Medico

felt this would be unfair to those retail druggists who must buy through wholesalers--and refused the chain's request on the grounds that such a discount would be illegal.

Do you agree with Medico? Why or why not? Be sure to identify what type(s) of discounts or allowances and which law(s) are involved.

2. Libby Corporation produces a wide line of canned foods--including "Early," one of the leading brands of canned corn. The wholesale selling price for a case (48 cans) of Early corn is $9.60--which includes a 5 percent trade discount for the wholesaler. Libby also gives a 10 percent quantity discount to wholesalers who buy in carload quantities. Wholesalers normally pass the quantity discount along to their customers in the form of lower prices. The identical corn is also sold to a few large food chains for use as dealer brands. The cans are sold under different labels at $8.00 per case (minus the 10 percent quantity discount if earned). Libby allocates 3 percent of its net sales of Early corn toward national advertising.

Suppose the Federal Trade Commission were to take a close look at Libby's pricing methods to see whether the manufacturer was violating federal pricing legislation. What aspects of Libby's pricing policies do you think the FTC might question based on what is presented above? Why? What laws might be involved?

3. Quality Dairy produces a line of milk products and sells them directly to retailers in a three-state area. Recently, one of Quality's major competitors-- a large national firm--offered to sell one of Quality's retail accounts its brand of white milk for $1.50/half gallon, which was 10 cents less than Quality charged for its brand. When the retailer threatened to stop carrying Quality half gallons--and instead stock only the national brand--Quality offered to sell that retailer its regular white milk for $1.40 per half gallon. When the national firm accused Quality of "price discrimination with predatory intent," Quality replied that it was simply "meeting competition in good faith."

Who is right in this case--Quality or its competitor? What law(s) would apply?

4. The Better Business Bureau (BBB) recently received a telephone call from an angry consumer who wished to complain about Fast Eddie's--an electronics discount chain with nine stores in the surrounding four-state area. The consumer had gone to Eddie's to buy some items listed in an "inventory clearance sale" advertisement. The first item was a "top-name" color TV marked down from $450 to $200. Upon arrival at the store, he found only one of the featured TVs in stock--a floor model in very poor condition. The salesclerk apologized--and suggested that the customer buy one of the store's other models at "regular everyday low prices" ranging from $199 on up. The consumer then asked to see a video camera that--according to the ad--was "originally priced at $1,295" and "now reduced to only $795." The salesclerk pointed to a dusty camera in a case near the back of the store. On closer inspection, the customer realized that the camera was a three-year-old model that did not have any of the features found on new cameras--even one that regularly sold for less than $795. An official from BBB sympathized with the consumer and said that his agency had received many similar complaints about Fast Eddie's. He went on to say, however, that there was very little anyone could do--other than to avoid shopping at such stores.

Comment on the Better Business Bureau's analysis of the above situation. Are Fast Eddie's pricing practices deceptive and/or illegal? Can anything be done in such situations?

Question for Discussion

According to one point of view, the Robinson-Patman Act benefits consumers by prohibiting pricing practices which may tend to injure competition. Another point of view, however, holds that the act only serves to protect inefficient competitors and thus may actually be harmful to consumers. Which view do you agree with? Why? How can we determine which view is "right"?

Name: _____ Course & Section: _____

Exercise 18-3

Cash discounts

This exercise is based on computer-aided problem number 18--Cash Discounts. A complete description of the problem appears on pages 31-32 of *Computer-Aided Problems to Accompany Basic Marketing.*

1. Tulkin has several variables to consider as he tries to decide what cash discount terms to offer. One thing he has noticed about his current situation (with 90 percent of his customers taking the cash discount) is that his ratio of cash discounts to total invoice amounts is .027--or about 3 percent. It occurred to him that another alternative might be to leave his terms the way they are for the short term, but increase his prices by about 3 percent. If he does this--so that the average invoice is about $927 instead of $900--and everything else stays the same, what will happen to his total <u>net</u> sales (after the cash discounts are taken)?

    $_____ net sales without price increase (120 customers)

    $_____ net sales with 3 percent price increase (120 customers)

2. Tulkin realizes that if he increases his list price some price-sensitive retailers will switch to other wholesalers. If he increases the price, how many customers can he "afford" to lose before his net sales are back to the level he had before the price increase?

    _____ number of customers after the price increase to earn about the same net sales as before the price increase

3. In thinking about price-sensitive customers, Tulkin feels he may be able to promote his favorable invoice terms to attract customers away from other wholesalers who have already changed to less favorable terms. He recognizes that drawing attention to his invoice terms will probably mean that more customers will take the cash discount. He also knows he might still have to change his terms of sale later--but thinks he could hang on to some of the new customers once they become aware of his good service and quality products. If he keeps his invoice terms the same--and 95 percent of the customers take the cash discount--how many new customers will Tulkin have to attract to increase his net sales by about $5,000? What will his expected gross sales and total monthly cash discount amount be in this case?

$_____ net sales with 120 customers, 90 percent taking discount

plus $___5,000.00___ target increase in net sales

$_____ new target for net sales

_____ = number of customers required to achieve target net sales, assuming 95 percent take the discount

$_____ expected gross sales with that many customers

$_____ expected cash discount amount with that many customers

4. Tulkin feels this plan may work--so he wants to see how things might look later if and when he reduces his terms closer to what competitors are charging--2/10, net 30. He figures he wouldn't lose customers at that point-- since others would already be offering similar terms. He is not certain how many customers will take the cash discount with the new terms--but he estimates that it will be between 40 percent and 60 percent. He is uncertain how his net sales might vary over that percentage range. To help answer this question, prepare a table that shows how his net sales, the total dollar value of cash discounts, and the ratio of cash discounts to invoice face value would change as the percentage of customers that take the discount varies between 40 percent and 60 percent.

Percent Taking Cash Discount	Net Dollar Sales	Total Cash Discounts	Ratio of Discounts to Face Value
40	$_____	$_____	_____
42	$_____	$_____	_____
44	$_____	$_____	_____
46	$_____	$_____	_____
48	$_____	$_____	_____
50	$_____	$_____	_____
52	$_____	$_____	_____
54	$_____	$_____	_____
56	$_____	$_____	_____
58	$_____	$_____	_____
60	$_____	$_____	_____

Appendix B

Marketing arithmetic

What This Chapter Is About

Appendix B provides a brief introduction (or review) of some important accounting terms which are useful in analyzing marketing problems.

The content of an operating statement (profit-and-loss statement) is reviewed first. Accounting terms are used in a technical sense--rather than a layman's sense--and should be studied with this in mind. Accountants try to use words precisely--and usually try to place the same kinds of data in the same places in their statements. So try to capture the "model" which they are using. Basically, it is: sales minus costs equals profit.

It also is useful to be able to calculate stockturn rates, operating ratios, markups, markdowns, and ROI and ROA--to fully understand some of the concepts in the text chapters.

This material should be "easy review" for those who have had some accounting. But regardless of your background, it probably will be helpful to study this material--to deepen your understanding of accounting statements and tools. Familiarity with these ideas is assumed in the text!

Important Terms

operating statement, p. 469
gross sales, p. 472
return, p. 472
allowance, p. 472
net sales, p. 472
cost of sales, p. 472
gross margin (gross profit), p. 472
expenses, p. 472
net profit, p. 473

purchase discount, p. 473
stockturn rate, p. 474
operating ratios, p. 476
markup, p. 477
markdown ratio, p. 478
markdown, p. 479
return on investment (ROI), p. 479
balance sheet, p. 479
return on assets (ROA), p. 480

True-False Questions

_T_ 1. An operating statement is a simple summary of the financial results of a company's operation over a specified period of time.

_F_ 2. The three basic components of an operating statement are sales, costs, and return on investment.

3. Net sales equals gross sales minus returns and allowances.

4. The "cost of sales" is the total value (at cost) of the sales during the operating period.

5. Gross margin (or gross profit) equals net sales minus operating expenses.

6. Net profit equals net sales minus the cost of sales minus operating expenses.

7. To calculate the net profit accurately, purchase discounts and freight charges should be added to the cost of sales.

8. Expenses do not include the cost of sales.

9. The stockturn rate is a measure of how long it takes a certain inventory of goods to be sold.

10. Stockturn rate may be calculated as the cost of sales divided by the average inventory at cost.

11. The various components of an operating statement should always be expressed in absolute numbers rather than in percentages.

12. If a store takes a 50-cent markup on a certain product, then its net profit for that item is also 50 cents.

13. A 25 percent markup on cost equals a 20 percent markup on selling price.

14. A markdown ratio equals dollar markdowns divided by net sales; returns and allowances are not included.

15. Markdowns are generally shown on a firm's operating statement.

16. Return on investment is not shown on the firm's operating statement.

17. To increase return on investment, a firm *must* increase sales.

18. Although return on investment is calculated in the same way as return on assets, the two ratios are trying to show different things about the company's use of resources.

Answers to True-False Questions

1. T, p. 469	7. F, p. 473	13. T, p. 478
2. F, p. 470	8. T, p. 474	14. F, p. 479
3. T, p. 472	9. F, p. 474	15. F, p. 479
4. T, p. 472	10. T, p. 475	16. T, p. 479
5. F, p. 472	11. F, p. 476	17. F, p. 480
6. T, p. 473	12. F, p. 477	18. F, p. 480

Multiple-Choice Questions (Circle the correct response)

1. The primary purpose of the operating statement is:
   a. to determine which products or customers are most profitable.
   b. to determine the net profit figure for the company.
   c. to present data to support the net profit figure.
   d. to indicate the source of the firm's assets.
   e. both b and c above.

2. The essential components of an operating statement are:
   a. gross sales, gross margin, and net profit.
   b. net sales, cost of sales, and profit or loss.
   c. sales, costs, and profit or loss.
   d. gross sales, gross margin, expenses, and net profit.
   e. sales, markdowns, and ROI.

3. Which of the following statements is *true*?
   a. "Gross sales" is equal to revenue actually received and kept.
   b. "Cost of sales" means the cost value of goods on hand at any given time.
   c. Expenses are included in the "Cost of sales" section of the operating statement.
   d. "Gross margin" less the "Cost of sales" equals "Net profit."
   e. None of the above statements is true.

4. Given the following data for the XYZ Company for the year 198X, calculate XYZ's net profit.

Gross sales	$157,000
Returns	-3,000
Allowances	-4,000
Purchases	60,000
Beginning inventory	50,000
Freight-in	3,000
Cost of sales	-100,000
Expenses	-30,000

   a. $10,000
   b. $12,000
   c. $17,000
   d. $20,000
   e. $27,000

5. Which of the following statements is *false*?
   a. Stockturn rate equals cost of sales divided by average inventory at cost.
   b. Stockturn rate equals gross sales divided by average inventory at selling price.
   c. Stockturn rate equals net sales minus gross margin divided by average inventory at cost.
   d. Stockturn rate equals sales in units divided by average inventory in units.
   e. Stockturn rate equals net sales divided by average inventory at selling price.

Use the following data to answer questions 6 and 7.

(handwritten: 510,00   450,00)

Gross sales	$1,020,000	
Markdowns	50,000	
Cost of sales	510,000 *(handwritten)*	50%
Beginning inventory	150,000	
Returns and allowances	20,000	
Expenses		30%
Purchases	400,000	

6. Calculate the net profit (or loss) for the firm described above.
   a. $150,000
   b. $190,000
   c. $204,000
   d. $200,000 *(circled)*
   e. Cannot be determined without more information.

7. Assume that the average stockturn rate for this industry is 4. How does this firm compare to its competitors?
   a. The firm has an above-average turnover rate. *(circled)*
   b. The firm has a below-average turnover rate.
   c. The firm has an average turnover rate.
   d. Cannot be determined.

Use the following data from a company's last accounting period to answer questions 8-10.

Sales returns	$ 10,000	
Sales allowances	15,000	
Expenses		25%
Closing inventory at cost	50,000	
Markdowns	45,000	
Freight-in	5,000	
Purchases	150,000	
Net profit	30,000	10%

8. The cost of sales is:
   a. $225,000
   b. $105,000
   c. $145,000
   d. $195,000 *(circled)*
   e. $ 75,000

9. The stockturn rate is:
   a. 6.0
   b. 3.9
   c. 4.3
   d. 2.8 *(circled)*
   e. 1.5

10. The markdown ratio is:
    a. 20 percent
    b. 11 2/3 percent
    c. 18 1/3 percent
    d. 10 percent
    e. 15 percent

11. Joe's Shoe Store uses a traditional markup of 25 percent for all of its shoes. If a pair of shoes costs him $6, what should Joe *add* to this cost to determine his selling price?
    a. $1.50
    b. 33 1/3 percent of $6.00
    c. 125 percent of $6.00
    d. $3.00
    e. 25 percent of $6.00

12. Knowledge of departmental markdown ratios for a given period would be useful in:
    a. preparing an operating statement for that period.
    b. determining the value of goods on hand.
    c. measuring the efficiency of the various retail departments.
    d. computing the stockturn rate for that period.
    e. All of the above.

13. To increase its return on investment (ROI), a firm could:
    a. increase its profit margin.
    b. increase its sales.
    c. decrease its investment.
    d. increase its leveraging.
    e. All of the above.

14. *Given the following information, calculate the ABC Company's ROI.*

Net sales	$1,000,000
Gross margin	200,000
Markdowns	200,000
Assets	300,000
Net profit (after taxes)	10,000
Owner's investment	100,000

    a. 3.3 percent
    b. 1,000.0 percent
    c. 10.0 percent
    d. 2.5 percent
    e. 5.0 percent

15. In Question 14, the ABC Company's ROA was:
    a. 3.3 percent.
    b. 2.5 percent.
    c. 30.0 percent.
    d. 150.0 percent.
    e. Some negative number--because the assets were larger than the owners' investment.

Answers to Multiple-Choice Questions

1. e, p. 469	6. d, p. 473	11. b, p. 478
2. c, p. 470	7. a, p. 474	12. c, p. 478
3. e, p. 472	8. d, p. 472	13. e, p. 480
4. d, p. 473	9. d, p. 474	14. c, p. 480
5. b, p. 474	10. a, p. 478	15. a, p. 480

McCarthy and Perreault

Exercise B-1

Marketing arithmetic

Introduction

A firm's financial records contain much useful information for a marketing manager. An effective marketing manager will make regular use of them in his planning. This exercise is designed to improve your understanding of the operating statement and the information it contains.

Assignment

Answer each of the following questions about the financial records of ABC Corporation.

1. Complete ABC's operating statement.

ABC CORPORATION
Operating Statement
For the Year Ending December 31, 198X

Gross sales			$52,000
Less: Returns and allowances			4,000
Net sales			a) _____
Cost of sales			
Beginning inventory at cost		$12,000	
Purchases at billed cost	$25,000		
Less: Purchase discounts	2,000		
Purchases at net cost	b) _____		
Plus freight-in	2,000		
Net cost of delivered purchases		c) _____	
Cost of goods available for sale		d) _____	
Less: Ending inventory at cost.		8,000	
Cost of sales			e) _____
Gross margin (gross profit)			f) _____
Expenses			
Selling expense			
Sales salaries	7,000		
Advertising expense	2,200		
Delivery expense	2,300		
Total selling expenses		g) _____	

Administrative expense
    Office salaries $ 3,800
    Office supplies   900
    Miscellaneous   300
        Total admin. expense   h) _____
General expense
    Rent expense   1,100
    Miscellaneous   100
        Total general expense   i) _____
            Total expense   j) _____
Net profit from operation   k) _____

2.   Calculate the stockturn rate (using cost figures).

3.   Calculate the following operating ratios. (Round each answer to one decimal place.)

    a)   Net sales   100%

    b)   Cost of sales   _____

    c)   Gross margin   _____

    d)   Expenses   _____

    e)   Net profit   _____

Question for Discussion

What additional financial information would help the marketing manager of ABC Corporation to improve his operation?

Chapter 19

Price setting in the real world

What This Chapter Is About

Price setting is challenging--but deciding on the right price is crucial to the success of the whole marketing mix.

Chapter 19 treats cost-oriented pricing in detail--because it is commonly used and makes sense for some firms. But cost-oriented pricing doesn't always work well. You should study this approach carefully, so you can better understand its advantages and disadvantages.

Pay special attention to the relationships of the various cost curves. Notice how costs vary at different levels of operation.

Some business managers have recognized the problems with average-cost pricing and have tried to bring demand into their price-setting. Demand-oriented pricing requires some estimate of demand--and ideally a whole demand curve. But demand curves are not easy to estimate. This is one reason why demand-oriented pricing has not been widely used. But it is possible to *estimate* demand curves. And it is probably better to try to estimate a demand curve than ignore it. Some examples of how this is being done are presented at the end of the chapter.

By estimating demand, it is possible to estimate the likely profit of various quantities--and find the most profitable price and quantity. Although this approach is not as widely used as cost-oriented pricing, it deserves careful study. Demand must be considered when setting price--unless you are willing to leave making a profit to chance. Demand-oriented pricing can be done--and can be very useful in helping to carry out the marketing concept--that is, satisfying customers *at a profit*.

Important Terms

markup, p. 483
markup (percent), p. 484
markup chain, p. 484
stockturn rate, p. 485
average-cost pricing, p. 487
total fixed cost, p. 488
total variable cost, p. 489
total cost, p. 489
average cost (per unit), p. 489
average fixed cost (per unit), p. 489
average variable cost (per unit), p. 489
experience curve pricing, p. 491
target return pricing, p. 492
long-run target return pricing, p. 492
break-even analysis, p. 492
break-even point (BEP), p. 493
fixed-cost (FC) contribution per
   unit, p. 494

marginal analysis, p. 496
marginal revenue, p. 496
marginal cost, p. 497
rule for maximizing profit, p. 498
marginal profit, p. 501
price leader, p. 503
value in use pricing, p. 504
leader pricing, p. 505
bait pricing, p. 505
psychological pricing, p. 506
odd-even pricing, p. 506
prestige pricing, p. 506
price lining, p. 507
demand-backward pricing, p. 507
full-line pricing, p. 508
complementary product pricing, p. 509
bid pricing, p. 509

True-False Questions

1. Markup (dollars) means the dollar amount added to cost of products to get the selling price--or markup (percent) means a percentage of the selling price which is added to the cost to get the selling price.

2. Considering the large number of items the average retailer or wholesaler carries--and the small sales volume of any one item--a markup approach to pricing makes sense.

3. According to the definition of markup given in the text, a product which a retailer buys for $2.00 would be priced at $3.20 if the retailer applied a markup of 60 percent.

4. A producer--whose product sells for $24--distributes its product through wholesalers and retailers who traditionally use a "markup chain" of 20 percent and 40 percent, respectively. Therefore, the retail selling price of this product is $50.

5. A wholesaler or retailer concerned with increasing profits should consider using a smaller markup as a way of achieving a substantial increase in turnover.

6. "Stockturn rate" means the number of times a firm's beginning inventory is sold in a year.

7. Producers commonly use a cost-oriented pricing approach--adding a standard markup to obtain their selling price.

F 8. Because average-cost pricing consists of adding a "reasonable" markup to the average cost of a product, it assures the producer of earning a profit at any level of output.

T 9. Total fixed cost is the sum of those costs that are fixed in total--no matter how much is produced.

F 10. Total variable cost would include items such as wages paid to workers, sales commissions, and salaries paid to top executives.

T 11. The rate of growth of total cost as output increases is not affected by total fixed cost.

T 12. Average cost is obtained by dividing total cost by the related total quantity.

F 13. Average fixed cost increases as the total quantity produced increases.

T 14. Average variable cost is obtained by dividing total variable cost by the number of units produced.

F 15. Because of economies of scale, all average and total costs tend to decline as the quantity produced increases.

F 16. Average-cost pricing works best when demand conditions are changing rapidly and substantially.

T 17. Experience curve pricing is like average-cost pricing--except that prices are based on an estimate of future average costs.

F 18. Unlike the average-cost curve approach, target return pricing assures that the target return is achieved--even if the quantity that is actually sold is less than the quantity used in setting the price.

T 19. Those who use long-run target return pricing assume that short-run losses and above-normal profits will average out in the long run--thus allowing the firm to achieve its long-run target return objectives.

F 20. Break-even analysis suggests that once a firm reaches its break-even point, profit will keep increasing with every additional unit sold.

T 21. Although break-even analysis considers the relationship of total revenue and total cost, it may not solve the firm's pricing problem because the assumed price may not be tied to realistic demand estimates.

T 22. The traditional goal of economic analysis--to maximize profits--is a reasonable one because if you know how to make the biggest profit, you can always adjust your price to pursue other objectives--while knowing how much profit you are giving up.

___ 23. Marginal analysis helps the marketing manager make the best pricing decision by focusing on the last unit which would be sold--to determine how total revenue and total cost would be affected.

___ 24. Since marginal revenue is the change in total revenue which results from the sale of one additional unit of a product--and since this extra unit will be sold while charging a positive price for all items--marginal revenue can never be negative.

___ 25. The marginal revenue curve is the same as the demand curve when the demand curve is down-sloping.

___ 26. Marginal cost--which is the change in total cost that results from producing one more unit--might also be defined as the change in total variable cost that results from producing one more unit.

___ 27. If an average-cost curve first drops and then rises, the related marginal cost curve would also start rising--but at a greater level of output.

___ 28. To maximize profit--the firm should produce that output where the difference between marginal revenue and marginal cost is the greatest.

___ 29. When using a graph to determine the most profitable output and price for a firm, the best price is obtained by going from the MR-MC intersection over to the price axis.

___ 30. Marginal analysis indicates that--to maximize profits--a firm should be willing to increase the quantity it will sell until the marginal profit of the last unit is at--or near--zero.

___ 31. If marginal costs can be covered in the short run--even though all fixed costs cannot--the firm should remain in operation.

___ 32. A firm in an oligopoly situation cannot use marginal analysis to maximize its profits because of the "kinked" demand curve facing the firm.

___ 33. A price leader in an oligopoly situation should have a very good understanding of its own and its competitors' cost structures--as well as an estimate of the industry demand curve.

___ 34. Value in use pricing is setting prices which will capture some of what customers will save by substituting the firm's product for the one currently being used.

___ 35. Leader pricing is most common in oligopoly situations--where most firms will raise or lower their price only after the industry leader raises or lowers its price.

___ 36. Items featured in "bait pricing" are real bargains priced low to get customers into the store to buy these and other items.

_____ 37. Psychological pricing assumes that some price changes will not affect the quantity sold.

_____ 38. Retailers who use "odd-even pricing" seem to assume that they face a rather jagged demand curve--that slightly higher prices will substantially reduce the quantity demanded.

_____ 39. Prestige pricing is possible when target customers think that high prices mean high quality or high status--and the demand curve for this market slopes down for a while and then bends back to the left again.

_____ 40. Although price lining may result in higher sales, faster turnover, and simplified buying--it also increases the retailer's total inventory requirements and often leads to greater markdowns.

_____ 41. Henry Ford's decision to build a car for the "masses"--setting "a price so low as to force everybody to the highest point of efficiency"--is an example of demand-backward pricing.

_____ 42. A manufacturer that offers a complete line (or assortment) of products should not be overly concerned about full-line pricing if it is aiming at different target markets for each of its products.

_____ 43. Complementary product pricing is setting prices on several products as a group.

_____ 44. The major job in bid pricing is assembling all of the costs--including the variable and fixed costs--that should apply to each job.

Answers to True-False Questions

1. T, p. 483-84	16. F, p. 490	31. T, p. 502
2. T, p. 484	17. T, p. 491	32. F, p. 503
3. F, p. 484	18. F, p. 492	33. T, p. 504
4. T, p. 485	19. T, p. 492	34. T, p. 504
5. T, p. 485	20. T, p. 492	35. F, p. 505
6. F, p. 485	21. T, p. 494	36. F, p. 505
7. T, p. 486	22. T, p. 496	37. T, p. 506
8. F, p. 487	23. T, p. 496	38. T, p. 506
9. T, p. 488	24. F, p. 496	39. T, p. 506
10. F, p. 489	25. F, p. 497	40. F, p. 507
11. T, p. 489	26. T, p. 497	41. T, p. 507
12. T, p. 489	27. F, p. 498	42. T, p. 508
13. F, p. 489	28. F, p. 498	43. T, p. 509
14. T, p. 489	29. F, p. 500-01	44. T, p. 510
15. F, p. 489-90	30. T, p. 501	

Multiple-Choice Questions (Circle the correct response)

1. A certain product retails for $100. How much does this product cost the retailer if his markup is 33 1/3 percent?
   a. $25.00
   b. $33.00
   c. $50.00
   d. $75.00
   e. $66.67

2. A certain item is sold at retail for $50. The retailer's markup is 25 percent *on cost*. The wholesaler's markup is 25 percent. What is the manufacturer's selling price?
   a. $30.00
   b. $32.00
   c. $28.10
   d. $35.11
   e. $25.00

3. With respect to markups and turnover, a marketing manager should be aware that:
   a. although supermarket operating expenses run 16-20 percent of sales, items sold at lower markups (i.e., less than 12 percent) still may be very profitable.
   b. depending on the industry, a stockturn rate of 1 or 2 may be quite profitable.
   c. high markups don't always mean big profits.
   d. speeding turnover often increases profits because the firm's operating costs are a function of time and the volume of goods sold.
   e. All of the above are true statements.

4. Which of the following statements about average-cost pricing is *true*?
   a. The chief merit of this approach is that it is based on well-researched pricing formulas.
   b. It consists of adding a "reasonable" markup to the average cost of a product.
   c. This method takes into consideration cost variations at different levels of output.
   d. It assumes that the average cost for the next period will be different from that of the last period.
   e. All of the above are true statements.

5. Total cost usually:
   a. is zero at zero quantity.
   b. grows at a rate determined by increases in total variable cost.
   c. is the sum of total fixed and total marginal costs.
   d. grows at a rate determined by increases in total fixed cost.
   e. None of the above is a true statement.

6. The *major* weakness of average-cost pricing is that:
   a. it always leads to losses instead of profits.
   b. costs decline and rise at different levels of output.
   c. demand is ignored.
   d. average fixed cost increases as the quantity increases.
   e. All of the above.

7. Average cost pricing will result in *larger* than expected profit:
   a. most of the time.
   b. if the average fixed cost estimate is based on a quantity that is smaller than the actual quantity sold.
   c. if the average total cost is higher than expected.
   d. only if the manager makes arithmetic errors in computing average variable cost.
   e. None of the above is correct.

8. Trying to find the *most profitable* price and quantity to produce:
   a. requires average-cost pricing.
   b. requires an estimate of the firm's demand curve.
   c. is easy once the average fixed cost is known.
   d. is only sensible if demand estimates are exact.
   e. All of the above are true.

9. When a firm seeks to obtain some specific percentage return on its investment (or a specific total dollar return), it is using:
   a. break-even pricing.
   b. experience curve pricing.
   c. "what the traffic will bear" pricing.
   d. target return pricing.
   e. average-cost pricing.

10. A manufacturer who uses "target return" pricing sold 1,000 units of his product last year. He wants to earn a profit of at least $20,000 in the coming year. If his fixed costs are $40,000 and his variable costs equal $20 per unit, what price would he charge (assuming that he could still sell 1,000 units)?
    a. $60
    b. $40
    c. $80
    d. $120
    e. Cannot be determined with information given.

11. Break-even analysis assumes that:
    a. variable cost is constant per unit but varies in total.
    b. average fixed costs increases as quantity increases.
    c. the demand curve slopes downward and to the right.
    d. average variable cost first decreases and then increases as quantity increases.
    e. All of the above.

12. Assume that a producer's fixed costs amount to $240,000, its variable costs are $30 per unit, and it intends to sell its portable washer to wholesalers for $50. Given this information, the break-even point is:
   a. 8,000 units.
   b. 12,000 units.
   c. 14,000 units.
   d. 20,000 units.
   e. almost 50,000 units.

13. Given the following data, compute the BEP *in dollars*:
   Selling price = $1.25
   Variable cost = $ .75
   Fixed cost   = $45,000
   a. $36,000
   b. $60,000
   c. $90,000
   d. $112,500
   e. None of the above.

$$1.25x - .75x - 45,000 = 0$$
$$1.25x - .75x = 45,000$$
$$.5x =$$

14. Break-even analysis can be used for:
   a. relating prices to potential demand.
   b. comparing various assumed pricing alternatives.
   c. finding the most profitable price.
   d. estimating future sales.
   e. All of the above.

15. A monopolistic competitor's "marginal revenue":
   a. is always positive.
   b. is always shown above the corresponding down-sloping demand curve on a graph.
   c. is the change in total revenue that results from the sale of one more unit of a product.
   d. All of the above are true statements.
   e. Only a and c above are true statements.

16. The change in total cost that results from producing one more unit is called:
   a. average variable cost.
   b. marginal cost.
   c. average fixed cost.
   d. total variable cost.
   e. average total cost.

17. To maximize profit, a firm should:
   a. produce that output where marginal revenue is at a maximum.
   b. produce that output where marginal cost is just less than or equal to marginal revenue.
   c. produce that output where marginal cost is greater than marginal revenue.
   d. try to maximize the difference between marginal revenue and marginal cost.
   e. produce that output where marginal profit is at a maximum.

18. A marketing manager should be aware that the most profitable level of output:
    a. is where total revenue equals total cost.
    b. is where the difference between marginal revenue and marginal cost is the greatest.
    c. is where the vertical difference between total revenue and total cost is the greatest.
    d. is where marginal revenue is at a maximum.
    e. Both b and c are correct.

Use the following figure to answer questions 19-21.

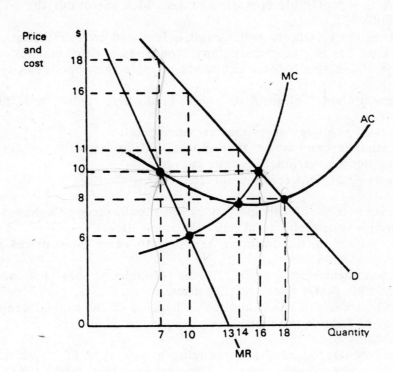

19. The most profitable quantity to sell would be:
    a. 7
    b. 10
    c. 13
    d. 14
    e. 18

20. The most profitable price would be:
    a. $6
    b. $8
    c. $10
    d. $16
    e. $18

21. The break-even point is:
    a. 10 units
    b. 13 units
    c. 14 units
    d. 16 units
    e. 18 units

22. In applying traditional economic analysis, a firm has discovered *two* break-even points--rather than a single break-even point. This means that:
    a. the firm's demand curve cannot be down-sloping.
    b. there is a profitable operating range which surrounds the point of maximum profit.
    c. seeking the maximum profit point is likely to prove fruitless.
    d. the firm has not experienced any economies or diseconomies of scale.
    e. None of the above--there can never be more than one break-even point.

23. Profit-maximizing oligopolists will find that their marginal cost curves intersect:
    a. marginal revenue curves that are horizontal.
    b. marginal revenue curves that appear to drop vertically at some prices.
    c. down-sloping marginal revenue curves.
    d. negative marginal revenue curves.

24. A "price leader" in an oligopoly situation should recognize that:
    a. "conscious parallel action" has been ruled illegal.
    b. other firms in the industry are sure to raise their prices if he raises his first.
    c. price cutting may occur if the "followers" are not able to make a reasonable profit at the market price.
    d. marginal analysis is not applicable because of the kinked demand curve.
    e. All of the above are true.

25. An equipment producer is introducing a new type of paint sprayer to sell to automobile body-repair shops. The sprayer saves labor time in painting the car, makes it possible to get as good a job with less expensive paint, and requires less work polishing after the car is painted. This company should use:
    a. leader pricing.
    b. bait pricing.
    c. complementary product pricing.
    d. odd-even pricing.
    e. value in use pricing.

26. Setting relatively high prices on products with perceived high status is known as:
    a. price lining.
    b. odd-even pricing.
    c. leader pricing.
    d. prestige pricing.
    e. bait pricing.

27. The manager of Green's Dress Shop has concluded that her customers find certain prices very appealing. Between these prices are whole ranges where prices are apparently seen as roughly equal--and price cuts in these ranges generally do not increase the quantity sold (i.e., the demand curve tends to drop vertically within these price ranges). Therefore, the manager has decided to price her dresses as close as possible to the top of each price range. This is known as:
    a. prestige pricing.
    b. bait pricing.
    c. leader pricing.
    d. psychological pricing.
    e. odd-even pricing.

28. The practice of setting different price levels for different quality classes of merchandise--with no prices between the classes--is called:
    a. full-line pricing.
    b. prestige pricing.
    c. price lining.
    d. odd-even pricing.
    e. psychological pricing.

29. "Demand-backward" pricing:
    a. is like leader pricing.
    b. has been called "market-minus" pricing.
    c. requires no demand estimates.
    d. is usually performed by retailers.
    e. All of the above are true statements.

30. Which of the following statements about "full-line pricing" is *true*?
    a. A marketing manager usually attempts to price products in the line so that the prices will seem logically related and make sense to potential customers.
    b. Most customers seem to feel that prices in a product line should be somewhat related to cost.
    c. The marketing manager must try to recover all his costs on the whole product line.
    d. Not all companies that produce a variety of products must use full-line pricing.
    e. All of the above are true statements.

31. With regard to bid pricing, a marketing manager should be aware that:
    a. the customer is always required to accept the lowest bid.
    b. since it costs very little to submit a bid, most firms try to bid for as many jobs as possible.
    c. the same overhead charges and profit rates usually apply to all bids.
    d. the major task is assembling all the costs--including the variable and fixed costs that apply to a particular job.
    e. All of the above are true statements.

Answers to Multiple-Choice Questions

1. e, p. 484	12. b, p. 493	23. b, p. 503
2. a, p. 485	13. c, p. 493	24. c, p. 504
3. e, p. 485-86	14. b, p. 495	25. e, p. 504
4. b, p. 487	15. c, p. 496	26. d, p. 506
5. b, p. 489	16. b, p. 497	27. d, p. 506
6. c, p. 490	17. b, p. 498	28. c, p. 507
7. b, p. 490	18. c, p. 499	29. b, p. 507
8. b, p. 490	19. b, p. 501	30. e, p. 508
9. d, p. 492	20. d, p. 501	31. d, p. 510
10. c, p. 492	21. e, p. 501	
11. a, p. 493	22. b, p. 502	

Exercise 19-1

Elements of cost-oriented price setting

Introduction

This exercise is designed to familiarize you with the arithmetic of cost-oriented pricing. Because most firms use cost-oriented methods to set prices, it is important that you understand these methods. Retailers and wholesalers, for example, use traditional markups that they feel will yield a reasonable rate of profit. You should be aware of how markups are figured. And you should know how stock turnover is calculated. Further, you should understand how the various types of costs differ, how they relate to each other, and how they affect profits as the sales volume varies.

Note: It is highly recommended that you review Appendix B: Marketing Arithmetic on pages 469-81 of the text before starting this exercise.

Assignment

Answer the following set of problems. Show your work in the space provided.

1.   The usual retail price of an item is $100.00. The manufacturer's cost to produce the item is $40.00. Retailers take a 40 percent markup and wholesalers take a 10 percent markup. (Note: markup is calculated on selling price, unless otherwise indicated.)

   a)   What is the retailer's markup in dollars? _____

   b)   What is the wholesale price? _____

   c)   What is the manufacturer's price? _____

d) What is the manufacturer's markup percentage? _____

e) What is the manufacturer's markup percentage *on cost*? _____

2. The Zang Manufacturing Company is trying to set its price on an item that will sell at retail for $60.00.

   a) For retailers to earn a markup of 40 percent, what should the wholesale price be? _____

   b) For the wholesalers in 2a to earn a markup of 20 percent, what should the manufacturer's price be? _____

3. Complete the following table. *Hint:* start with the first column and work to the right, column by column.

Item	Quantity produced				
	0	1	2	3	4
Total cost					$90
Total fixed cost	$30				
Total variable cost			$30		
Average cost				$25	
Average fixed cost					
Average variable cost		$15			

4. a) Using the data from Question 3, plot the total cost, total fixed cost, and total variable cost curves on the following graph.

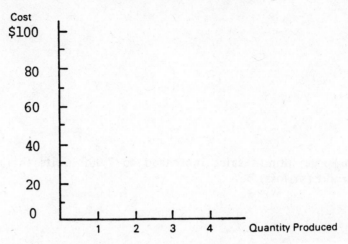

    b) Using the data from Question 3, plot the average cost, average fixed cost, and average variable cost curves on the following graph.

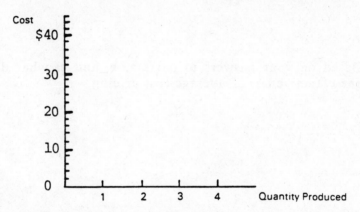

5. Mono Corp. has fixed costs of $3,000,000 and average variable costs of $100 per unit at all levels of output. It wishes to earn a profit of $300,000 this year--which is an increase of 10 percent over last year when Mono sold 5,000 units of its product.

    a) Use the average-cost pricing method to determine what price Mono should charge for its product.

b)   Suppose Mono were only able to sell 4,000 units this year because of increased competition. What would its profit (or loss) be?

c)   Suppose Mono's sales increased to 7,000 units this year. What would its profit (or loss) be?

d)   Based on your answers to parts a, b, and c, what do you conclude about the effectiveness of average-cost pricing?

6.   Suppose in Question 5 that Mono had decided to use "target return" pricing instead of average-cost pricing. Suppose further that it wished to earn a 20 percent return on its investment of $500,000.

a)   What price should Mono charge for its product?

b) What would Mono's return on investment be if it were only able to sell 4,000 units?

c) What would Mono's return on investment be if its sales increased to 7,000 units?

Question for Discussion

Why do so many firms use cost-oriented pricing methods when such methods have so many obvious shortcomings?

Exercise 19-2

Using break-even analysis to evaluate alternative prices

Introduction

Break-even analysis can be a very useful tool for evaluating alternative prices--especially when the prices being considered are fairly realistic from a demand point of view. Break-even analysis shows how many units would have to be sold--or how much dollar volume would have to be achieved--to just cover the firm's costs at alternative prices. A realistic appraisal of the likelihood of achieving the break-even point associated with each alternative price might show that some prices are clearly unacceptable--that is, there would be no way that the firm could even reach the break-even point, let alone make a profit.

The mechanics of break-even analysis are relatively simple--once you understand the concepts and assumptions of break-even analysis. This exercise reviews these ideas and then has you apply them to a fairly common decision-making situation.

Assignment

Read each of the following problems carefully--and fill in the blanks as you come to them. Where calculations are required, make them in the space provided--and show your calculations to aid review.

1. Study the break-even chart in Figure 19-2a and answer the following questions:

   a) According to Figure 19-2a, at what quantity, total revenue, and price will the firm break even?

      Quantity _____ Total Revenue _____ Price _____

   b) The firm's total fixed cost in this situation is: _____

   c) The firm's average variable cost (AVC) is: _____

   d) Using the information in Figure 19-2a, plot the firm's *demand curve* (D), *average fixed cost curve* (AFC), and *average variable cost curve* (AVC) in Figure 19-2b. Label each curve and both axes.

FIGURE 19-2a
Break-Even Chart

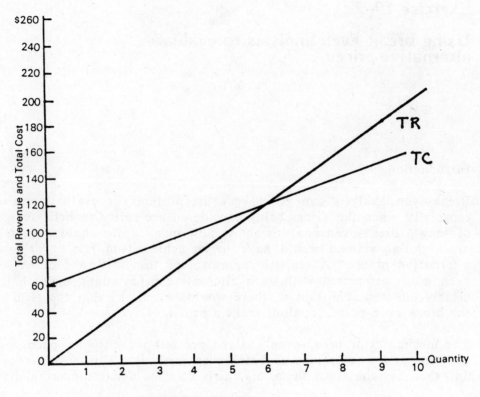

FIGURE 19-2b

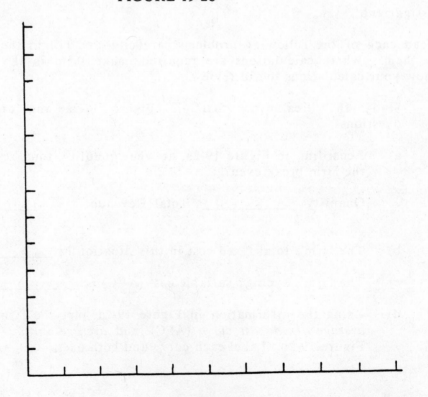

e) Using Figure 19-2a, draw the total revenue curve which would be relevant if the firm were considering a price of $35 per unit. Given this price of $35 per unit, at what quantity and total revenue would the firm break even?

Quantity _____ Total Revenue _____

f) What price should the firm charge to maximize profits--the price you calculated in (a) or $35? Why?

2. a) Suppose you were considering going into the car-washing business and investing in a new kind of car-washing unit which is more mechanized than the usual ones--but also has higher fixed costs. Calculate the break-even point in dollars and units if the usual price of $4.00 per car were charged. The variable cost per car is estimated at $2.00. The total fixed cost per year (including depreciation, interest, taxes, fixed labor costs, and other fixed costs) is estimated at $320,000.

BEP in $ _____ BEP in units _____

b) There is some possibility that there will be price cutting in your proposed market in the near future. Calculate the BEPs for the situation in (a) if the retail price drops to $3.50 per car.

BEP in $ _____ BEP in units _____

c) There is also a possibility that the new washing unit will deliver a better job for which some people will be willing to pay more. Calculate the new BEPs if it were possible to raise the retail price to $4.50.

BEP in $ _____ BEP in units _____

d) Should you go into the car-washing business in *any* of the above situations? Explain.

Question for Discussion

Looking at Figures 19-2a and 19-2b, what does break-even analysis assume about the nature of demand and about the competitive environment? Is break-even analysis relevant for monopolistic competition?

Exercise 19-3

Setting the most profitable price and quantity to produce

Introduction

Demand must be considered when setting prices. Ignoring demand curves does not make them go away. Usually, a market will buy more at lower prices--so total revenue *may* increase if prices are lowered. But this probably won't continue as the price gets closer to zero. Further, total cost--and perhaps average costs--will increase as greater quantities are sold.

So, if a firm is at all interested in making a profit (or avoiding losses), it should consider demand and cost curves *together*. This exercise shows how this can be done--and emphasizes that not all prices will be profitable.

Assignment

Figure 19-3 shows the XYZ Manufacturing Company's estimated total revenue and total cost curves for the coming year. Study this figure carefully and answer the questions which follow.

FIGURE 19-3

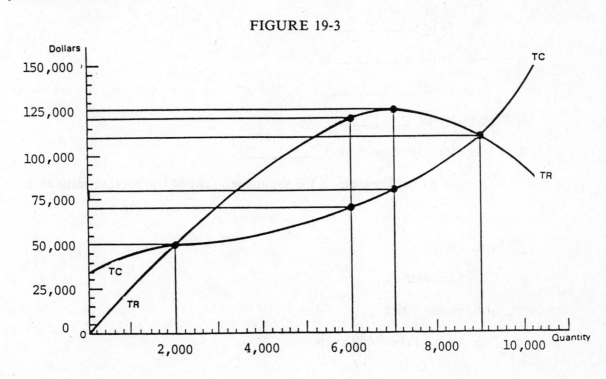

1. Complete the following chart by referring to Figure 19-3--the graph of XYZ's total costs and revenues.

Quantity	Total Cost	Average Cost	Total Revenue	Price*	Total Profit (Loss)
2,000	_____	_____	_____	_____	_____
6,000	_____	_____	_____	_____	_____
7,000	_____	_____	_____	_____	_____
9,000	_____	_____	_____	_____	_____

*Remember: Total Revenue = Price X Quantity
            Total Profit = Total Revenue - Total Cost

Using the information from Question 1, and Figure 19-3, answer Questions 2-11.

2. Given that Total Revenue = Price X Quantity, what should XYZ's price be if it wants to get the most total revenue it can and plans to sell:

    a.   2,000 units: _____

    b.   6,000 units: _____

    c.   7,000 units: _____

    d.   9,000 units: _____

3. What would XYZ's average cost per unit be at:

    a.   2,000 units: _____

    b.   6,000 units: _____

    c.   7,000 units: _____

    d.   9,000 units: _____

4. XYZ has total fixed costs of: $ _____

5. To maximize its *total revenue*, XYZ should sell (check the correct response):

    _____ a.   2,000 units.

    _____ b.   6,000 units.

    _____ c.   7,000 units.

    _____ d.   8,000 units.

    _____ e.   more than 9,000 units.

6. Figure 19-3 indicates that XYZ's demand curve is (check the correct response):

_____ a. horizontal.

_____ b. vertical.

_____ c. downward-sloping from left to right.

_____ d. upward-sloping from left to right.

7. XYZ's demand curve is (check the correct response):

_____ a. elastic.

_____ b. inelastic.

_____ c. unitary elastic.

_____ d. elastic up to 7,000 units and inelastic beyond 7,000 units.

_____ e. inelastic up to 7,000 units and elastic beyond 7,000 units.

8. XYZ's *average* cost curve is (check the correct response):

_____ a. horizontal.

_____ b. U-shaped.

_____ c. vertical.

_____ d. upward-sloping from left to right.

9. XYZ will *lose money* if it sells (check the correct response):

_____ a. less than 2,000 units.

_____ b. less than 9,000 units.

_____ c. more than 7,000 units.

_____ d. more than 9,000 units.

_____ e. both a and d are correct.

10. XYZ will *break even* if it sells (check the correct response):

_____ a.   2,000 units.

_____ b.   6,000 units.

_____ c.   7,000 units.

_____ d.   9,000 units.

_____ e.   both a and d are correct.

11. To *maximize profit*, XYZ should sell (check the correct response):

_____ a.   2,000 units.

_____ b.   6,000 units.

_____ c.   7,000 units.

_____ d.   9,000 units.

_____ e.   more than 9,000 units.

12. The maximum amount of profit XYZ can earn is: $ _____

Question for Discussion

Should a firm in monopolistic competition try to sell as many units as it can produce? Why or why not? State your assumptions.

Exercise 19-4

Using marginal analysis to set the most profitable price and quantity to produce

Introduction

Too many firms seem to ignore demand--depending almost blindly on cost-oriented pricing. A firm might operate quite profitably using cost-oriented pricing--but could it earn larger profits by charging a different price? The firm has no way of answering this question unless it also takes demand into consideration. When both costs and demand are known (or estimated), marginal analysis can be used to determine the most profitable price and the most profitable quantity to produce. Of course, in the short run the firm's objective may *not* be to maximize profit. In this case, marginal analysis can be used to show how much profit is "lost" when the firm pursues some other objective--such as maximizing sales.

This exercise uses the graphic approach to marginal analysis. You are asked to interpret--from a graph--the relationships among demand, price, quantity, average cost, marginal cost, and marginal revenue. (See page 496 in the text.)

Assignment

Use Figure 19-4 on the next page to answer the following questions:

1. At what price would 130 units be sold? _____

2. How many units would be sold if the firm priced its product at $40?
    _____

3. At what output (quantity) _____ and price _____ would the average cost per unit be *minimized*?

4. At what output _____ and price _____ would the firm break even?

5. At what output _____ and price _____ would the firm maximize its *total revenue*?

6. At what output _____ and price _____ would the firm maximize its *total profit*?

7. What will the average profit per unit be when the firm maximizes its total profit? _____

8. What is the maximum amount of profit this firm can earn? _____

FIGURE 19-4

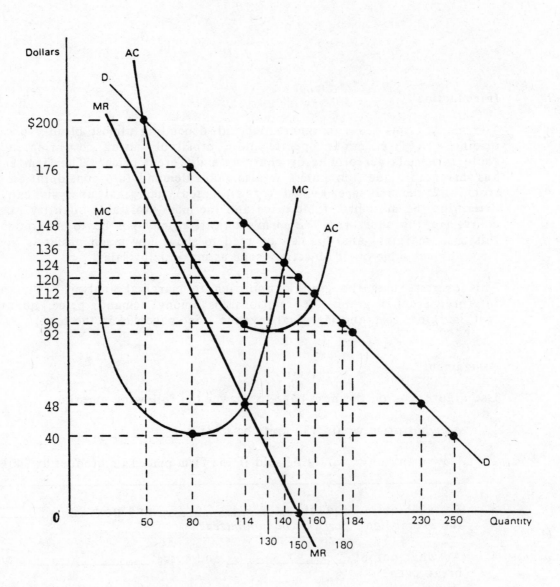

Question for Discussion

Why do so few firms use demand-oriented pricing? Is it an impossible task?

Exercise 19-5

Break-even/profit analysis

This exercise is based on computer-aided problem number 19--Break-even/Profit Analysis. A complete description of the problem appears on pages 32-33 of *Computer-Aided Problems to Accompany Basic Marketing.*

1. The marketing manager is interested in how the break-even point--in both units and sale dollars--changes as fixed costs vary. Do a What If analysis (using the break-even column on the left side of the spreadsheet) to vary fixed costs between $27,000 and $33,000 (that is, plus or minus 10 percent from the initial $30,000 level). See how the break-even point changes and fill in the missing numbers in the table below. Then, briefly explain the pattern you observe.

Fixed Cost Level	Break-Even (units)	Break-Even (sales)
$27,000	_____	$_____
$_____	72,000	$_____
$30,000	_____	$_____
$_____	_____	$95,400
$33,000	_____	$_____

Explanation: _____

_____

_____

_____

_____

2. The marketing manager is also interested in how variable cost changes affect break-even. If fixed cost remains at $30,000 and price and other variables stay the same, what happens to the break-even points (units and dollar sales) as the variable cost varies between $.72 and $.88--that is, plus or minus 10 percent from the initial value of $.80 a unit? As you did above, fill in the missing values in the table on the next page, and briefly explain the pattern you observe.

Average Variable Cost	Break-Even (units)	Break-Even (sales)
$.72	_____	$_____
$_____	68,182	$_____
$.80	_____	$_____
$_____	_____	$105,882.10
$.88	_____	$_____

Explanation: _____

_____

_____

_____

_____

3. The marketing manager is also considering what happens if fixed costs and variable costs change at the same time. For the two combinations of fixed cost and variable cost shown below, what are the break-even points in units and dollars?

Fixed Cost	Variable Cost	Break-Even (units)	Break-Even (dollars)
$27,000	$.84	_____	$_____
$33,000	$.76	_____	$_____

In the first situation above, fixed cost decreased and variable cost increased from the original (spreadsheet) situation. In the second, fixed cost increased and variable cost decreased. Once the break-even point is achieved, which of these combinations would earn profits the fastest as additional units are sold? Briefly explain why.

_____

_____

_____

_____

Chapter 20

Planning and implementing marketing programs

What This Chapter Is About

Chapter 20 emphasizes that marketing strategy planning requires creative *blending* of all the ingredients of the marketing mix. And, eventually, a marketing manager must develop a time-related *plan* that spells out the implementation details for a strategy. Then, since most companies have more than one strategy, marketing managers should develop a whole marketing *program* which integrates the various plans.

You need an estimate of potential sales to know if a marketing plan will be profitable. So this chapter explains different methods for forecasting sales. You should become familiar with the different methods and their likely accuracy-- because each has advantages *and* disadvantages. Some firms make several forecasts on the way to developing one final estimate of future sales.

Sales forecasting must consider not only market potential but also the firm's (and competitors') marketing plans--and how customers might respond to those plans. The concept of a response function is introduced to show the kind of thinking that applies here. Unfortunately, the shapes of response functions must be estimated in each particular situation. But just as with demand curves, which do not go away if they are ignored, response functions *should be* considered in strategy planning-- because they show the potential effectiveness of alternative strategies. Even crude estimates of response functions are better than none.

Since Chapter 9, we have been discussing various aspects of the four Ps. The product classes and the product life cycle are integrating themes which have been running through these chapters. This chapter highlights these ideas. A product's class and stage in the life cycle can suggest some "typical" marketing mixes. In addition, some special factors are discussed which should help you understand why and when typical mixes might be suitable--and when it would be desirable to modify the typical to develop the firm's own unique marketing strategy.

Following selection of a firm's marketing program, implementation efforts may be helped by some flow-charting techniques, which are explained toward the end of the chapter.

Important Terms

market potential, p. 517
sales forecast, p. 517
trend extension, p. 517
factor method, p. 519
factor, p. 519
time series, p. 521

leading series, p. 521
indices, p. 521
jury of executive opinion, p. 523
response function, p. 527
threshold expenditure level, p. 530
task method, p. 541

True-False Questions

___ 1. A marketing strategy is a "big picture" of what a firm will do in some target market--while a marketing plan includes the time-related details for that strategy--and a marketing program is a combination of the firm's marketing plans.

___ 2. Market potential is an estimate of how much a whole market segment might buy.

___ 3. A major limitation of trend extension is that it assumes that conditions in the past will continue unchanged into the future.

___ 4. National economic forecasts available in business and government publications are often of limited value in forecasting the potential of a specific market segment.

___ 5. The factor method of sales forecasting tries to find a relation between a company's sales and data on some other factor which is readily available.

___ 6. A factor is a variable which shows the relation of some other variable to the item being forecasted.

___ 7. The main problem with the "buying power index" (BPI) is that it is based on just one factor--population.

___ 8. A leading series is a time series which, for some reason, changes in the opposite direction but ahead of the series to be forecasted.

___ 9. Indices are statistical combinations of several time series.

___ 10. "Trend-projecting" forecasting techniques should probably be supplemented by a "jury of executive opinion" or some other type of judgmental approach.

___ 11. Instead of relying heavily on salespeople to estimate customers' intentions, it may be desirable for a firm to use marketing research techniques such as surveys, panels, and market tests.

___ 12. Annual forecasts of national totals such as GNP are likely to be more accurate than industry sales forecasts--and in turn industry sales forecasts will almost always be more accurate than estimates for individual companies and individual products.

___ 13. When marketers fully understand the needs and attitudes of their target markets, they may be able to develop marketing mixes which are obviously superior to "competitive" mixes.

___ 14. A response function shows (mathematically or graphically) how a firm should respond to changing customer needs and attitudes.

___ 15. The response functions for each of the four Ps tend to have the same shapes for all firms--regardless of the target market.

___ 16. The typical general marketing effort response function shows that there is a straight-line relationship between marketing expenditures and sales.

___ 17. Usually there is some threshold expenditure level which is needed just to be in a market--and therefore that expenditure level may be necessary to get any sales at all.

___ 18. Typical marketing mixes are a good starting point for developing possible marketing mixes--and estimating their response functions.

___ 19. Even if you don't know as much as you would like about potential customers' needs and attitudes, knowing how they would classify your product--in terms of the product classes--can give you a starting point in developing a marketing mix.

___ 20. Even low-priced items such as newspapers may be distributed directly if they are purchased frequently and the total volume is large.

___ 21. Some products--because of their technical nature, perishability, or bulkiness--require more direct distribution than is implied by their product class.

___ 22. Aggressive, market-oriented middlemen usually are readily available and eager to handle the distribution of any new products.

___ 23. Distribution through national middlemen will generally guarantee a new producer fairly uniform coverage in all geographic markets.

___ 24. Some wholesalers enter a channel of distribution mainly because they can give financial assistance to other channel members.

___ 25. A company's own size affects its place in a channel system--because size affects discrepancies of quantity and assortment.

___ 26. Typically, marketing variables should change during a product's life cycle.

___ 27. Finding the best marketing program requires some juggling among the various plans--comparing profitability versus resources needed and available.

___ 28. Budgeting for marketing expenditures as a percentage of either past or forecasted sales leads to larger marketing expenditures when business is good and sales are rising--and to reduced spending when business is poor.

___ 29. The most sensible approach to budgeting marketing expenditures is the "task method."

___ 30. Marketing program implementation efforts can be greatly aided by use of PERT--which stands for Product Evaluation and Rating Techniques.

Answers to True-False Questions

1. T, p. 516	11. T, p. 524	21. T, p. 533
2. T, p. 517	12. T, p. 524	22. F, p. 534
3. T, p. 518	13. T, p. 527	23. F, p. 534
4. T, p. 518	14. F, p. 527	24. T, p. 535
5. T, p. 519	15. F, p. 529	25. T, p. 535
6. T, p. 519	16. F, p. 530	26. T, p. 535
7. F, p. 521	17. T, p. 530	27. T, p. 540
8. F, p. 521	18. T, p. 531	28. T, p. 541
9. T, p. 521	19. T, p. 532	29. T, p. 541
10. T, p. 523	20. T, p. 533	30. F, p. 542

Multiple-Choice Questions (Circle the correct response)

1. The main difference between a "strategy" and a "marketing plan" is:
   a. that a plan does not consider the firm's target market.
   b. that a plan includes several strategies.
   c. that time-related details are included in a plan.
   d. that resource commitments are made more clear in a strategy.
   e. There is no difference.

2. As defined in the text, market potential is:
   a. what a market segment might buy (from all suppliers).
   b. how much a firm can hope to sell to a market segment.
   c. how much the firm sold to a market segment in the last year.
   d. the size of national income for the coming year.

3. The trend-extension method often can be useful for forecasting annual sales, but it depends upon the assumption that:
   a. the forecast is for a new product.
   b. sales during the coming period will be about the same as the previous period.
   c. there will be big changes in market conditions.
   d. the general growth (or decline) which has been seen in the past will continue in the future.
   e. the firm will continue to improve its marketing mixes.

4. You have been asked to develop a sales forecast for one of your company's major products. What would be the most logical *starting point*?
   a. Determine why the company's sales fluctuate the way they do.
   b. Consider the prospects for the economy as a whole.
   c. Determine your industry's prospects for the near future.
   d. Analyze regional sales for this product for last year.
   e. Perform marketing research into consumer buying habits.

5. *Sales & Marketing Management* magazine's "Buying Power Index" is based on:
   a. each market's share of the total U.S. population.
   b. each market's share of the total income in the United States.
   c. each market's share of the total retail sales in the United States.
   d. All of the above.
   e. Only a and b above.

6. Given the complexity of buyer behavior, sales forecasts for established products are likely to prove more accurate if based on:
   a. market tests.
   b. trend extension.
   c. a single factor.
   d. several factors.

7. Sales forecasters often try to find business indicators which change before sales and thus will help predict future sales. These indicators are called:
   a. correlation coefficients.
   b. time series.
   c. leading series.
   d. trend extenders.
   e. input-output measures.

8. Q.R. Smith Specialist, Inc., has developed a new product about which it is quite excited. Which of the following sales forecasting methods would be *least appropriate*?
   a. Market tests
   b. Sales force estimates
   c. Trend extension
   d. Jury of executive opinion
   e. A survey of customers

9. Which of the following sales forecasting techniques would be most useful for the marketing manager of an industrial products manufacturer facing intense competition?
   a. Sales force estimates
   b. Jury of executive opinion
   c. Use of a national economic forecast
   d. Trend extension of past sales
   e. Multiple-factor method

10. A company which wants to *objectively* estimate the reaction of customers to possible changes in its marketing mix should use:
   a. trend extension.
   b. jury of executive opinion.
   c. sales force estimates.
   d. surveys, panels, and market tests.
   e. None of the above.

11. Generally, the *largest* percentage error in a forecast should be expected when forecasting:
   a. sales for well-established products.
   b. industry sales.
   c. sales for a new product for a company.
   d. a company's total sales.
   e. national economic forecasts.

12. Developing a "marketing plan":
   a. means selecting a target market and developing a marketing mix.
   b. involves nothing more than assembling the four Ps better than your competitors.
   c. is easy--and profits are virtually guaranteed--provided that a firm fully understands the needs and attitudes of its target market.
   d. All of the above are true statements.
   e. None of the above is a true statement.

13. A "response function":
   a. shows how target customers are expected to react to changes in marketing variables.
   b. measures the firm's performance in responding to customer needs.
   c. generally focuses on the whole marketing mix--not each of the four Ps.
   d. is usually shown on a graph in the form of a U-shaped curve.
   e. All of the above are true statements.

14. The following response function for product quality indicates that:

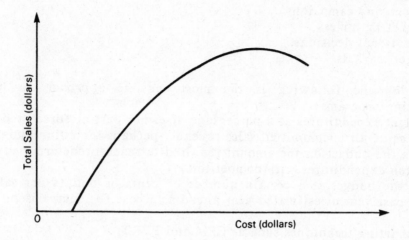

a. consumers want as much product quality as it is possible to provide.
b. product quality is the most important element in a firm's marketing mix.
c. the ideal level of expenditure for product quality is at the point where sales are at a maximum.
d. expenditures to increase product quality can produce diminishing or negative returns.
e. there is no "threshold expenditure level" for product quality.

15. Marketing strategy planners should keep in mind that:
a. there will be different response functions for different target markets.
b. different response functions for alternative marketing mixes can be compared to select the "best" mix.
c. response functions for each of the four Ps are useful--but the firm also needs a general marketing effort response function.
d. there usually is not a straight-line relationship between marketing expenditures and sales.
e. All of the above are true statements.

16. A manufacturer of a consumer product is trying to establish brand recognition and preference in monopolistic competition. The firm places considerable emphasis on channel development and is becoming somewhat less selective in its choice of middlemen. Promotion is both informative and persuasive--as the firm is seeking to increase both primary and selective demand. Prices in the industry are competitive--but there has been little price-cutting to date. What stage of the product life cycle is this firm's situation characteristic of?
a. Market introduction
b. Market growth
c. Market maturity
d. Sales decline

17. A marketing program can be best described as consisting of several:
    a. marketing plans.
    b. advertising campaigns.
    c. marketing mixes.
    d. operational decisions.
    e. target markets.

18. Which of the following is the most sensible approach to budgeting for marketing programs?
    a. Budget expenditures as a percentage of either past or forecasted sales.
    b. Set aside all uncommitted sales revenue--perhaps including budgeted profits.
    c. Base the budget on the amount required to reach predetermined objectives.
    d. Match expenditures with competitors.
    e. Set the budget at a certain number of cents or dollars per sales unit--using the past year or estimated year ahead as a base for comparison.

19. Flow-charting techniques such as CPM and PERT:
    a. require that all marketing activities must be done in sequence.
    b. do not indicate how long a project will actually take to complete.
    c. identify the tasks which must be performed to achieve predetermined objectives.
    d. require complex mathematical tools and analysis.

Answers to Multiple-Choice Questions

1. c, p. 516	8. c, p. 523	15. e, p. 529
2. a, p. 517	9. a, p. 523	16. b, p. 536
3. d, p. 517	10. d, p. 524	17. a, p. 539
4. b, p. 518	11. c, p. 524	18. c, p. 541
5. d, p. 520	12. e, p. 524-27	19. c, p. 542-43
6. d, p. 521	13. a, p. 527	
7. c, p. 521	14. d, p. 528	

Exercise 20-1

Using the "Survey of Buying Power" to estimate market and sales potential

Introduction

All marketers are faced with the ongoing problem of forecasting market and sales potentials. Forecasting is as much an art as a science--and many different forecasting methods can be used. Regardless of which method is used, the forecast should be based on data that is accurate, reliable, and up to date.

Many forecasters rely very heavily on data published in *Sales and Marketing Management's* annual "Survey of Buying Power" (see pages 520-21 of the text). The "Survey" provides data on three important market characteristics--population, "Effective Buying Income," and retail sales. Population is reported by age group. "Effective Buying Income" (comparable to disposable income) is broken down into four income groups, and retail sales are shown for six store categories. Further, the data is broken down geographically according to Metropolitan Statistical Areas, counties, and cities.

While similar U.S. census data is published every 10 years, the "Survey of Buying Power" data is published each year. Moreover, "Survey" estimates have been shown to do a good job updating the census data on which they are based. A disadvantage, however, is that "Survey" data, like all published data, may not be available in the exact form a particular firm desires. Most firms find it necessary to modify the data or supplement it with other data--before making their forecasts.

Probably the most widely used part of the "Survey" is the "Buying Power Index" (BPI), a weighted index of three variables--population, Effective Buying Income, and retail sales--which measures a market's *ability* to buy as a percentage of the total U.S. potential. The BPI is calculated by giving a weight of 5 to the market's percent of the U.S. Effective Buying Income, a weight of 3 to its percent of U.S. retail sales, and a weight of 2 to its percent of the U.S. population. The sum of those weighted percents is then divided by 10 to arrive at the BPI--as shown in the formula below:

$$BPI = \frac{5(\% \text{ U.S. Effective Buying Income}) + 3(\% \text{ U.S. Retail Sales}) + 2(\% \text{ U.S. Population})}{10}$$

For example, suppose Anytown, U.S.A., had about 5 percent of the total U.S. Effective Buying Income, about 4 percent of U.S. retail sales, and about 1 percent of the U.S. population. Then the BPI for Anytown is found by substituting these percentages into the formula above:

$$\frac{5(5) + 3(4) + 2(1)}{10} = 3.9$$

Thus Anytown's market potential--relative to the entire United States--would be 3.9 percent. So if Americans were expected to buy $10,000,000 worth of "widgets" during the coming year, the population of Anytown might be expected to buy 3.9 percent X $10,000,000, or $390,000 worth of widgets.

FIGURE 20-1

Sample Tables from *Sales and Marketing Management's* "Survey of Buying Power"

CAL. S&MM ESTIMATES			POPULATION—12/31/85							RETAIL SALES BY STORE GROUP 1985					
METRO AREA County City	Total Population (Thousands)	% Of U.S.	Median Age of Pop.	% of Population by Age Group				House-holds (Thousands)	Total Retail Sales ($000)	Food ($000)	Eating & Drinking Places ($000)	General Mdse ($000)	Furniture/ Furnish./ Appliance ($000)	Auto-motive ($000)	Drug ($000)
				18–24 Years	25–34 Years	35–49 Years	50 & Over								
ANAHEIM - SANTA ANA	**2,124.0**	**.8819**	**31.4**	**12.9**	**19.1**	**21.2**	**21.8**	**755.0**	**15,352,829**	**2,829,803**	**1,824,914**	**1,828,476**	**825,230**	**3,600,576**	**454,459**
Orange	2,124.0	.8819	31.4	12.9	19.1	21.2	21.8	755.0	15,352,829	2,829,803	1,824,914	1,828,476	825,230	3,600,576	454,459
• Anaheim	238.6	.0991	30.7	14.2	19.6	19.5	22.1	87.1	1,776,605	330,393	279,948	221,045	130,782	331,156	53,481
Buena Park	66.4	.0276	30.1	14.2	17.6	21.4	20.0	22.2	650,811	100,406	49,620	87,982	18,970	219,746	29,986
Costa Mesa	87.4	.0363	30.9	16.4	23.1	19.2	21.3	34.7	1,400,325	130,851	110,095	214,919	69,676	429,614	14,779
Cypress	42.5	.0176	31.0	12.1	14.9	27.4	16.7	13.3	157,584	43,613	23,643	13,547	5,532	33,652	5,808
Fountain Valley	56.1	.0233	31.2	9.7	15.5	29.3	14.8	16.5	338,298	103,093	34,920	60,640	23,439	16,033	12,069
Fullerton	109.0	.0453	31.5	15.3	19.1	19.5	23.7	40.5	799,911	148,918	95,528	120,904	28,695	220,438	28,775
Garden Grove	131.9	.0548	30.7	13.4	18.2	20.1	22.1	45.0	807,705	198,897	94,165	57,861	34,453	211,838	27,605
Huntington Beach	183.1	.0760	30.6	13.1	20.6	23.1	17.7	65.9	1,183,465	223,768	115,182	171,585	84,597	260,242	37,526
Irvine	84.7	.0352	30.3	11.3	23.9	25.4	13.4	29.8	562,767	115,036	76,467	3,279	10,494	259,170	17,367
La Habra	48.2	.0200	31.6	13.8	17.8	19.2	24.8	17.7	304,293	50,165	35,601	29,281	23,517	71,350	17,651
Newport Beach	67.1	.0279	37.6	12.4	18.0	23.3	31.1	29.8	812,014	107,984	156,276	97,530	18,361	214,678	18,941
Orange	99.1	.0411	31.1	12.8	18.4	21.4	21.5	34.4	984,229	133,455	111,975	139,869	56,723	217,162	24,524
• Santa Ana	226.4	.0940	28.1	14.7	21.3	16.8	18.5	71.4	1,578,004	285,582	157,653	129,542	116,271	458,436	43,645
Westminster	74.5	.0309	31.4	12.1	17.4	22.1	21.6	25.4	682,920	116,066	43,082	116,845	44,350	184,200	13,185
SUBURBAN TOTAL	1,659.0	.6888	32.0	12.4	18.7	22.1	22.2	596.5	11,998,220	2,213,828	1,387,313	1,477,889	578,177	2,810,984	357,333
BAKERSFIELD	**475.8**	**.1976**	**30.3**	**11.8**	**17.6**	**18.2**	**23.6**	**169.5**	**2,676,721**	**620,314**	**278,631**	**253,242**	**128,177**	**606,436**	**90,703**
Kern	475.8	.1976	30.3	11.8	17.6	18.2	23.6	169.5	2,676,721	620,314	278,631	253,242	128,177	606,436	90,703
• Bakersfield	142.8	.0593	29.8	12.9	20.6	17.6	21.7	54.2	1,462,078	213,980	143,190	203,907	94,324	443,057	54,699
SUBURBAN TOTAL	333.0	.1383	30.6	11.3	16.3	18.4	24.4	115.3	1,214,643	406,334	135,441	49,335	33,853	163,379	36,004
CHICO	**166.7**	**.0692**	**33.2**	**14.5**	**17.2**	**15.6**	**31.3**	**67.4**	**929,536**	**250,530**	**91,207**	**96,499**	**40,120**	**171,040**	**51,368**
Butte	166.7	.0692	33.2	14.5	17.2	15.6	31.3	67.4	929,536	250,530	91,207	96,499	40,120	171,040	51,368
• Chico	30.8	.0128	24.9	34.2	20.3	11.4	17.9	12.5	395,025	97,466	49,062	18,444	25,450	84,107	13,230
SUBURBAN TOTAL	135.9	.0564	35.7	10.1	16.5	16.4	34.4	54.9	534,511	153,064	42,145	78,055	14,670	86,933	38,138
FRESNO	**578.8**	**.2403**	**30.3**	**12.6**	**18.2**	**17.8**	**23.7**	**207.2**	**3,071,465**	**655,537**	**267,519**	**339,962**	**155,910**	**727,178**	**151,982**
Fresno	578.8	.2403	30.3	12.6	18.2	17.8	23.7	207.2	3,071,465	655,537	267,519	339,962	155,910	727,178	151,982
• Fresno	280.2	.1163	29.9	13.9	20.3	16.1	23.7	107.5	1,977,194	336,497	169,795	314,443	117,623	452,890	93,514
SUBURBAN TOTAL	298.6	.1240	30.8	11.3	16.3	19.4	23.7	99.7	1,094,271	319,040	97,724	25,519	38,287	274,288	58,468

CAL. S&MM ESTIMATES	EFFECTIVE BUYING INCOME 1985							CAL. S&MM ESTIMATES	EFFECTIVE BUYING INCOME 1985						
METRO AREA County City	Total EBI ($000)	Median Hsld EBI	% of Hslds by EBI Group (A) $10,000–$19,999 (B) $20,000–$34,999 (C) $35,000–$49,999 (D) $50,000 & Over				Buying Power Index	METRO AREA County City	Total EBI ($000)	Median Hsld EBI	% of Hsids by EBI Group (A) $10,000–$19,999 (B) $20,000–$34,999 (C) $35,000–$49,999 (D) $50,000 & Over				Buying Power Index
			A	B	C	D					A	B	C	D	
ANAHEIM - SANTA ANA	**31,573,345**	**33,131**	**17.2**	**25.8**	**20.5**	**26.3**	**1.0702**	Huntington Beach	2,823,617	35,247	15.4	25.6	21.8	28.7	.0911
Orange	31,573,345	33,131	17.2	25.8	20.5	26.3	1.0702	Irvine	1,585,747	45,209	8.8	21.6	24.0	41.7	.0474
• Anaheim	3,235,765	29,312	20.0	28.0	19.4	20.6	.1158	La Habra	669,927	30,683	18.5	28.3	21.0	21.1	.0225
Buena Park	875,501	33,035	16.2	28.2	23.4	22.7	.0351	Newport Beach	1,641,295	39,045	14.7	21.0	15.7	38.5	.0523
Costa Mesa	1,271,269	28,724	20.5	28.5	18.1	20.4	.0601	Orange	1,388,762	32,545	18.2	25.1	20.9	24.9	.0542
Cypress	617,532	40,566	11.1	23.2	25.3	34.1	.0180	• Santa Ana	2,378,405	26,809	21.9	29.5	19.6	14.7	.0952
Fountain Valley	810,777	43,597	10.1	20.6	26.7	38.7	.0264	Westminster	1,018,794	34,025	16.3	25.8	23.4	24.8	.0391
Fullerton	1,686,906	31,435	18.3	26.1	18.6	25.5	.0564								
Garden Grove	1,709,010	31,655	17.7	28.0	22.3	21.3	.0588	SUBURBAN TOTAL	25,959,175	34,613	16.3	25.0	20.8	28.5	.8592

It should be noted that there is nothing sacred about the weights used to calculate the BPI. Many firms tailor the index to their own needs by applying a different set of weights or adding additional variables to the index based on their past experience. A manufacturer of snowmobiles, for example, might add a weather variable, such as average inches of snowfall, to the BPI. A potential pitfall in applying the BPI is that because it is broadly based, the BPI is said to be most useful for "mass products sold at popular prices." Thus, for more expensive products, the BPI may need to be modified by taking additional buying factors into account.

Assignment

The purpose of this exercise is to familiarize you with the Buying Power Index and to show its use in forecasting market and sales potential. Answer each of the following questions and show your work in the space provided.

1.   Suppose that Apex, U.S.A., accounts for 3 percent of the U.S. population, 5 percent of the nation's Effective Buying Income, and 3 percent of U.S. retail sales. Calculate Apex's "Buying Power Index."

2.   Reading from Figure 20-1, what is the Buying Power Index for:

   a)   the Anaheim-Santa Ana metropolitan area: _____

   b)   Orange county: _____

   c)   the city of Anaheim: _____

3.   a)   About 8,000,000 electric toasters are sold in the United States each year. Based on the Buying Power Index, estimate the number of toasters that are sold in the Anaheim-Santa Ana metropolitan area each year. Label your calculations.

b)   Assume that your firm has captured a 10 percent share of the electric toaster market. About how many electric toasters should your firm sell in the Anaheim-Santa Ana metropolitan area?

c)   Suppose your firm sold 4,000 electric toasters last year in the Anaheim-Santa Ana metropolitan area. Given your answer to part (b) above, what does this fact indicate?

4.   Assume that a firm with an annual sales of $2,000,000 sells its products *only* in the Anaheim-Santa Ana metro area. In order to allocate its sales force to different cities within the Anaheim-Santa Ana metro area, the firm's sales manager wants to know what volume of sales the firm can expect in each city. Use the BPI to estimate the firm's sales volume in dollars *for the city of Anaheim only*. (Hint: Although the percentages reflected in the BPI are relevant for the entire United States--not just the Anaheim-Santa Ana metro area--the *relative positions* of the different cities within this area remain the same.) Explain your answer.

5.   Suppose a national manufacturer of expensive diamond jewelry wanted to estimate its sales potential in the Anaheim-Santa Ana metropolitan area. Would the BPI be useful for this purpose? Why or why not?

Question for Discussion

Would the "Survey of Buying Power" data be more useful to "mass marketers" or "target marketers"? Why?

Exercise 20-2

Using response functions to help plan marketing mixes

Introduction

A "response function" shows (mathematically and/or graphically) how a firm's target market is expected to respond to changes in marketing variables. This concept may seem rather "academic"--but it is not. Marketing managers must make judgments about the likely responses of their potential customers to alternative marketing mix variables. Whether they actually attempt to draw such curves--or only have "gut feelings"--is not important. What *is* important is that they must have *some* feeling for how marketing expenditures affect sales or profits if they are to have any hope of making effective use of the firm's resources. Just as demand curves do not "go away" if they are ignored--response functions will not "go away" either.

At the same time, it is only fair to say that estimating response functions is not easy. A lot of information and judgment is needed--and even then the results are only "guesstimates." For this reason, most marketers have not done much with response functions. However, most do try to make rough estimates of how sales would increase if a few more salespeople were added, or an additional $50 thousand was allocated to advertising, and so on. Basically, they are attempting to estimate one or a few points on the relevant response function. This is all they feel they need--so they do not bother to estimate the whole function. This may be a practical approach--but it also may cause the marketing manager to under- or overuse some variables--perhaps missing their most productive range, where sales rise sharply with small increases in marketing effort.

This exercise seeks to deepen your understanding of response functions. You are asked to identify the shapes of response functions for several different markets and marketing mixes. Also, you are asked to analyze a few response functions and decide which ones you would use in different budget situations.

Assignment

1. The marketing manager of a large consumer products firm has not yet selected a target market--and is in the process of estimating how different market segments would respond to different marketing mix variables. She is focusing on how each of four segments would respond to variations in advertising expenditures (other marketing expenditures remaining constant). Her descriptions of each segment are summarized on the next page. Study each

description and then indicate which of the response functions shown in Figure 20-2 is most relevant for each segment. (Note: use all the choices.)

FIGURE 20-2

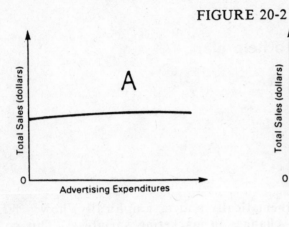 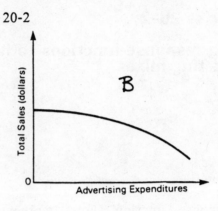

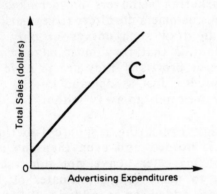 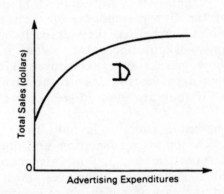

a) ____ This group relies on advertising for information about products. They are open to persuasion when the product appears to satisfy their needs reasonably well. Once they become aware of a product, they tend to make a fairly quick decision about whether to purchase--and repurchase--it.

b) ____ This group buys on "impulse" and responds well to the "power of suggestion." They have much exposure to mass media--and their buying behavior is described very well by the classical stimulus-response model.

c) ____ This group is antiestablishment, nonmaterialistic, and hostile toward "big business." They believe that producers use advertising to manipulate consumers--and are likely to boycott firms that try to "shove products down our throats." Members of this group have very strong negative feelings, for example, about children's TV shows being sponsored by cereal or toy manufacturers.

d) ____ This group behaves like "economic men." Advertising has little influence on their purchases. They watch relatively little TV--spending much of their time reading books, scientific journals, and consumer-oriented publications such as *Consumer Reports*.

2. Use Figure 20-3 in answering the following questions:

FIGURE 20-3

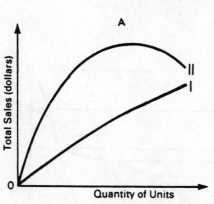

A

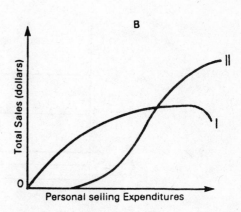

B

a) Graph A shows two response functions for the same target market. Each curve indicates a different price/quantity relationship--i.e., the response functions are alternative total revenue curves. Assuming that one response function suggests "skimming pricing"--while the other suggests "penetration pricing"--indicate which is which. Explain your answer.

b) Graph B shows two response functions for the same target market--one shows the use of manufacturers' agents to sell a firm's new product--and the other shows the use of the firm's own sales force to sell the new product (with all other marketing expenditures held constant). Indicate which response function reflects the use of manufacturers' agents and which shows the use of the firm's own sales force. Explain your answer.

FIGURE 20-4

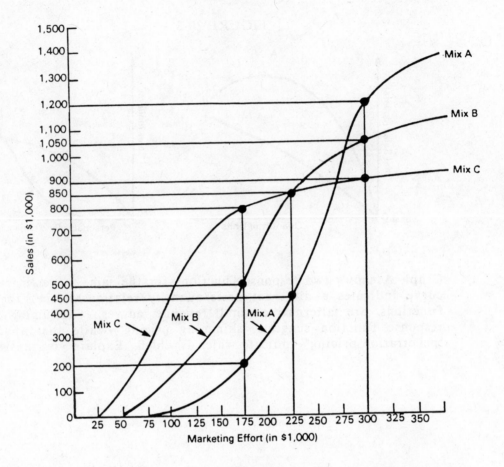

3.   Figure 20-4 shows three estimated response functions which show how a firm's target market is likely to respond to each of three alternative marketing mixes. Explain which marketing mix the firm should choose and *why* if:

a)   its budget for the coming year provides $175,000 for marketing expenditures:

b)   its budget for the coming year provides $225,000 for marketing expenditures:

c)   its budget for the coming year provides $300,000 for marketing expenditures:

Question for Discussion

Do response functions *really* have any value for marketing strategy planners--given the difficulty of estimating the shape of response functions for individual marketing variables and for alternative marketing mixes?

Name: _____ Course & Section: _____

Exercise 20-3

Adjusting marketing strategies over the product life cycle

Introduction

A marketing manager must take a dynamic approach to marketing strategy planning. Markets are continually changing--and today's successful strategy may be tomorrow's failure. Competitive advantages are often achieved and maintained by firms who are best able to anticipate and respond positively to changes in their uncontrollable environments. Some changes may be completely unpredictable, of course--but other changes may be somewhat predictable and should be planned for in advance. Otherwise, by the time the planner realizes that some important changes have taken place, it may be too late to adjust an existing strategy or, if necessary, to plan a new strategy.

Among the changes that are more predictable--and which should be considered when developing marketing plans--are the typical changes in marketing mix variables which are often made over the course of a product life cycle. Exhibit 20-10 on page 536 of the text shows some of these typical changes.

Assignment

This exercise stresses how marketing strategies may need to be adjusted over the product life cycle. Read the following case and follow the instructions.

ELECTRO, INC.

Electro, Inc. manufactures a broad line of electric equipment for industrial buyers. Its sales and profits have stopped growing in recent years--and the firm's top executives are anxious to diversify into the consumer products market. However, they do not want to enter a new market with just another "me too" product. Instead, they hope to discover a real "breakthrough opportunity"--an unsatisfied market with large profit potential.

For several years, Electro's marketing research and product planning departments have been working together in search of an innovative new product for the firm's entry into the consumer market. Now, the top executives believe that they have finally found such a product. The new product is an "electric breakfast cereal maker" for do-it-yourselfers. The cereal maker can use "commodity-type" ingredients (milk, eggs, oats, rice, oil, fruits, and nuts) which are available at most

Learning Aid to Accompany Basic Marketing

20-17

FIGURE 20-5
Planned Changes in Marketing Strategy for Cereal Maker
over the Course of Its Product Life Cycle

Item	Market Introduction Stage
Target market dimensions	
Nature of competition	
Product	
Place	
Promotion	
Price	

McCarthy and Perreault

Market Growth Stage	Market Maturity Stage

supermarkets. It has the capacity to mix and cook up to two-pound batches of "your own blend of cereal" for about half the price of similar store-bought cereal. It is expected to retail for about $100.

Electro's marketing manager believes the new product will appeal to budget-minded families and individuals--and also health-conscious people who want to eat a nutritious, "natural" food with no preservatives added. He feels the product has almost unlimited potential--citing the recent success of electric yogurt makers in what is probably a much smaller market (i.e., many more people eat cereal than yogurt in the United States). Further, the firm's research and development staff is sure that it will take any potential competitors at least a year to introduce a similar product.

The electric breakfast cereal maker is really a revolutionary new concept--and will probably require a major promotion effort to gain consumer acceptance. Moreover, Electro has no established channels of distribution in the consumer products market--and middlemen may be reluctant to handle an unproven product which lacks a well-known brand name. Also, the firm is not sure what pricing policies to adopt, because it has no previous experience in the consumer products market.

To further complicate his strategy planning efforts, Electro's marketing manager recognizes that he will probably need to modify his marketing strategy over time-- as the new product passes through the various stages of its life cycle. So that the firm will be in a position to adjust quickly to changing market conditions, he wishes to plan his future marketing strategies for the cereal maker--as well as his beginning strategy.

1. Assume the role of marketing manager for Electro, Inc. and fill in Figure 20-5 to show how your marketing strategy for the electric cereal maker would vary over the stages of its product life cycle. (See Exhibits 20-10 and 20-11 on pages 536-37 of the text for some general ideas about what you might include in your answers.) Be specific.

Question for Discussion

What kind of product will the "electric breakfast cereal maker" be--that is, what product class--and what type of marketing mix would be typical for such a product? Are there any other factors that should be taken into account in planning the marketing mix for this product?

McCarthy and Perreault

Exercise 20-4

Comparing marketing mixes

This exercise is based on computer-aided problem number 20--Comparing Marketing Mixes. A complete description of the problem appears on page 33 of *Computer-Aided Problems to Accompany Basic Marketing*.

Sunco's marketing manager wants to do some additional analysis of Marketing Mix B and Marketing Mix C--beyond the situation on the initial spreadsheet.

1. As a starting point, he is interested in how much gross margin is earned by the sale of one unit with either marketing mix. While he did not program this on the spreadsheet, it is simple to calculate--by subtracting the unit cost from the selling price per unit. What is the gross margin per unit for each mix?

	Mix B			Mix C
	_____ selling price		_____	selling price
minus	_____ unit cost	minus	_____	unit cost
equals	_____ unit gross margin	equals	_____	unit gross margin

2. Will a marketing mix with a higher unit gross margin always be more profitable? Briefly explain your answer.

_____

_____

_____

_____

_____

3. Neither proposed marketing mix uses newspaper advertising. But Sunco's marketing manager is considering adding it. The cost of the newspaper ads will vary depending on the number and size of the ads--but could add up to $10,000 of total advertising expense. Sunco's marketing manager is wondering what the effect of the added advertising expense will be on the break-even point for each marketing mix. For Marketing Mix B, do a What If analysis in which advertising expense varies between $20,000 and $30,000 (that is, a possible increase of up to $10,000). Then answer the following questions.

What is the break-even point (in units) if advertising expense is $23,000?

_____ units needed to break even with $23,000 advertising

What is the break-even point (in units) when advertising increases to $24,000?

_____ units needed to break even with $24,000 advertising

Now, look at this analysis from a different perspective. How many additional units must be sold to break even each time an additional $1,000 is spent on advertising?

_____ increase in units required to break even each time $1,000 of advertising expense is added

4. Do a What If analysis varying advertising expense for Marketing Mix C from $30,000 to $40,000 (that is, a possible increase of up to $10,000). Then answer the questions below.

For Marketing Mix C, what is the break-even point (in units) if advertising expense is $35,000?

_____ units needed to break even with $35,000 advertising

What is the break-even point (in units) when advertising increases to $36,000?

_____ units to break even with $36,000 advertising

For Marketing Mix C, how many additional units must be sold to break even each time an additional $1,000 is spent on advertising?

_____ increase in units required to break even each time $1,000 of advertising expense is added

Think about the results you have reported above, and then briefly explain why each additional dollar of advertising expense has a different effect--in terms of additional units required to break even--with the two different marketing mixes.

_____

_____

_____

_____

_____

Chapter 21

Controlling marketing plans and programs

What This Chapter Is About

Chapter 21 shows that a wealth of information may be available from a firm's own records. But it will be useless unless the marketing manager knows how it can be obtained and used--and then asks for it!

Various sales and cost analysis techniques are presented in this chapter. They can be useful for evaluating and controlling the marketing activities of a firm. These techniques are not really complicated. They require only simple arithmetic, and perhaps a computer if a large volume of adding and subtracting is required.

Be sure to distinguish between straightforward sales or cost analysis and performance analysis. Also, be sure to distinguish between the full-cost approach and the contribution-margin approach to cost analysis. Each can be useful in certain situations. But uncritical use of either method might lead to the wrong decision.

This is an important chapter. Marketing plans are not always easy to implement. The marketing manager must know how to use these control-related tools. They help keep a plan on course--and point to situations where a new plan is needed.

Important Terms

control, p. 547
sales analysis, p. 548
performance analysis, p. 549
performance index, p. 551
iceberg principle, p. 556

natural accounts, p. 557
functional accounts, p. 557
full-cost approach, p. 562
contribution-margin approach, p. 563
marketing audit, p. 569

True-False Questions

_____ 1. Control is the feedback process that helps the marketing manager learn how ongoing plans are working and how to plan for the future.

_____ 2. Because of the 80/20 rule--traditional accounting reports are usually of great help to marketing managers in controlling their plans and programs.

_____ 3. Routine sales analyses are best done by manually reviewing data stored in sales invoice files.

___ 4. The best way to analyze sales data is to break it down by geographic region and customer type.

___ 5. Sales analysis provides a detailed breakdown of company sales records, but with no attempt to compare them against standards. Performance analysis seeks exceptions or variations from planned performance.

___ 6. A performance index is a number--such as a baseball batting average--which shows the relation of one value to another.

___ 7. A well-designed performance analysis will not only solve marketing problems--but may also be used to forecast sales.

___ 8. The "iceberg principle" suggests that while averaging and summarizing data can be helpful to managers--they should be sure that these summaries do not hide more than they reveal.

___ 9. Because most marketing expenditures are made for the general purpose of "increasing sales," detailed marketing cost analysis is all but impossible--and most marketing expenditures should be treated as general overhead costs.

___ 10. While *functional* accounts are the categories to which various costs are charged in the normal accounting cycle--*natural* accounts are set up to indicate the *purpose* for which the expenditures are made.

___ 11. The first step in marketing cost analysis is to reclassify all the dollar cost entries in the functional accounts into natural accounts.

___ 12. Marketing cost analysis can be used to analyze not only total company profitability--but also the profitability of territories, products, customers, salespeople, or any other breakdowns desired.

___ 13. Marketing cost analysis is NOT performance analysis--but if the marketing manager has budgeted costs to various tasks, it would be possible to extend the cost analysis to a performance analysis.

___ 14. The full-cost approach requires that difficult-to-allocate costs be split on some basis.

___ 15. Although the contribution-margin approach focuses management attention on variable cost--rather than total cost--it is likely to lead to the same marketing decisions as the full-cost approach.

___ 16. While full-cost analysis is especially useful for evaluating alternatives, the contribution-margin approach does a better job of showing individuals within the firm how much they have actually contributed to general overhead and profit.

___ 17. For most firms, the biggest obstacle to using marketing cost analysis is not the amount of data processing that is required--but rather the need for marketing managers to insist that the necessary data be collected.

___ 18. Ideally, a marketing audit should not be necessary because a good manager should continually evaluate the effectiveness of his operation--but, in practice, a marketing audit is probably needed because too many managers are "so close to the trees that they can't see the forest."

Answers to True-False Questions

1. T, p. 547	7. F, p. 552	13. T, p. 562
2. F, p. 548	8. T, p. 556	14. T, p. 563
3. F, p. 548	9. F, p. 557	15. F, p. 563
4. F, p. 549	10. F, p. 557	16. F, p. 566
5. T, p. 549	11. F, p. 557	17. T, p. 567
6. T, p. 551	12. T, p. 558	18. T, p. 569

Multiple-Choice Questions (Circle the correct response)

1. According to the "80/20 rule":
   a. marketing accounts for 80 percent of the consumer's dollar.
   b. only 20 out of every 100 firms use formal marketing control programs.
   c. about 20 percent of a typical firm's customers are unprofitable to serve.
   d. even though a firm might be showing a profit, 80 percent of its business might be coming from only 20 percent of its products or customers.

2. A marketing manager who wants to analyze his firm's sales should be aware that:
   a. sales invoice files contain little useful information.
   b. the best way to analyze sales data is according to geographic regions.
   c. sales analysis involves a detailed breakdown of a company's sales forecasts.
   d. sales analysis may not be possible unless he has made arrangements for collecting the necessary data.
   e. a manager can never have too much data.

3. Performance analysis differs from sales analysis in that performance analysis involves:
   a. detailed breakdowns of a company's sales records.
   b. analyzing only the performance of sales representatives.
   c. comparing performance against standards--looking for exceptions or variations.
   d. analyzing only people--not products or territories.
   e. budgeting for marketing expenditures on the basis of contribution margins.

4. If Salesperson X had a performance index of 80 and Salesperson Y had a performance index of 120, then:
   a. Salesperson X may be having some problems and his sales performance should be investigated.
   b. the two would average out to 100--and this would suggest that "all is well."
   c. Salesperson X's performance should be investigated as a guide to improving everyone's performance.
   d. Salesperson Y probably should be fired.
   e. Salesperson Y obviously had higher sales than Salesperson X.

5. Which of the following statements best describes the "iceberg principle"?
   a. Problems in one area may be offset by good performances in other areas--and thus the problems may not be visible on the surface.
   b. Ten percent of the items in inventory usually account for 80 percent of the sales.
   c. Within a company's sales force there are usually one or two sales reps who don't carry their weight.
   d. Many sales reps do not make their quotas because they ignore certain clients.
   e. Airfreight is less risky than shipping by boat.

6. Which of the following statements regarding marketing cost analysis is *false*?
   a. Functional accounts include items such as salaries, social security, taxes, raw materials, and advertising.
   b. The costs allocated to the functional accounts will be equal in total to those in the natural accounts.
   c. Functional accounts can be used to show the profitability of territories, products, customers, sales representatives, and so on.
   d. Cost analysis is not performance analysis.
   e. Traditional accounting methods do not show the purpose for which marketing expenditures are made.

7. If one were using the "full-cost" approach to marketing cost analysis, then allocating fixed costs on the basis of sales volume would:
   a. make some customers appear more profitable than they actually are.
   b. not be done--because only variable costs would be analyzed.
   c. make some products appear less profitable than they actually are.
   d. decrease the profitability of the whole business.
   e. Both a and c are true statements.

8. Which of the following statements about the contribution-margin approach is *false*?
   a. It is concerned with the amount contributed by an item or group of items toward covering fixed costs.
   b. This approach suggests that it is not necessary to consider all functional costs in all situations.
   c. It is not used by many accountants because the net profit obtained using this approach is misleading.
   d. This approach frequently leads to data which suggest a different decision than might be indicated by the full-cost approach.
   e. It focuses on controllable costs--rather than on total costs.

9. Which of the following statements about a "marketing audit" is *true*?
   a. A marketing audit should be conducted only when some crisis arises.
   b. It probably should be conducted by someone inside the marketing department who is familiar with the whole program.
   c. A marketing audit should evaluate the company's whole marketing program-- not just some parts of it.
   d. A marketing audit should be handled by the specialist most familiar with each of the marketing plans in the program.
   e. All of the above are true statements.

Answers to Multiple-Choice Questions

1. d, p. 548	4. a, p. 552	7. e, p. 565
2. d, p. 548	5. a, p. 556	8. c, p. 565
3. c, p. 549	6. a, p. 557	9. c, p. 569

Exercise 21-1

Sales and performance analysis

Introduction

This exercise shows how sales analysis and performance analysis might be used to help plan and control marketing programs. *Sales analysis* begins with a detailed breakdown of the company's sales records and can take many forms--since there is no one best way to analyze sales data. As outlined in the text, any one of several sales breakdowns may be appropriate--depending on the nature of the company, its products, and which strategies are being evaluated.

Performance analysis seeks exceptions or variations from planned performance. In contrast to simple sales analysis--where facts and figures are merely listed--performance analysis involves the use of predetermined standards against which actual results are compared. Here, the purpose is to determine where--and why--performance was better or worse than expected.

Sales analysis and performance analysis can be useful in pinpointing operating problems which may require corrective action--or in identifying areas in which the company may be performing exceptionally well. Such analyses will *not* reveal *what* is causing a given problem--nor will they provide a *solution* to the problem. This requires sound management judgment--both in interpreting the data and in developing solutions. By using sales and performance analyses, however, marketing managers can rely on factual evidence--rather than guesswork--when problems do arise--and thereby improve the quality of their decision making. Better yet, by continually auditing their marketing programs--by analysis of well-chosen data--they may be able to anticipate problems and take action *before* they become serious.

Assignment

Assume you are the marketing manager for a small manufacturer of electrical products. Your company's products are sold by five sales reps--each serving a separate territory--who earn a straight commission of 10 percent of sales. The company's accountant has just given you the data shown on the next page describing last year's sales. Actual sales were less than expected, so you decide to analyze the data further to help you decide what to do.

TABLE 21-1

Sales Territory	Sales Quota	Actual Sales	Total Calls	Total Orders	Total Customers
A	$ 960,000	$ 480,000	1,200	360	420
B	600,000	600,000	1,320	780	300
C	720,000	360,000	480	300	240
D	900,000	1,080,000	1,560	1,200	480
E	360,000	540,000	720	360	120
Total	$3,540,000	$3,060,000	5,280	3,000	1,560

1. a) Calculate a *sales performance index* for each sales territory. Show your work. One answer is provided as an example:

Territory A:

Territory B:

Territory C:

Territory D: ($1,080,000 / 900,000) X 100 = 120.0

Territory E:

b) What do the performance indices indicate about the relative selling performance of each salesperson? One answer is provided as an example.

Territory A:

Territory B:

Territory C:

Territory D: This salesperson's actual sales were much higher than expected for some reason. We should try to find out why.

Territory E:

McCarthy and Perreault

2. Some additional sales analysis would be desirable to help you decide *why* the sales reps performed as they did. Therefore, using the data in Table 21--1, make the necessary calculations to complete the following table. Some answers have been provided as a check on your work.

TABLE 21-2

Sales Territory	Order/Call Ratio	Average Sale per Order	Average Sale per Customer	Sales Commissions
A	30.0%			
B			$2000	
C				$36,000
D		$900		
E				
Average for All Territories	56.8%			

3. On the basis of your sales and performance analyses, what do you conclude about the sales performance of each salesperson? What factors would you want to investigate further before taking any corrective action?

Territory A:

Territory B:

Territory C:

Territory D:

Territory E:

Question for Discussion

Does the above analysis suggest any specific management action which was not clearly indicated by a review of Table 21-1? How does this illustrate the "iceberg principle"?

Exercise 21-2

Controlling marketing plans and programs with marketing cost analysis

Introduction

This exercise shows the importance of marketing cost analysis in controlling marketing plans and programs. Our focus will be on analyzing the profitability of different *customers*--but marketing cost analysis could also be used to determine the profitability of different *products*. (Try it!)

The first step in marketing cost analysis is to reclassify all the dollar cost entries in the natural accounts into functional cost accounts. This has already been done for you in this exercise--to simplify your work. The next step is to reallocate the functional costs to those customers (or products) for which the expenditures were made. Here, careful judgment is required--because although no single basis of allocation is "correct," in some cases one may be better (i.e., make more sense) than others. Further, the basis of allocation selected can have a very significant effect on the profitability of a customer (or product).

Assignment

1. Using the data in Tables 21-3 and 21-4, calculate profit and loss statements for each of three customers. Show your answers in Table 21-5. Where you must make allocations of costs to products or customers, indicate under "Comments" the basis of allocation you selected and why. (See the example on pages 558-62 of the text for suggestions.)

TABLE 21-3
Sales by Product

Product	Cost/Unit	Selling Price per Unit	Number of Units Sold	Items/Unit	Items Packaged
A	$11	$22	5,000	1	5,000
B	6	12	10,000	3	30,000
C	10	17	6,000	2	12,000

TABLE 21-4
Sales by Customer

			Number of Units of Each Product Ordered		
Customer	Number of Sales Calls	Number of Orders	A	B	C
1	20	10	500	4,000	1,000
2	25	20	2,000	3,500	3,000
3	15	10	2,500	2,500	2,000
Total	60	40	5,000	10,000	6,000

Other expenses from functional cost accounts:

Sales salaries	$48,000
Clerical expenses (order and billing)	12,000
Advertising	33,000
Packaging expenses	11,750
Administrative expenses	36,000

Comments:

TABLE 21-5
Profit and Loss Statement by Customer

	Customer 1	Customer 2	Customer 3	Whole Company
Net Sales:				
Product A				
B				
C				
Total Sales				
Cost of Sales				
Product A				
B				
C				
Total Cost of Sales				
Gross Margin				
Expenses:				
Sales Salaries				
Clerical Expenses				
Advertising				
Packaging Expenses:				
Product A				
B				
C				
Total Expenses . . .				
Net Profit (or Loss)				

2. What do you conclude from your analysis? Should any of the customers be dropped? Why or why not? What factors must you consider in answering this question?

Question for Discussion

Which of the two basic approaches to cost analysis--full cost or contribution margin--was used in the above exercise? Would your conclusions have been different if the other approach had been used? If so, which approach is "correct"?

McCarthy and Perreault

Exercise 21-3

Marketing cost analysis

This exercise is based on computer-aided problem number 21--Marketing Cost Analysis. A complete description of the problem appears on pages 33-34 of *Computer-Aided Problems to Accompany Basic Marketing*.

Tapco's marketing manager is considering changing the price of one or both products. He has decided to use the spreadsheet to analyze his idea more carefully.

1. At present, Tapco is selling 5,000 units of Product A for $10.00 each. Based on the full-cost approach, how much profit does Product A contribute to the company? What is its allocated administrative expense? Its allocated advertising expense?

    $_____ Net profit or loss-Product A

    $_____ Administrative expense-Product A

    $_____ Advertising expense-Product A

2. The marketing manager is considering raising the price of Product A to $12.00. He estimates that the quantity demanded will be only 3,725 at $12.00--but he is not certain how that will affect profits from Product A. Given his price and quantity estimates, use the full-cost approach column of the spreadsheet to compute the following information for this situation (a price increase).

    $_____ Net profit or loss-Product A

    $_____ Administrative expense-Product A

    $_____ Advertising expense-Product A

3. Based on these two analyses (1 and 2 above), is it a good idea to increase the price of Product A to $12.00? Briefly explain your answer.

    _____

    _____

    _____

    _____

    _____

    _____

4. Now, evaluate the same pricing change using the contribution-margin approach. What happens to the contribution margin for Product A at the higher price and lower quantity?

_____ contribution margin based on 5,000 units at $10 each

_____ contribution margin based on 3,725 units at $12 each

5. Based on the change in the contribution margin, is it a good idea to increase the price of Product A to $12.00? Briefly explain your answer.

_____

_____

_____

_____

6. Briefly explain why the effect of the price increase appears to be attractive using the full-cost approach--but unattractive using the contribution-margin approach. Be specific. (Be sure to consider Tapco's total profitability before answering.)

_____

_____

_____

_____

_____

7. Based on this analysis, Tapco's marketing manager decided not to increase the price of Product A. But he is also considering lowering the price of Product B to $5.50--because he thinks that the lower price will stimulate increased unit sales. But he is not certain exactly how much the quantity sold would increase. What (minimum) quantity should Tapco expect to sell to make a price reduction on Product B a good idea?

a minimum of _____ units of Product B at $5.50 each

Chapter 22

Marketing strategy planning for international markets

What This Chapter Is About

Chapter 22 highlights the types of opportunities that are available in international marketing. The typical evolution of corporate involvement in international marketing is explained. It is noted that some corporations become so deeply involved with international marketing that they become "multinational corporations."

Six stages of economic development are discussed--to suggest the varying marketing opportunities in different economies. The trend toward cooperation among neighboring countries is discussed--pointing up the need for marketers to think of running multinational operations.

This chapter stresses that much that has been said about marketing strategy planning throughout the text applies directly in international marketing. The major stumbling block to success in international marketing is refusal to learn about and adjust to different peoples and cultures. Try to see that making such adjustments is not impossible and that, therefore, your marketing strategy planning horizon probably should be broadened from domestic marketing to international marketing.

Important Terms

exporting, p. 575
licensing, p. 576
contract manufacturing, p. 576
management contracting, p. 577
joint venturing, p. 577

wholly-owned subsidiary, p. 578
multinational corporations, p. 578
tariffs, p. 584
quotas, p. 584
gross national product (GNP), p. 590

True-False Questions

____ 1. The United States is the largest exporter and importer of products in the world.

____ 2. When a manufacturer moves into exporting, it usually is primarily concerned with selling some of what the firm is currently producing to foreign markets.

____ 3. Licensing is a relatively easy--but risky--way to enter foreign markets.

____ 4. Management contracting--in international marketing--means turning over production to others, while retaining the marketing process.

_____ 5. A domestic firm wishing to enter international marketing can use a joint venture--which simply involves entering into a partnership with a foreign firm.

_____ 6. If a foreign market looked really promising, multinational corporations might set up a wholly-owned subsidiary--which is a separate firm owned by a parent company.

_____ 7. A multinational company is one that earns over 30 percent of its total sales or profits by exporting domestic production to foreign markets.

_____ 8. One reason for the movement of some multinational firms into the United States is that labor costs in other countries are rising.

_____ 9. The typical approach to becoming involved in international marketing is to start with the domestic firm's current products and the needs it knows how to satisfy.

_____ 10. Most industrial products tend to be near the "insensitive" end of the continuum of environmental sensitivity.

_____ 11. If the risks of getting into international marketing are difficult to evaluate, it usually is best to start with a joint venture.

_____ 12. Segmenting international markets is usually easy because so much good data is available.

_____ 13. Tariffs are simply quotas on imported products.

_____ 14. A nation in the first stage of economic development offers little or no market potential.

_____ 15. An excellent market for imported consumer products exists among countries or regions which are experiencing the second (preindustrial or commercial) stage of economic development.

_____ 16. When a nation reaches the primary manufacturing stage of economic development, it will begin to export a large portion of its domestic production of consumer products.

_____ 17. Once a nation reaches the fourth stage of economic development, it will usually manufacture most of its consumer durables--such as autos and televisions.

_____ 18. When a nation reaches the stage of capital equipment and consumer durable products manufacturing, industrialization has begun--but the economy still depends on exports of raw materials.

_____ 19. A nation which reaches the sixth stage of economic development normally exports manufactured products which it specializes in producing.

___ 20. A mass distribution system is desirable for any country--regardless of its present stage of economic development.

___ 21. The population of the United States is about 15 percent of the world's population.

___ 22. With the exception of a few densely populated cities around the world, most of the world's population is fairly evenly distributed in rural areas.

___ 23. The best available measure of income in most countries is gross national product (GNP).

___ 24. An analysis of literacy in various countries shows that only one tenth of the world's population can read and write.

___ 25. A basic concern in organizing for international marketing is to be sure that the firm transfers its domestic know-how into international operations.

Answers to True-False Questions

1. T, p. 574	10. T, p. 581	19. T, p. 587
2. T, p. 575	11. F, p. 582	20. F, p. 588
3. F, p. 576	12. F, p. 583	21. F, p. 588
4. F, p. 577	13. F, p. 584	22. F, p. 589
5. T, p. 577	14. T, p. 584	23. T, p. 590
6. T, p. 578	15. F, p. 585	24. F, p. 592
7. F, p. 578	16. F, p. 585	25. T, p. 593
8. T, p. 579	17. F, p. 586	
9. T, p. 580	18. T, p. 586	

Multiple-Choice Questions (Circle the correct response)

1. Marketing managers should be aware that:
   a. U.S. manufacturers export only about 3 percent of the goods they produce.
   b. customers in foreign markets are not much different from American customers.
   c. the United States is the largest exporter and importer of products in the world.
   d. most foreign trade involves the less-developed, less-industrialized nations.
   e. All of the above are true statements.

2. When a business firm in one country sells a firm in another country the right to use some process, trademark, or patent for a fee or royalty--this practice is called:
   a. exporting.
   b. contract manufacturing.
   c. joint ventures.
   d. licensing.
   e. management contracting.

3. To minimize its own risks, the Boomtown Petroleum Corp. of Houston, Texas, operates a South American oil refinery which is wholly owned by residents of that country. Boomtown is engaged in an activity known as:
   a. management contracting.
   b. a joint venture.
   c. exporting.
   d. licensing.
   e. contract manufacturing.

4. A multinational corporation:
   a. is any U.S.-based corporation with direct investments in several foreign countries.
   b. is one which sells the right to use some process, trademark, patent, or other right for a fee or royalty to foreign firms.
   c. is a worldwide enterprise which makes major decisions on a global basis.
   d. is any firm which earns over 30 percent of its sales and profits in foreign markets.
   e. All of the above are true statements.

5. An American firm trying to sell to customers in a foreign market should:
   a. use the same product and promotion it uses in the United States.
   b. keep its product the same--but adapt its promotion to meet local needs and attitudes.
   c. adapt both its product and its promotion to meet local needs and attitudes.
   d. develop a whole new product and a whole new promotion blend.
   e. Any of the above might be effective--depending on the opportunity.

6. According to the "continuum of environmental sensitivity":
   a. industrial products need to be adapted to foreign markets more than consumer products.
   b. faddy or high-style consumer products are easily adaptable to foreign markets and thus involve very little risk in international marketing.
   c. it is extremely risky to market basic commodities in international markets.
   d. some products are more adaptable to foreign markets than others--and thus may be less risky.
   e. All of the above are true statements.

7. International marketing:
    a. usually involves simply extending domestic marketing strategies to foreign countries.
    b. always involves a great deal of risk.
    c. requires far less attention to segmenting than domestic marketing.
    d. usually involves very complex and often unfamiliar uncontrollable variables.
    e. All of the above are true statements.

8. What stage of economic development is a country in when small local manufacturing of products such as textiles has begun and the dependence on imports for nondurable products is declining?
    a. Capital products and consumer durable products manufacturing stage
    b. Exporting of manufactured products stage
    c. Non-durable consumer products manufacturing stage
    d. Commercial stage
    e. Primary manufacturing stage

9. A multinational manufacturer will usually find the biggest and most profitable foreign markets for its products in countries that are in which of the following stages of economic development?
    a. Primary manufacturing
    b. Capital products and consumer durable products manufacturing
    c. Preindustrial or commercial
    d. Non-durable and semi-durable consumer products manufacturing
    e. Exporting manufactured products

10. Which of the following countries has the *highest* GNP per capita?
    a. United States
    b. India
    c. Sweden
    d. Israel
    e. Japan

Answers to Multiple-Choice Questions

1. c, p. 574
2. d, p. 576
3. a, p. 577
4. c, p. 578

5. e, p. 580
6. d, p. 581
7. d, p. 582
8. c, p. 585

9. e, p. 587
10. c, p. 592

Exercise 22-1

Strategy planning for international markets:
Consumer products

Introduction

Today, more and more firms are turning to international markets in search of new profit opportunities. Basically, marketing strategy planning is no different for international markets than for domestic markets. The firm should choose a target market and develop a marketing mix to satisfy the needs of that target market.

International marketing strategy planning can be much more difficult, however. Strategy planners must deal with unfamiliar, uncontrollable variables. And there may be big differences in language, customs, beliefs, religion and race, and even income distribution from one country to another. Even identical products may differ in terms of which needs they satisfy, the conditions under which they are used, and people's ability to buy them.

Further, reliable data for market analysis may be harder to obtain when a firm moves into international markets. The wealth of published data which American marketers tend to take for granted may not exist at all. And consumers in some countries are far less willing to take part in market research studies than most Americans.

This exercise shows how some market analysis might be done for international markets--and shows some of the common mistakes a marketer is likely to make in planning international marketing strategies.

Assignment

Read the following case and answer the questions which follow:

NATURAL BEVERAGE CORPORATION

The Natural Beverage Corporation recently developed a new beverage named "Constant Delight" which was expected to appeal to almost anyone who drinks beverages with meals. Constant Delight met with instant success when introduced for sale in the United States a year ago. Weekly sales far exceeded all previous forecasts--and at first the company had trouble producing enough of the product to satisfy demand.

Constant Delight did not appeal equally well to all Americans. According to a survey conducted by a market research firm, Constant Delight attracted about 30 percent of the tea drinkers in the country, 20 percent of the coffee drinkers, and about 25 percent of those who normally drink soft drinks. In each case, the Constant Delight buyers switched about 10 percent of their meal beverage purchases to Constant Delight. Little acceptance was achieved among wine, milk and water drinkers.

Encouraged by the success of Constant Delight, Natural Beverage Corporation decided to expand its market coverage overseas. The following four countries were being considered as potential new markets: England, France, Spain, and West Germany. However, only *one* of these countries could be chosen at the present time because of limited company resources. Therefore, the marketing manager of Natural Beverage was asked to decide which of the four countries would offer the highest dollar sales potential.

As a start, he obtained the market data shown in Table 22-1 by looking up the populations of the four countries in the *U.S. Statistical Abstract* and then asking a market research firm to estimate the average per capita expenditures in these countries for tea, coffee, and soft drinks. Next, he was able to determine the dollar sales potential for each country by estimating the percentage of tea drinkers, coffee drinkers, and soft drink users who could be expected to purchase Constant Delight. For example, if 30 percent of the tea drinkers in a country can be expected to switch 10 percent of their beverage purchases to Constant Delight, then the per capita expenditures on Constant Delight will be 3.0 percent (30 percent X 10 percent) of the per capita expenditure on tea, and so on.

TABLE 22-1
Estimated Average Annual per Capita Expenditures on
Selected Meal-Time Beverages in Four Countries

Country	Population	Per Capita Beverage Expenditures		
		Tea	Coffee	Soft Drinks
United Kingdom	56,400,000	$80	$40	$10
France	55,000,000	10	20	40
Spain	38,800,000	30	10	40
West Germany	60,900,000	20	60	80

1. Using the switching rates for domestic tea, coffee and soft drink drinkers, determine the dollar sales potential for Constant Delight in France, Spain, and West Germany by completing Table 22-2. The sales potential for the United Kingdom has already been calculated for you as an example.

TABLE 22-2
Per Capita Expenditures and Total Sales Potential for
Constant Delight in Four Countries

| Country | Per Capita Expenditures for Constant Delight by Beverage Switchers | | | Total per Capita Expenditure for Constant Delight | Total Sales Potential in Country |
	Tea	Coffee	Soft Drinks		
United Kingdom	$2.40	$.80	$.25	$3.45	$194,580,000
France					
Spain					
West Germany					

Calculations:

2. Which one of the four countries would offer the highest dollar sales potential for Constant Delight?

3. What do the above calculations assume about the Natural Beverage Corporation's potential target markets for Constant Delight?

4. Will Natural Beverage Corporation have to change its marketing mix when it expands overseas? Why or why not?

5. What type of involvement would you recommend for Natural Beverage Corporation in its efforts to expand into international markets--exporting, licensing, contract manufacturing, management contracting, joint ventures, or a wholly-owned subsidiary? Why?

Question for Discussion

The per capita beverage expenditures shown in Table 22-1 are just imaginary--but an actual market research study would no doubt show that beverage expenditures do in fact vary considerably among these and other countries. What factors might explain such differences in per capita beverage expenditure patterns? Should a firm's marketing strategy planning be based solely on such data *and* U.S. experience--or would further study or even test marketing be desirable?

Exercise 22-2

Strategy planning for international markets: Industrial products

Introduction

In Chapter 8, we saw that industrial products marketers should consider the number, kind, size, and location of potential customers--as well as the nature of the buyer and the buying situation. These same dimensions apply in both domestic *and* international markets. A key difference, however, is that the international marketer must first consider in which nation(s) the firm wishes to market its products.

The first step in segmenting international markets, therefore, is to conduct a *preliminary screening* of all prospective markets to determine in which regions or countries the firm may wish to operate.[1]

Although this preliminary screening should be as complete as possible--using all available information--it need not become a complex task. Some nations may be quickly ruled out as potential markets due to unfavorable climatic conditions, unfriendly political and legal environments, or the wrong stage of economic development.

For the remaining countries, published import-export data can be useful in sifting out attractive marketing opportunities from a wide choice of international markets. One excellent source of such data is the United Nations' *Commodity Trade Statistics* series. It provides import-export data for most countries on a quarterly basis-- broken down by commodity according to the Standard International Trade Classification (SITC).[2]

Assignment

This exercise shows the use of import-export data during the "preliminary screening" phases of international marketing. The exercise focuses on international markets for metalworking machinery (SITC #736.1). Read the following case and answer the questions that follow.

---

[1]Franklin R. Root, *Strategic Planning for Export Marketing* (Scranton, Pa: International Textbook Company, 1966), pp. 20-23.

[2]Standard International Trade Classification, Revised, *United Nations Statistical Papers*, Series M, No. 34.

TUCKER MACHINE WORKS

Tucker Machine Works of Smithfield, Ohio, manufactures a broad line of standard and custom-made metalworking machine tools. The firm has experienced a sharp decline in sales and profits in recent months--in part due to changes in tax laws which have made it less attractive for U.S. companies to invest in capital equipment.

In hopes of discovering new profit opportunities, Tucker's marketing manager is exploring the possibility of marketing the firm's products to customers outside the United States. Because of the firm's limited resources, the marketing manager plans to restrict the firm's international efforts to one region of the world at first--and to only a few countries within that region. Further--to avoid the intense competition often found in *developed* economies--he plans to focus on *developing* economies which offer considerable market potential.

As a first step in determining which regions or countries might be attractive markets for Tucker's products, the marketing manager turned to the most recent issue of the United Nations' *Commodity Trade Statistics* to locate data concerning U.S. exports of metalworking machinery to foreign nations. He discovered that U.S. exports for his commodity classification (SITC #736.1) totaled about $397 million for the previous year. Developed economies accounted for approximately 55 percent of this total, developing economies about 44 percent, and central planned economies only about 1 percent. The dollar value of U.S. machinery exports to *developing* economies was about $176,000,000--the bulk of which was distributed by region or trading group as follows:

Destination	Value of U.S. Exports
Africa	$ 28,678,000
Asia	31,738,000
Caribbean Nations	1,776,000
Central American Common Market	681,000
Latin American Free Trade Association	104,943,000
Middle East	8,941,000

From the above data, the marketing manager concluded that Tucker should concentrate its initial international marketing efforts on the Latin American Free Trade Association (LAFTA)--since its member nations accounted for almost 60 percent of the U.S. exports to developing economies. His next task was to select those LAFTA member nations which appeared to offer the most attractive market potential for metalworking machinery--using *Commodity Trade Statistics* export data for individual nations, as shown below.

LAFTA Member Nations	Value of U.S. Exports
Argentina	$ 6,611,000
Brazil	16,149,000
Chile	636,000
Colombia	2,282,000
Ecuador	419,000
Mexico	71,418,000
Peru	773,000
Venezuela	6,655,000

1. Based on the above data, which nations probably offer the most market potential for Tucker's metalworking machinery? Why? (Note: For the sake of simplicity, assume that all of these nations are equally "friendly" toward the U.S. firms. In an actual situation, a firm would, of course, have to carefully consider the political and legal environments in each country before selecting its target markets. But, for now, include any relevant text or classroom discussion as "input" to your answer to this and following questions.)

2. The data used in the above analysis include only U.S. exports of metalworking machinery to various regions or individual nations. Do these data accurately reflect the market potential offered by each region or nation? What very important uncontrollable variable would Tucker's marketing manager be overlooking if he based his preliminary screening on these data alone? How might he avoid making such an error?

3. In conducting his preliminary screening, should Tucker's marketing manager consider only those nations whose machinery imports have been relatively *high*--or should he also consider other nations whose machinery imports have been relatively *low*? Explain your answer, emphasizing what (specifically) you would want to know about each potential market.

4. Once Tucker's marketing manager has decided in which regions or countries the firm might wish to market its products, what else must he do *before* selecting the marketing strategy he will implement?

Question for Discussion

Some multinational firms reorganize themselves as worldwide operations to achieve foreign sales--instead of just exporting their domestic production. Would import-export data be useful to these firms? How?

Exercise 22-3

Export opportunities

This exercise is based on computer-aided problem number 22--Export Opportunities. A complete description of the problem appears on pages 34-35 of *Computer-Aided Problems to Accompany Basic Marketing*.

1. Weavco has found that one of the better import agents in Country B is already very knowledgeable about textile firms. This agent has assured Weavco's marketing manager that Weavco will not have to spend any money on marketing research if he is selected as Weavco's agent. On the other hand, this agent wants a 20 percent commission--not the 13 percent Weavco had expected to pay. Weavco still thinks that other agents are available at the 13 percent commission--but they might need marketing research assistance. What quantity would this (20 percent) agent have to sell for Weavco to break even in Country B? To earn its target profit of $50,000?

    _____ units to break even   _____% = share of market

    _____ units to reach target   _____% = share of market

2. Briefly discuss the main advantage and disadvantage of the proposed arrangement (in question 1) compared to Weavco's original plan.

    _____

    _____

    _____

    _____

    _____

3. Although he would like to avoid the "up-front" marketing research costs, Weavco's marketing manager is unwilling to pay the import agent a 20 percent commission. However, he thinks the agent might be willing to negotiate. Weavco's marketing manager is trying to decide what commission to offer. As a starting point, he has decided to determine the commission percent that would achieve Weavco's target profit with about the same unit sales as would have been required if the company paid some other agent a 13 percent commission, but paid for the research ($38,000). What commission percent would meet that requirement?

    _____ percent commission (which he might propose to import agent)

4. Weavco worked out an arrangement with the import agent. After some negotiation, the agent agreed to a 15.5 percent commission. However, the agent suggests that the Weavco machine would be more competitive--and sell faster--if the price were $1,000 lower. If Weavco were to lower the price, how many machines would it have to sell to break even in Country B? To reach its target profit?

_____ units to break even _____ units to earn target profit

Chapter 23

Marketing in a consumer-oriented society: appraisal and challenges

What This Chapter Is About

Chapter 23 provides an evaluation of the effectiveness of both micro- and macro-marketing. The text explains the authors' views, but their answers are far less important than their reasoning. It is extremely important to understand the arguments both pro and con--because the effectiveness of marketing is a vital issue. How well you understand this material--and how you react to it--may affect your own feelings about the value of business and the contribution you can make in the business world. Do not try to memorize the "right" answers. Rather, try to understand and evaluate the authors' reasoning. Then, develop your own answers.

When you have studied this chapter, you should be able to defend your feelings about the worth of marketing--using reasoned arguments rather than just "gut feelings." Further, you should have some suggestions about how to improve marketing--if you feel there are any weaknesses. Perhaps you yourself--as a producer and/or consumer--can help improve our market-directed system.

True-False Questions

____ 1. Although our economic objectives may change in the future, at the present time marketing probably should be evaluated according to the basic objective of the American economic system--which is to satisfy consumer needs--as *consumers see them*.

____ 2. Since individual consumer satisfaction is a very personal concept, it probably does not provide a very good standard for evaluating macro-marketing effectiveness.

____ 3. At the micro-level, marketing effectiveness can be measured--at least roughly--by the profitability of individual marketers.

____ 4. According to the text, macro-marketing does not cost too much, but micro-marketing frequently does cost too much, given the present objective of the American economic system--consumer satisfaction.

____ 5. One reason why micro-marketing often costs too much is that many firms are still production-oriented and not nearly as efficient as they might be.

____ 6. Companies should encourage dissatisfied customers to complain--and should make it easy for them to do so.

___ 7. According to the text, greater use of cost-plus pricing would result in better, more efficient, micro-marketing decisions.

___ 8. Our present knowledge of how consumers behave confirms the view that pure competition is the ideal way of maximizing consumer welfare.

___ 9. The performance of micro-marketing activities in monopolistic competition probably leads to the same allocation of resources that would be found in a pure competition economy--and no difference in consumer satisfaction.

___ 10. Despite its cost, advertising can actually *lower* prices to the consumer.

___ 11. According to the text, it is probably fair to criticize the marketplace for fulfilling consumers' "false tastes" because marketing creates most popular tastes and social values.

___ 12. A good business manager might find it useful to follow the following rule: "Do unto others as you would have others do unto you."

___ 13. Consumer advocates have placed great emphasis on the need for *consumers* to behave responsibly to make our macro-marketing system work.

___ 14. The text suggests that socially responsible marketing managers should try to limit consumers' freedom of choice for the good of society.

___ 15. Given the role that business is supposed to play in our market-directed system, it seems reasonable to conclude that a marketing manager should be expected to improve and expand the range of goods and services made available to consumers.

___ 16. Market-oriented business managers may be even more necessary in the future if the marketing system is expected to satisfy more subtle needs--such as for the "good life."

Answers to True-False Questions

1. T, p. 598	7. F, p. 602	13. F, p. 614
2. F, p. 599	8. F, p. 604	14. F, p. 615
3. T, p. 599	9. F, p. 605	15. T, p. 615
4. T, p. 600	10. T, p. 606	16. T, p. 616
5. T, p. 601	11. F, p. 610	
6. T, p. 601	12. T, p. 612	

Multiple-Choice Questions (Circle the correct response)

1. Consumer satisfaction:
    a. is the basic objective of all economic systems.
    b. is easier to measure at the macro-level than at the micro-level.
    c. depends on one's own expectations and aspirations.
    d. is hard to define.
    e. is totally unrelated to company profits.

2. Which of the following statements about marketing does the text make?
    a. Micro-marketing never costs too much.
    b. Macro-marketing does not cost too much.
    c. Marketing is not needed in all modern economies.
    d. Micro-marketing always costs too much.
    e. Macro-marketing does cost too much.

3. According to the text, micro-marketing may cost too much because:
    a. some marketers don't understand their markets.
    b. prices are frequently set on a cost-plus basis.
    c. promotion is sometimes seen as a substitute for product quality.
    d. All of the above are true statements.
    e. None of the above--marketing never costs too much!

4. The text concludes that:
    a. pure competition should be the welfare ideal.
    b. advertising can actually lower prices to the consumer.
    c. marketing makes people buy things they don't need.
    d. marketing makes people materialistic.
    e. marketing's job is just to satisfy the consumer wants which exist at any point in time.

5. The future poses many challenges for marketing managers because:
    a. new technologies are making it easier to abuse consumers' rights to privacy.
    b. the marketing concept has become obsolete.
    c. it is marketing managers who have full responsibility to preserve our macro-marketing system.
    d. social responsibility applies only to firms--not to consumers.
    e. ultimately it is marketing managers who must determine which products are in the best interests of consumers.

Answers to Multiple-Choice Questions

1. c, p. 599   3. d, p. 601-03   5. a, p. 612-16
2. b, p. 600   4. b, p. 606

Exercise 23-1

Does micro-marketing cost too much?

Introduction

One reason that micro-marketing often *does* cost too much is that some production-oriented firms insist on clinging to their traditional ways of doing things--ignoring new marketing mixes and strategies. In a dynamic market, this can lead to higher than necessary costs--and perhaps even to the bankruptcy of the firm.

This can easily be seen in channels of distribution--where many inefficient and high-cost channels exist even today. High-cost channels are not *necessarily* evidence of inefficiency, however. If some target markets really do want some special service which is relatively expensive--then perhaps that is the best channel system for them. But this possible reason for "high-cost" channels of distribution does not explain all such systems. Some do appear to be more expensive than necessary because the established firms insist on buying from and selling to their usual sources and customers--even though other available channels would do as good a job (or maybe better), at lower cost.

This exercise shows how the use of alternative channels of distribution might lead to different--and in some cases higher--prices to final consumers. You are asked to calculate the probable *retail* prices which would result if a manufacturer were to use several different channels to distribute its product.

Assignment

1. A manufacturer of a new toothpaste is planning to use several different channels of distribution, as listed below. Each middleman in each of the alternative channels uses a cost-plus approach to pricing. That is, each firm takes a markup on its selling price to cover operating expenses plus profit. The manufacturer sells the toothpaste to the *next* member of each channel for $.86 per "large" tube.

   Using the data shown on the next page for markup estimates, calculate the *retail* selling price in each channel of distribution. Show your work in the space provided. The price for the first channel is calculated for you as an example.

	Operating Expenses*	Profit Margin*
Retail		
Small drugstores	39%	2%
Supermarkets	20%	1%
Chain drugstores	33%	3%
Mass merchandisers	29%	2%
Wholesale		
Merchant wholesalers	13%	2%
Rack jobbers	18%	2%

*Note: operating expenses and profit margin are given as a percentage of sales

a) Manufacturer to merchant wholesalers who sell to small drugstores:

$$13\% + 2\% = 15\% \quad = \text{Merchant wholesalers' markup on selling price}$$

$$\frac{\$.86}{100\% - 15\%} = \$1.01 = \text{Price to retailers}$$

$$39\% + 2\% = 41\% \quad = \text{Retailers' markup on selling price}$$

$$\frac{\$1.01}{100\% - 41\%} = \$1.71 = \text{Retail price}$$

b) Manufacturer directly to a national chain of drugstores:

c)   Manufacturer to merchant wholesalers who sell to supermarkets:

d)   Manufacturer directly to a regional chain of mass merchandisers:

e)   Manufacturer to rack jobbers who sell to supermarkets:

2. Consider the different retail prices that you calculated for Question 1. Assuming that it wanted to maximize profit, which channel(s) should the manufacturer choose to develop an effective marketing strategy or strategies? Why?

3. Assume that each of the five channels in Question 1 were to survive in the marketplace. From a *macro* viewpoint, should the "high-cost" channels be made illegal to "protect" consumers--and develop a "fair and efficient" marketing system? Why or why not?

Question for Discussion

What other reasons besides "tradition" help explain why micro-marketing often *does* cost too much? What can (should) be done to make sure that micro-marketing does *not* cost too much in the future?

Exercise 23-2

Does macro-marketing cost too much?

Introduction

All economic systems *must* have a macro-marketing system. The systems may take many forms, but all must have some way of deciding *what* and *how much* is to be produced and distributed *by whom, when,* and *to whom.*

Our macro-marketing system is basically a market-directed system. The key decisions are made fairly automatically and democratically--through the micro-level decisions made by individual producers and consumers. Together these individual decisions determine the macro-level decisions--and provide direction for the whole economy.

Does our macro-marketing system work in an efficient and fair way which achieves our social objectives? This question is very subjective, and we usually analyze the performance of our marketing system in terms of how well it satisfies consumer needs--as consumers see them. But remember that not all consumers have the same needs!

The marketing concept suggests that a firm should try to satisfy the needs of *some* consumers (at a profit). But, what is "good" for some producers or consumers may not be "good" for the whole society. This is the "micro-macro dilemma." It means that in running our macro-marketing system, some compromises must be made to balance the needs of society and the needs of individual producers and consumers. Making these compromises and still protecting individual freedom of choice is not easy. This exercise will help you understand the difficulty of resolving micro-macro dilemmas.

Assignment

Listed below are several imaginary situations which might be classified as "micro-macro dilemmas." For each situation, identify both sides of the dilemma--i.e., who benefits and who suffers in each situation--and state what action you would recommend.

1. Studies by the Consumer Product Safety Commission show that there are a large number of deaths each year among users of ATVs--"all terrain vehicles" which are intended for off-road use on sand, dirt, and packed snow. The death rate is especially high for 3-wheel ATVs. To reduce injuries and fatalities, Congress is about to pass a law making 3-wheel ATVs illegal.

2. A new state sales tax on wine and beer will be used to finance expansion of the state highway patrol and other highway safety programs in the state of Florida.

3. The Consumer Product Safety Commission is considering legal action that would force manufacturers of blow-type hair dryers to add a special safeguard to prevent electrical shocks if the dryer is accidentally dropped in a sink or tub full of water. The proposed safeguard would double the cost of most blow dryers.

4. Wanting to reduce pollution, Congress is about to pass a new law making it illegal to drive a gasoline or diesel-powered automobile between the hours of 7:00 a.m. and 7:00 p.m. in any city with a population of 500,000 or more--starting in three years (to allow time for appropriate adjustments).

5. The Federal Trade Commission is considering a proposal to stop all television advertising for children's toys. Critics argue that children do not understand the advertising and that it creates social pressure on low-income families to use their money unwisely.

6. To avoid the risks of nuclear accidents, Congress is about to pass a new law making it illegal to use nuclear reactors to generate power. Power companies would have five years before the law went into effect--to allow time for appropriate adjustments.

7. Wanting to encourage competition, Congress is considering a bill which would limit all firms to a maximum market share of 20 percent--requiring firms with larger shares to break apart or drop some customers.

8. Wanting to see more "equality of income," some U.S. legislators have introduced a bill proposing that all annual income over $200,000 be taxed at the rate of 100 percent.

Question for Discussion

Can "micro-macro dilemmas" such as those discussed above be resolved in any workable way? How? Be specific. Would "micro-macro dilemmas" be better resolved in a market-directed or a planned economic system? What implication does this have for answering the question: "Does macro-marketing cost too much?"